KNOWLEDGE MANAGEMENT

Also By

Database Analysis and Design Science Research Associates, Chicago, 1984
(2nd. edition February 1991, Macmillan, New York).

Introduction to Systems Analysis and Design Prentice-Hall, Sydney, 1987.
Translated into Spanish and German (2nd. edition, November 1990)
(3rd edition August, 1994), 490 pages. Fourth edition 1998, Fifth edition, 2001.

Relational Database Design: An Introduction (Prentice-Hall, Australia, 1990),
297 pages.

Designing the Networked Enterprise (Artech House, 1997), 342 pages.

Knowledge Management

Organizing Knowledge Based Enterprises

Igor Hawryszkiewycz

*Head of the School of Systems, Management and Leadership
at the University of Technology, Sydney, Australia*

palgrave
macmillan

First published 2010 by
PALGRAVE MACMILLAN

Palgrave Macmillan in the UK is an imprint of Macmillan Publishers Limited, registered in England, company number 785998, of Houndmills, Basingstoke, Hampshire RG21 6XS.

Palgrave Macmillan in the US is a division of St Martin's Press LLC, 175 Fifth Avenue, New York, NY 10010.

Palgrave Macmillan is the global academic imprint of the above companies and has companies and representatives throughout the world.

Palgrave® and Macmillan® are registered trademarks in the United States, the United Kingdom, Europe and other countries.

ISBN-13: 978–0–230–23027–9

This book is printed on paper suitable for recycling and made from fully managed and sustained forest sources. Logging, pulping and manufacturing processes are expected to conform to the environmental regulations of the country of origin.

A catalogue record for this book is available from the British Library.

A catalog record for this book is available from the Library of Congress.

10   9   8   7   6   5   4   3   2   1
19 18 17 16 15 14 13 12 11 10

Printed and bound in Great Britain by
CPI Antony Rowe, Chippenham and Eastbourne

To Nicholas, Matthew, Isabella and Michael

Contents

Part III   Organizing for Knowledge Management

Part IV   Supporting Technologies

List of Figures and Tables

Figures

Tables

Foreword

This book describes how to organize business processes that use knowledge for competitive advantage in today's changing environment. It is written for students in business management and information systems design, as well as business managers and information systems designers, to describe how to set up business processes that create and use knowledge.

Business enterprises today recognize that knowledge sharing is essential for business innovation in today's organizations. They no longer see knowledge as a separate activity but as integrated in everyday business activities. People follow processes where they collaborate and use each other's knowledge to create innovative products, services and ways of working.

Lightweight methods are used to organize processes to support the collaboration and knowledge sharing. The organization of the processes is described in terms of perspectives commonly seen as important in business organization. The perspectives are the business activity itself, social structure, knowledge management and technology. They are combined to provide the best support for sharing and knowledge creation in business environments.

The book is composed of four parts. The first part begins by describing the basic concepts of business processes, social networks, collaboration, innovation and knowledge management. It emphasizes methods to reduce the socio-technical gaps that often exist when technology does not match the task or the way people work. The emphasis here is to remove such gaps and create designs where technology, social structures and business activities are combined to facilitate knowledge creation and innovation.

Typical business processes are described in the second part, current business systems. They include Enterprise Resource Planning (ERP) systems and e-business systems and the creation of value networks by integrating processes of many enterprises. Examples of processes include outsourcing, product development or alliance formation and management. Services for knowledge workers and integration of ERP systems with knowledge activities are included.

The third part, organizing for knowledge management, describes a blueprint to create a business architecture that combines business activities with social networking and knowledge management. Guidelines are provided to specify requirements of the business architectures. The guidelines include matching social structures to process activities and the knowledge needed to support such structures. The design methods include collaboration and knowledge management and how to provide the connectivity and interactivity to get such advantage.

The last part, supporting technologies, describes how to implement business architectures. It covers alternate implementations for creating electronic workspaces that support collaboration and facilitate knowledge management. It emphasizes lightweight technologies to assist knowledge workers to use technology to fit in with their emerging work practices and to define requirements for business applications.

Preface

This book is for students and practitioners interested in designing business processes for today's competitive environment. It goes beyond optimizing workflows or providing easy access to information but describes process design from a number of perspectives now found in any business system. It particularly focuses on combining perspectives from process workflows, business activities, knowledge management, social structures and technology to build a business system that takes all aspects of business into account. It focuses on collaborative processes especially those that leverage technology to create knowledge.

Why is process design seen as important? The book sees process design as important because really it is the design of how the whole business works. Designers must consider all business perspectives in process designs. They must consider the tasks in business activities; the knowledge needed in the activities, their social structures and information flows and put them together in a way that creates an effective and productive process. The book particularly sees social structures as central to creating the knowledge in today's business environment. This book brings social structures into prominence as the way to bring knowledge and business activity together and put them together into a smooth running process.

In particular the book emphasizes how social structures and technology can support collaboration and encourage knowledge sharing and innovation in business processes. The book then develops design methods to create a process that takes all business perspectives into account to align the process to the business. Then in the last part the book describes the ways different technologies can be used to support the process. The book's approach to design is how to bring the perspectives together for competitive advantage through innovation.

Technology has also evolved and now provides many options to support networking and collaboration. In the emerging environment, technology must go beyond improving a workflow or providing better access to information. It must support all aspects of a process including the collaboration needed to create new knowledge and integrate it into everyday operations. The book describes how the technologies now becoming available through what is commonly referred to as Web 2.0 can be integrated into business processes to provide competitive advantage.

Primarily the focus of the book is on teaching but it also provides ways for business process managers to organize their processes in today's complex business environments to get value from knowledge management through collaborative work by sharing knowledge across networks. It is the potential of changing each perspective on its own to provide a better process outcome.

It introduces perspectives in an organized way while stressing relationships between the perspectives.

The book initially covers business issues but from Chapter 9 onwards it looks at implementations using technology. This begins with modelling methods to define requirements and then proceeding through design in Chapters 10–12 to create a business architecture that combines social structure, business activity, knowledge and technology. The choice of available technologies for the business architecture is described in Chapter 13. The treatment of technology is more from a technology capability viewpoint rather than detailed implementation. The book is divided into four parts starting with business aspects and describing some evolving business processes. This is followed by business design and then choosing technologies. The design process focuses on most effective design method as here the business not the technology is the driving factor.

- Part I of the book focuses on describing processes from all perspectives. It describes processes from each perspective in turn showing how they can be combined in ways that align business activities and social structures that match the organizational task. It describes knowledge management and ways to promote knowledge sharing by the choice of social structures and business activities.
- Part II of the book describes a range of current business applications including the role of Enterprise Resource Planning (ERP) systems and Web technologies and ways to get value through their integration to create a business architecture that facilitates knowledge sharing. It shows the trend from the focus on activities to include knowledge management and lately the emphasis on business networking.
- Part III of the book provides the design methods to identify the business requirements and to use the requirements to organize business processes. It considers all business perspectives in the design and creates a business architecture that integrates knowledge sharing into all parts of the business. The design methods provide the flexibility to choose the best design method given a business requirement.
- Part IV of the book provides an overview of technologies that can be used to support knowledge-based processes and provides guidelines for selecting them. It describes technologies to create the workspaces that support the social relationships and business activities

The book has a number of case studies. These are introduced early to stress the different perspectives and their role in process design. The case studies can be continued through the book, especially in the later parts to choose the technical support for the business activities.

Acknowledgements

The author and publishers wish to thank the following for permission to reproduce copyright material.

Justin Chen for permission to publish an image of his site titled 'I left my heart in the Aegean', www.justin-photo.idv.tw.

Every effort has been made to trace rights holders, but if any have been inadvertently overlooked, the publishers would be pleased to make the necessary arrangements at the first opportunity.

Part I
Knowledge Management within Business Communities

The Business Environment

Processes as the way to conduct your business

Learning objectives

- Processes as a way of doing business
- Delivering value to customers
- Evolving business environment
- Perspectives of process design
- Why process innovation is important
- Service delivery as part process design
- Dynamic change and complexity.

1 Introduction

This book provides students and practitioners in business information systems with the methods needed to design business processes in today's competitive business environment. It focuses on ways to be innovative in process design and create processes that use knowledge to deliver value to business clients. This chapter introduces the role of processes in business.

Most people see a business process from the perspective shown in Figure 1.1. Here it is a collection of activities that take a number of inputs and create an output that provides value and experience to the business customers at a cost-efficient way. There are many other perspectives used to design a process. The book identifies these major perspectives and applies them in process design. The

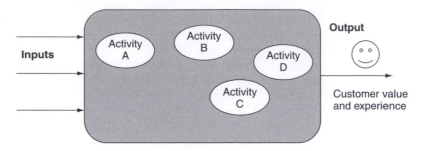

Figure 1.1   A process

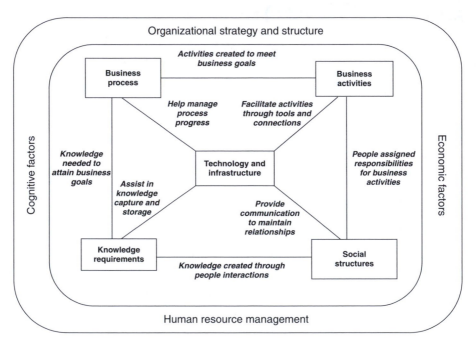

Figure 1.2   The process perspectives

major perspectives, which provide the choices for creating processes, are shown in Figure 1.2. These are the following:

- The process perspective that sees the process as a set of steps;
- Business activities or what people do in a processes and the outcomes produced by the activities;
- Knowledge and learning or what knowledge people create and use to continually improve the process;

- Social structure and networking that describes how people communicate to create and share knowledge and the way to organize people to encourage knowledge sharing; and
- Technology to facilitate the business activities and support the relationships in the social structure.

The first chapters in the book cover these perspectives and the relationships between them. Business activities are covered in Chapter 2, social structure in Chapter 3, knowledge is covered in Chapters 4 and 5. Chapter 6 introduces social software and its role in knowledge capture. The next two chapters cover typical business applications and show the gradual trend from emphasis on the process perspective, through the knowledge perspective and now the social perspective. Chapter 7 describes applications that primarily focus on business activities, whereas Chapter 8 describes the more dynamic business networks and their social structures. Then Chapters 10 and 11 show how the perspectives can be combined in design processes that create business architectures. Chapters 12 and 13 then describe how to choose supporting technologies for these architectures.

There are of course other perspectives as, for example, economic and cost factors, human factor issues, organizational structure that are not given prominence in this book and are shown on the outer shell in Figure 1.2. These are important in design but often cannot be changed in process design. Their impact on design is, however, discussed throughout the book.

The book also provides lightweight modeling tools to help readers better understand and design processes. These tools provide ways to model the perspectives and put them together to create a new process. The term 'lightweight' is used to imply that the methods are relatively user-friendly and address the major rather than detailed aspects of design. For business students without any technology minor these may require developing some familiarity. The tools are introduced gradually in the book, with a formal description given in Chapter 9. Some readers may wish to read this chapter earlier. A glossary of the notation is also provided at the end of the book.

1.1 Business and strategy

The book focuses on processes and the way they are used to implement business strategy. Strategy often revolves around a business model, which defines the kind of business customers, how they will be served, what markets will be addressed and the costs and financial issues related to the business. The book sees the development of business strategy as important but focuses on designing processes within the strategic framework. It describes the way strategy impacts on the design process and also how process design can effect strategy.

2 Processes as a way of doing business

One may ask – Why is there an increasing emphasis on process design? Basically because processes define ways we do business, which in turn must continually innovate to maintain competitive advantage. Innovation calls for products to be continually improved to provide new kinds of services, often at less cost than the services they replace. The services themselves add value to customer experiences, as, for example, the continual improvement of services found using mobile phones. Services combined with business processes are seen as delivering customer value in the most cost-efficient way.

2.1 Business process innovation

Businesses are continually changing to achieve competitive advantage through innovation and productivity improvements. As a result, ways to design and change processes are becoming increasingly important. Such process change almost takes place continuously and is called process innovation. Process innovation differs from business process re-engineering (BPR), which was common in the 1990s. BPR focused on improving the process flow dimension and reduce costs. Now process innovation has a different goal – it is to create processes that encourage innovation throughout the business. Hamel (2006) describes the emergence of new management methods to evaluate business performance. Process design becomes important here in order to support the new management methods. Processes must be chosen to fit the problem. Hall and Johnson (2009) describe the differences between typical processes. One are standard processes that provide similar services for each customer; the other are processes that continually change or emerge to provide services, which must be customized to highly variable customer needs. Traditionally improvement in standard processs was based on improving the process itself – the steps that it follows and reducing the cost at each step. Emerging processes especially in knowledge-based environments require more than that. They require social interaction to generate new ideas, continuous innovation through knowledge and learning, and technologies that support these other perspectives.

3 The emerging nature of business

The term 'Enterprise 2.0', as defined by McAfee (2006), is being increasingly used to describe new business systems and the way they will have to leverage the emerging facilities of the World Wide Web to create the social structure needed in such enterprises. Tapscott and Williams in 2008 describe the kind of advantages that can be leveraged using collaborative technologies to create the new enterprise. In such environments processes will need to be flexible and people to continuously network to obtain value through utilizing the best available expertise. The key is the ability to create flexible processes that support enterprise-wide people networking to quickly bring together the expertise needed to create innovative products. Prahalad and Krishnan (2008) further build on this idea and the important role of social structures in facilitating innovation in business processes.

3.1 Business activities

Business processes are made up of business activities. These activities include all aspects of the business. They include input logistics, or the purchase of input parts, the manufacturing and distribution of products and services, and internal processes such as payroll.

Business activities now encourage innovation and deliver better services, and innovative products. Innovation is seen as crucial to today's business success. Products are increasingly changing and it is increasingly important to develop new and competitive products and services. Business processes that support innovation in most cases include activities like:

- Generating ideas to provide eventual customer solutions with its focus on social relationships;
- Managing knowledge and use it to come up with new ideas with an emphasis on knowledge management;
- Putting the ideas into practice with its emphasis on process;
- Finding experts with the knowledge of 'what works and what does not'. Often this knowledge is called tacit knowledge and cannot be easily stored. Hence it becomes important to develop systems and processes that can bring people with such tacit knowledge into a process.

It is often difficult to quantify the business value of innovation although the benefits can be easily identified. Business benefits of innovation processes, however, are often expressed in qualitative rather than quantitative ways. It is realized that innovation requires people to share knowledge throughout the process. However, the way to do this is not clear and often depends on the organization itself and its culture. For example, most people see the benefit of arranging a meeting to exchange ideas and experiences. However, it is difficult to place an exact value on the resulting benefit. One measure can be estimates of potential new products or improvements to products and potential sales but again these are often estimates.

3.2 Processes in business networking

Business networking is another change in the way business is conducted. There are fewer and fewer enterprises that create their own service or product and sell it. It is now more common for enterprises to be made up of many businesses each contributing its expertise to provide a service or to manufacture a product. Much of this change has come about because of increasing globalization and the ability of firms to harness expertise from many parts of the world and to market its products globally. Business networking has gone beyond transaction-based systems to a more collaborative approach to get competitive advantage by sharing expertise and knowledge found in a number of firms. The change is continuing with greater emphasis on alliances, and the sharing of knowledge to create yet new and innovative services to people.

Virtually all product development involves businesses working together and people sharing ideas and knowledge. The iPod, for example, is made from disk drives, display modules, video processors and memory all produced by different manufacturers in different countries. Tapscott and Williams (2008) in their book titled *Wikinomics* outline the benefits to business through net-working. The term 'Business Web' is being coined to describe such business networking relationships. The goal of a business is to find partners who can add value by contributing specialized knowledge to the work of the business. There are now many ways business value can be obtained through network-ing. Perhaps the most common is to add the specialized expertise possessed by other businesses, especially where it would take considerable time to build this expertise yourself. This way you can put new products together much faster than developing your own components. There is also a wide variety of work in managing such relationships and in carrying out tasks together. This includes design work, meetings to set plans and managing joint projects among other activities.

3.3   Greater emphasis on knowledge

There is increasing emphasis on using knowledge more productively. Enter-prises are developing new ways to capture and reuse knowledge, as for example capturing experiences to guide future work, or ways to use captured knowl-edge to quickly respond to new issues. In a concrete sense, knowledge creation usually requires the capture and combination of both tacit and explicit knowl-edge from a number of specialized areas (Grant, 1996). Examples include formulation or response to proposals, planning and strategy development or the production of internal reports. Such knowledge-intensive processes do not necessarily produce 'knowledge' objects. More often new knowledge is found in reports, product designs, procedures, plans, proposals and responses to proposals. Within public enterprises these include devising ways to pro-vide new services at ever-lower costs, which in turn call for a range of expert knowledge.

The term 'knowledge worker' is now increasingly used to define the kind of work carried out by people in the emerging enterprise. Such workers bring together their expertise to develop products and services. They require flexible work environments to come up with ideas, evaluate them and put them into practice. The term 'knowledge-based processes' is often used to describe the work carried out by knowledge workers. The work of knowledge workers is covered in Chapter 3.

4   The emerging nature of knowledge-based processes

Business processes are also changing as a result of changes in the business environment. A general idea of the emerging environment is illustrated in Figure 1.3, which is a generic illustration that shows customers always looking for products with new features whereas organizations need the agility to respond to these needs.

The driver in this new environment is changing customer needs. What was good today can be improved tomorrow as people learn and identify new ways of using services. Take for example the value of word processors. First they were simply used to make typing amendments easier. Now once people learn to use the technology ways of improving the quality of the documents are continually evolving.

Figure 1.3 also illustrates the linkage between the four perspectives. The social perspectives are important for business to keep track of customer needs and be agile enough to quickly adapt to the changing needs. Such agility requires an organization to quickly bring people together to come up with ideas of how to respond to customer needs and to develop the required response. It requires not only technology, but also the organizational flexibility to bring such teams together, support them with resources that can include travel or meetings as well as use of technology.

The book addresses the question on what kind of process is needed in such environments. The four perspectives provide a way to answer this question. The question is decomposed into what social relationships are to be supported, what knowledge is needed, what steps will be followed and how will technology

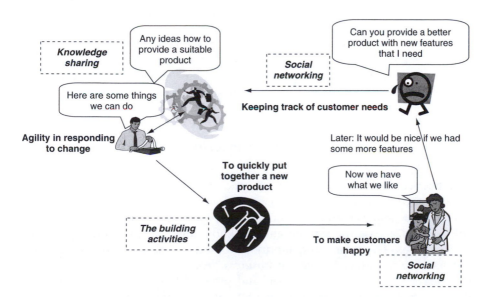

Figure 1.3   The emerging dynamic environment

support these perspectives. The other aspect is that the process must be designed in ways that can change.

> Hence we can define one important requirement for knowledge-based pro-
> cesses. They must be flexible and easy to change as new ways of doing business
> are identified.

4.1   Providing services to customers

An emerging business activity is service provision. Most products now come with associated services to clients. Social structures also play an important role here. They are important in identifying client preferences, and establishing the social relationships that are needed to deliver services to clients and businesses. The idea of service goes beyond simply providing one-off responses to requests such as, for example, easier ways to manage reservation or purchases. The best example is the kind of services provided to customers of mobile devices. These go beyond simply contacting people but now include finding location of local restaurants, access to internet, games and many others. Customer service is now a terminology that defines the value a business delivers to its customers. It refers to greater customization of services to individual needs to enable individuals to improve their personal activities and business work practices.

The increasing importance of service provision requires greater emphasis on the social and knowledge perspectives to understand the knowledge needs within innovative environments. Service provision has a major role in changing environments where knowledge processes also need to continually change. Such change can be accomplished by rearranging services, changing existing ones or creating new ones. The way products and services are being delivered is also changing with greater emphasis on delivery across computer networks. New ways of service delivery calls for further changes to business processes to get competitive advantage.

4.2   Collaboration and knowledge management

Processes now increasingly support collaboration between people to bring together people's individual knowledge and enable them to use their collective experience to develop new products and services.

Hence one important question in business processes design is how to facilitate collaboration to use the vast amounts of knowledge, which is found in global organizations. This requires organizations to develop social groups and establish the social relationships, as part of business processes, to collectively use their knowledge to develop new products and services. Knowledge management in this sense goes beyond simply storing information, but includes the facilitation of people networks that lead to innovative use of knowledge outcomes. At the same time it is necessary to provide the tools needed to both communicate and direct their effort to enterprise goals. The importance of social networks in business is also stressed by Prahalad and Krishnan (2008), who give numerous examples of their importance in business.

> Hence we can define one important requirement for knowledge-based processes. The processes must integrate social networking into business activities.

One might argue that social relationships existed virtually ever since civilization began. However, although personal relationships have always existed they are now more intense and often transient. Often such relationships are now conducted over computer networks. Communication over computer networks impacts on individuals, social groups and work teams. The communication often follows the norms people use in their work, sometimes known as culture. Culture can apply to national preferences, organizational processes or local teams. Any design of a new system must ensure that any new collaborative processes create minimal disturbance to cultural norms, or at least change them in an acceptable way. Chapter 5 covers cultural issues with suggestions to designers of how to change the nature of communication while preserving cultural norms.

5 Dynamic environments and complex adaptive processes

The changing environment often means that processes emerge as the environment changes. Emergent processes are opportunistic as they evaluate current situation and may initiate new tasks if new opportunities are identified. Usually this can result in many islands of disconnected work, which must be eventually coordinated. Emergent processes introduce a further dimension as the process goal itself may now change. This often occurs when working in knowledge-intensive environments. The emphasis here is on methods that support the more complex and unpredictable processes. The term 'complex adaptive processes' is now increasingly used to describe emergent processes.

This complexity arises from the interdependencies of knowledge workers (Davenport, 2005), organizational structure, technology and tasks. Such interdependencies can often be reduced into structured forms when designing predefined systems. The relationships in complex adaptive processes cannot usually be structured. They emerge over time and their nature itself changes. Here processes can change quickly and unexpectedly and the change cannot be predicted. They can adapt any of the collaboration structures defined in Chapter 4. Complexity theory (Merali and McKelvey, 2006) provides a number of guidelines for the modeling of complex adaptive systems (Holland, 1995). These introduce new criteria for developing design methodologies. These criteria include the following:

- The ability to self-organize at local levels in response to a wide variety of external changes. The reorganization can focus on social structure, knowledge, process or technology

- The definition and quick establishment of self-contained units that address well-defined parts of the environment,
- Loose connections between system elements and a way to reorganize the structure to respond to external change,
- The ability to organize connections between units and support the changed connections and interactivity.
- The aggregation of smaller units into larger components with consequent changes to the connectivity and interactivity,
- The realization of simple interfaces between model components.

The design methods described in this book focus on developing business activities that are self-contained and provide users with the ability to reorganize their activity. They also maintain connections with other activities through the social perspective to work towards a common goal.

5.1 Businesses as collections of processes

The degree of complexity increases as the number of business processes grows. Some authors see businesses as process ecosystems (Vidgen and Wang, 2006) which must be integrated throughout the business. This becomes even more important in business networking where processes may be owned by different organizations. As links between the different processes become more detailed, so the business relationships become more complex. As a result there is the danger of creating unnecessary chaos (Boisot, 2006) as the relationships between processes become less structured. The systematic design methods in this book create business architectures that provide greater flexibility in supporting evolving in relationships through changes in the different perspectives.

6 Summary

By the end of this introductory chapter the reader should be aware of the importance of process design, especially in matching processes to business objectives in innovative ways. The reader should also be aware that process design must be approached from more than one perspective and that the perspectives must be combined to create a business process. The next four chapters describe the perspectives and relationships between them in more detail. Chapter 2 describes the kind of processes and the way they are composed of business activities. Then Chapter 3 continues by describing the kinds of social structures for different activity types and Chapter 4 continues with the choice of social structure to support knowledge sharing. Chapter 5 then deals in greater depth on the influence of culture on knowledge sharing.

Readers should also be aware that design must consider increasingly complex environments. The complexity arises from an increase in business networking, the increasing relationships between processes and continual change within the business environment.

7 Questions and exercises

Question 1

Discuss the different perspectives of process design. Do you think some perspective can become the dominant perspective in design? Nominate some processes and their dominant perspective?

Question 2

What do you understand by the term 'process innovation'? What strategic goals would emphasize the need for process innovation?

Question 3

Why is the social perspective important in designing processes that facilitate innovation?

Question 4

Would you agree that greater emphasis on services places greater importance in combining social and knowledge perspectives in process design? Explain why.

Some further readings

Boisot, M. (2006) 'Moving to the Edge of Chaos: Bureaucracy, IT and the Challenge of Complexity' *Journal of Information Technology*, 21, pp. 239–248.

Grant, R.M. (1996) 'Prospering in Dynamically-competitive Environments: Organizational Capability as Knowledge Integration' *Organization Science*, Vol. 7, No. 4, July, pp. 375–387.

Hamel, C.G. (2006) 'The Why, What, and How of Management Innovation' *Harvard Business Review*, Vol. 84, No. 2, February, pp. 1–11.

Hall, J.M., Johnson, M.E. (2009): "When Should a Process Be Art" *Harvard Business Review*, Vol. 87, No. 3, March, pp. 58–65.

McAfee, A.P. (2006) 'Enterprise 2.0: The Dawn of Emergent Collaboration' *MIT Sloan Management Review*, Vol. 47, No. 3, Spring, pp. 21–28.

Prahalad, C.K., Krishnan, M.S. (2008) *The New Age of Innovation* (McGraw-Hill).

Tapscott, D., Williams, A.D. (2008) *Wikinomics: How Mass Collaboration Changes Everything* (Penguin Books, London, UK).

Vidgen, R., Wang, X. (2006) 'From Business Process Management to Business Process Ecosystem' *Journal of Information Technology*, 21, pp. 262–271.

Business Processes and Activities

2

Learning objectives

- Processes as a collection activities
- Criteria for combining business process perspectives
- Processes and technology
- Socio-technical issues in selecting technologies

- Technology and knowledge sharing
- Social structures and knowledge sharing
- Good process characteristics.

1 Introduction

This chapter continues from Chapter 1 by broadly describing the way the perspectives provide choices to create a good process design. It focuses on the main perspective, namely the business process, but defines in broad terms its relationship to the other perspectives in process design. Details of the different perspectives and the way they are used in design are outlined in the subsequent chapters.

The chapter begins by describing processes as a set of business activities that are combined to provide services to process clients. It then broadly describes the other perspectives and the broad criteria they must satisfy when used in process design. The main objective is on the importance of social structures in knowledge management and the broad objectives of using technology to realize this objective.

2 Describing a process as a set of connected business activities

A business process defines the way businesses organize their business activities. Many processes in business deal with simple transaction exchanges. Recording bank transactions or updating inventory records are some examples. But more and more processes now include considerable negotiation and collaboration. Figure 2.1 is an example of a process where a recruitment company finds employees for a client. It uses a very simple notation where each process activity is represented by an ellipse. Arrows indicate the sequence in which the activities are followed.

Recruting a manager

The process looks simple at first – it is made up of four steps as shown in Figure 2.1.

- Get requirements usually defined in terms of required skills. These can include personal management skills, financial knowledge, as well as knowledge about the department to be managed.
- Find candidates in a variety of ways including advertising and contact lists.
- Hold interviews and select one candidate for presentation to client.
- Arrange employment after interviews and discussion with the client.

Each of these, however, is a complex step requiring discussion, small changes, negotiations and agreements.

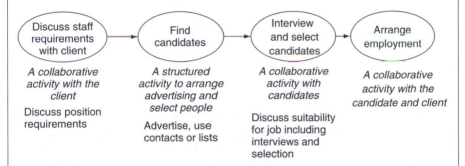

Figure 2.1   Recruiting a manager

Knowledge is also gathered and created throughout the process. Such a process can be organized in many different ways. We can get different people to carry out each of the steps, or we can make one person responsible for the one hiring request. The people can carry out their work in different ways. First there is information about the manager position and the qualifications, which are needed in the position. There are then alternate ways to find candidates. Much of this is often knowledge possessed by people experienced in this area. The organization, for example, may have a list of people seeking work and may select candidates from that list. Alternatively, they may advertise. Finally they may know potential candidates. Knowledge of successful ways to find good candidates can be captured here and used later. Candidates then provide information about themselves and this is discussed during the interviews to create knowledge about the suitability of candidates for the position.

Technology can of course assist many such activities but only if it is properly chosen to match the ways people work in the activity, and it allows knowledge to move between the activities.

This book will develop ways to define such processes and to organize them. Then the technology to manage the knowledge and transfer it between the different people in the process must be identified and installed.

The terms 'information' and 'knowledge' are used almost interchangeably here. The distinction will be described later in Chapter 5, but primarily information is something that is recorded and readily available whereas knowledge is created by interpreting this information. Still another process that is primarily collaborative is shown in Figure 2.2.

Assessing market opportunities

The process shown in Figure 2.2 usually commences with collecting market information. The collected information is assessed and then decisions are made as to what actions if any to take.

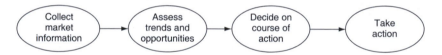

Figure 2.2   Assessing market opportunities

Each of the steps is itself a detailed activity. A team may be created to collect the information. Team creation may be a process in itself as it requires a search for people with expert knowledge in the area. The team then develops the sales report. To do this it may need to organize surveys and sort the information into reports.

Again information and knowledge is developed at each step. First there is knowledge used in making decisions on how and when to collect information. Then people's knowledge is used to assess and interpret the collected information and make any decisions. Much of this knowledge is developed as the process proceeds. People in the process use their experiences to interpret new information and create new knowledge about its meaning and what is to be done. Usually roles are defined for each activity and people are assigned to these roles.

Technology even becomes more important here when the activities are carried out by people across distance. It becomes important to keep everyone aware what others are doing and to quickly transfer any knowledge between the different activities.

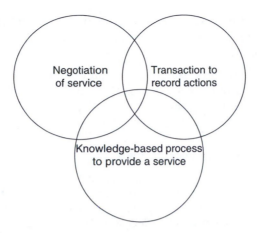

Figure 2.3   Different activity kinds

2.1 Business activities and processes

There is another interesting observation here. A process such as advertising for employees in any organization is almost a never-ending process. It goes on all the time and never stops. However, as far as one position goes, the process commences when a position is approved and terminates when a person is hired. Thus at any time there may be a number of processes or hirings going on. Each of these goes through a number of activities such as for example advertising or interviewing. All these activities also follow a process, which must be coordinated with the hiring process creating a process ecosystem as described earlier. A business must then be able to support any number of concurrent processes. The term *process choreography* is now increasingly used to describe more complex environments. We have activities that follow their internal ongoing processes and which combine with the more defined structured processes to achieve the best possible goals. Hiring the person is a goal; the activities define the best way to achieve the goal. The choreography defines the way all the activities together. A distinction is often made between three kinds of activities, which are shown in Figure 2.3. They are the following:

- Transaction-based activities, which usually result in simple actions such as recording outcomes or resource use. Often these activities concern financial transactions and are followed precisely to enable auditing to ensure financial accountability. These are described in detail in Chapter 7.
- Business processes, that require some negotiation, but where most activities take place on the WWW. These processes usually concern maintaining relationships across distance but often require some negotiation of service. Such relationships may be between clients and a business, or between one or more business. E-business processes are described in detail in Chapter 7.

- Knowledge-based processes, whose main goal is to design new products and services, develop businesses and business networks. They are described in detail in Chapter 4.

In fact most business processes often include all mix of the three activity types although often one predominates. Different parts of the process tend to emphasize one of the three types.

Business activities in recruitment

For example, consider Figure 2.4, which is a more detailed description of the recruitment process. It identifies a number of activities and whether they are collaborative, Web-based or transaction-based. Here there is initially some discussion or negotiation within a firm to decide on the kind of person required. This is usually a collaborative activity. Then approval is obtained from management. Once this is obtained the position is advertised on the Web and people apply through the Web. These activities are thus Web-based. Then there are a number of activities concerned with selecting candidates for interview, interviewing and then hiring someone. There are predominantly collaborative activities.

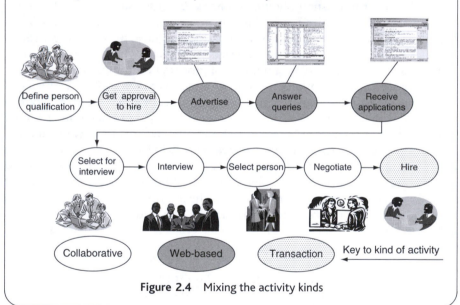

Figure 2.4   Mixing the activity kinds

2.2 Process emergence

Processes often do not follow a prescribed set of steps. Options are found even in a simple process like arranging travel for a group. This can be seen as a simple process that consists of three steps. One process step is to discuss preferences with group members. The next is to arrange airfares and the next to book the hotels. These steps are not necessarily sequential. It is of course possible to go back to previous steps or even carry out some steps concurrently. For example, while arranging airfares it may be necessary to go back to a discussion with a group to discuss alternative flights. Similarly arranging airfares and hotels may be carried out concurrently. There are often unexpected variants to the process. For example, difficulties in arranging accommodation can require changes to the flight schedule. Finding new knowledge, as for example lack of hotel vacancies, can impact on the way the process goes. In this example we may go back and plan a different trip. Finding new information often leads to what is known as *process emergence* – that is the next step taken depends on the current situation, especially as new information is discovered. This is where knowledge and learning about a situation comes into play and businesses over time must learn ways to deal with unexpected situations and respond to them.

Sometimes an emergent process may result in a change of plan altogether following discussion between travelers – for example, why travel by plane, maybe we can take a cruise instead. It is thus not often possible in knowledge-based processes to predict all steps before the process begins. Ways to describe such processes are described in Chapter 9.

2.3 Terminology for describing processes

Processes can be described at a number of levels as, for example, shown in Figure 2.5.

Process levels in arranging travel

Figure 2.5 characterizes the situation found in many businesses. It further underscores the need to ensure that processes at all levels are closely integrated and work together. The top-level process, which usually defines services provided to clients, must be well defined and must be supported to proceed smoothly. But at the same time the next level of the business must also work well. It is not good to promise clients to make hotel reservations and then find that the hotel booking system does not work well and results in unnecessary delays.

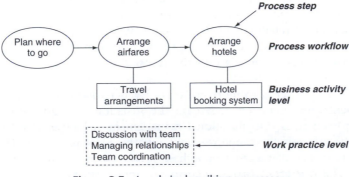

Figure 2.5   Levels in describing processes

These levels are the following:

- The process workflow level defines the process steps and their sequence in satisfying a client request. These are logical and basically describe what is happening – not how the process is carried out.
- The business application, which includes the business activities that support each process step. These are the activities that are usually ongoing and can support numerous instances of processes with individual outcomes. For example, a hotel booking system supports a number of individual reservations. An interview arrangement in the recruitment process occurs for many selection processes.
- The work practice level, which defines the actual detailed ways that people carry out individual tasks. It can be how we create a spreadsheet, how we get information about clients, or how we hold meetings. One goal here is to design the business activity level processes in ways that expedite the client process workflow. These define the work practices actually followed by people in the process.

Productivity improvements can be made at all levels. We can focus on the process and reduce the number of process steps. We can focus on organizing the activities by ensuring that each step is carried out in the best possible way. To do this, it may be necessary to go to the work practice level and improve the ways that people exchange information and knowledge, and provide tools and improved ways of interaction.

2.4 Processes in business networks

There is increasing evidence that businesses to remain competitive must increasingly operate as networks. In this way one organization can gain access to the expertise of another organization. Such networks emerge as new opportunities arise in the business and expertise must be quickly gathered to address the opportunity. Furthermore other research has shown that networks can access far diverse and expert knowledge and can in effect be more creative and innovative than highly structured local organizations. Networking can be simply exchanging transactions. A retailer in a network like that shown in Figure 2.6 can make an order to wholesalers, the ordered goods are delivered, an invoice is issued and payment is made. In this case the transactions do not need any human intervention.

The trend however is to more collaborative networking. Here many of the arrangements are negotiated based on the situation at the time rather than following fixed rules. Organizational management is increasingly required to manage the increasingly complex social networks. Here retailers negotiate with wholesalers or manufacturers to purchase products for sale to their customers using their knowledge of changing customer trends. Such arrangements require extensive collaboration between people in the organizations. They often require

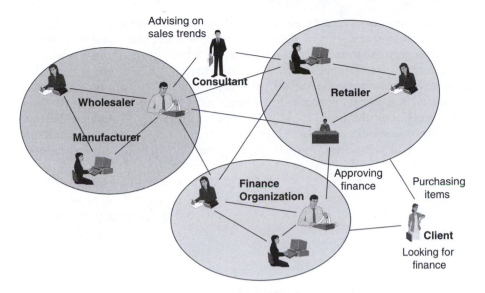

Advising on sales trends

Consultant

Wholesaler

Retailer

Manufacturer

Finance Organization

Approving finance

Purchasing items

Client

Looking for finance

Figure 2.6   Businesses as interacting communities

arranging finance for their clients or customers. Furthermore such arrangements can often quickly change. Again the emphasis is on process flexibility.

Process flexibility can mean many things. One is simply changing some activity, as for example how we place a customer order. An improvement here may be grouping orders to reduce delivery costs. Or we might get a new business partner to manage our orders while we focus on production processes. The term 'value networking' is now increasingly used to describe ways to form business networks that generate value to all networks participants. This will be discussed in more detail in Chapter 8.

One of the benefits of business networking is to extend knowledge sharing to business. Knowing how your partner's business works often makes it easier to explain product details to clients or alternatively to pass on innovative product requirements from customers to manufacturers. One example of this has been sharing of information in consulting companies, where large savings in report preparation were reported. These savings were obtained through the reduction of response preparation time from four to two months (Hansen, et al., 1999) by collecting knowledge from consultants and preparing guidelines and information for consultants arranging new consultancies.

Hence there is another process requirement here – that of business networking, sometimes referred to as building a business web. It is now virtually generally agreed that competitive advantage can be obtained by quickly setting up business webs made up of business each with their specialized expertise.

Many examples of such business networking can be found in the book titled *Wikinomics* by Tapscott and Williams (2008), who see the trend to networking gaining momentum. All these areas are then combined to make a product. Returning to the example of the iPod, marketed by Apple, it is constructed of components from many businesses – that supply the casing, disk and other components. Perhaps it is fair to say that if Apple were to develop the expertise in all these areas, then the iPod would have taken much longer to develop. It is the building of such business webs that enables enterprises to quickly respond to new demands. Again processes must be flexible and quickly bring such partnership together to create innovative products.

Networking often introduces further complexities into processes. When compared to hiring a manager or collecting information, networking often requires searching for partners, negotiating agreements and defining responsibilities in joint work.

Processes in business networking

Responding to a tender for developing a call center

The processes found in business networking must have a matching social structure. Figure 2.7 illustrates a process where one organization issues a tender for someone to provide call center services. A provider often needs to find partners that can provide the needed software, hardware and networking, and a location.

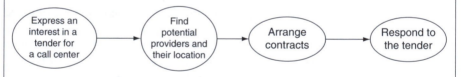

Figure 2.7   Finding partners for a tender response

Here the first step is to find business partners to bring their expertise to the project. This requires searches to get expressions of interest and arranging contracts or at least expressions of interest to enter into a contract should they be successful in the tender. Then a response to the tender is made.

Knowledge is the central issue. Knowing the partners to contact, how to approach them and develop expressions of interest is one kind of knowledge that is needed. What questions to ask when assessing tender responses? Preparing the tender response also requires knowledge on successful ways to run call centers economically and evaluate any risks involved in the response.

3 Introduction to knowledge management and process

Knowledge is an important perspective in process design. It is however important to keep in mind the difference between information and knowledge. Everyone knows that vast amounts of information can be found from the Internet using GOOGLE or other search engines. The question then becomes how to use this information to solve a problem – or how to cross the gap from information to knowledge. To do this the information must be interpreted and externalized to a problem at hand. This requires people to use their expert knowledge to interpret the information. Furthermore such interpretation becomes more effective as more people work together on the information. This is where teamwork and social groups become important. People with different expertise in a team often see ways to relate stored information to the problem at hand. The important part of team design especially across distance is to give the team the opportunity to provide such comments and discuss them with the whole team. One distinction found in knowledge management is between:

- Explicit knowledge, which is stored and accessible knowledge, such as documents, and
- Tacit knowledge, which is possessed by people, who may be expert in a particular field.

This difference between the two kinds of knowledge is important in many ways. It distinguishes between the knowledge, which is captured and stored using computers and the social aspects of interpreting this knowledge to solve new problems. Such interpretation is the tacit knowledge that is often personal and not easily captured. Often stored knowledge includes ways that problems were solved in the past and serves as what is sometimes called a knowledge base of good practices to help people solve today's problems. It is dealt with in considerable detail in Chapter 4.

3.1 Combining knowledge management and business activities

Ultimately the goal of process design is to use knowledge management to improve the quality of outputs and decision making in business activities. The goal is not to simply have a separate process or activity to manage knowledge. On the other hand, it is to increase emphasis on knowledge in every process, or to make the processes increasingly *knowledge intensive*. The goal is for people to continually improve the process by learning how to carry out their work better and raise the quality of their products. Furthermore such improvement should be carried out with least effort and not seen by people as extra work to be done. The goal is for the process to improve naturally with continuous contribution from its participants, who should develop a sense of ownership of the process.

One important issue here is the strategy to be chosen for knowledge management. It is, for example, possible to have separate knowledge management centers for each kind of business process. Alternatively one center can serve a number of processes. It is also possible to choose between personalized and codified strategies. The book suggests that knowledge should be captured during the process and social structures must be established to do so. Such choices are described later in the chapter on design. These alternatives are discussed in more detail in Chapter 4.

Designs must combine knowledge and process

Knowledge must be shared and created during process execution and made available throughout the business. Preferably knowledge should be captured at each business activity.

---

4 Technologies to support knowledge-based processes

Technology is an important perspective in process design. There is a range of technologies available for process support. There are technologies to support the flow of documents through business activities. There are numerous technologies available to support business activities processes. The ultimate goal is to use the technologies to support all the business activities and their interactions in forming a process. The four perspectives become important here. Technology must:

- Support the social relationships and keep people aware of what is happening;
- Provide the support to carry out the business activities; and
- Provide ways to capture and share knowledge.

There are technologies to support people working in communities, small groups working together or to support organization-wide collaboration. They range in sophistication from simple e-mail to multi-media structures. They are now increasingly mobile allowing collaboration to take place over vast distances. There is now increasing emphasis on what are commonly known as Web 2.0 technologies. These are technologies that increasingly support the development of shared objects such as blogs or Wikis. Although now commonly used in many personal sites it is not clear how they can be used to generate value in business processes. The book will cover social networking technologies in Chapter 6 and look at ways of using them to obtain business value in Chapter 12 onwards.

> ## Technology must support knowledge management at each business activity
>
> Technology must be chosen to support knowledge sharing, creation and utilization across the business and not individual business activities.

5 Collaboration and team work

The social networking perspective considers how people should work together to develop and provide new products and services. Thus processes must be designed in ways to help people exchange knowledge and be aware of each other's activities. They must also retain and pass on their accumulated knowledge between members or to new members, who may join the organization. In that case any new members will be able to quickly begin to contribute to the team. Additional services are often needed when team members are separated by distance or where teams are transitory with experts brought into teams as needed.

It is necessary to support collaboration between teams and not only between individual team members. An example of such a structure is shown in Figure 2.8 again using techniques found in rich pictures. Here there may be a market development team working with a client. Various suggestions by the market development team are sent for feedback from distant distributors, who themselves may also have ideas to contribute. Support must be provided internally within the development team as well as for coordination with distributors. One important consideration here is how to develop and maintain a collaborative culture with people working across distance. Some of these issues are described in Chapter 5.

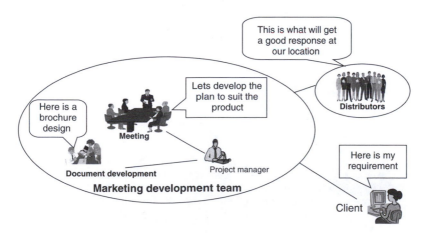

Figure 2.8 Working in teams

5.1 Teams and communities

Project communities differ from open communities as they usually have a goal to accomplish. Whereas open communities simply put information on the site for sharing, project communities work towards specific goals. Team work must thus be increasingly managed to ensure that goals are rapidly achieved.

The continually reducing cost of communication results in the emergence of new communities and networking within existing communities. Networks of people, who make up such communities, are becoming more complex and individuals are increasingly required to participate in many communities in their environment. As a result the more common work situation that most people find themselves in is like that shown in Figure 2.9. Here the person is networking for many different purposes. There is a community, the team, as well as the team within the context of a business process. People thus move between the different communities thus further adding to the sharing of knowledge.

More and more organizations are now seen as networks of communities. The question is how to support such communities to share the increasing volume of information and at the same time improve their productivity.

The increasing emphasis on community networking requires the development of a social culture where individuals, even if separated by distance, should see themselves as parts of social groups with a common purpose. Increasing complexity leads to more emphasis to social networking to use and create new knowledge to resolve issues that often come up suddenly. The book introduces knowledge issues and social networking in this chapter and describes their relationship in more depth in Chapter 4.

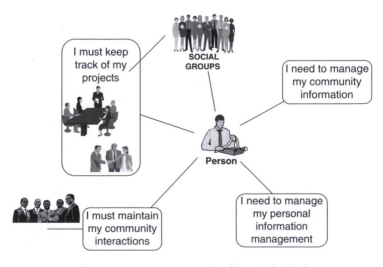

Figure 2.9 Current situation for an individual

6 Communities and knowledge management

Knowledge management usually serves some community and hence the relationship between knowledge and social structure is important. It also considers the way people make up the communities in industry and in society as well as the way they interact in these communities. These business communities often differ from social communities as they work towards a well-defined goal. Some descriptions of communities include the following:

- A group of people whose communication and collaboration over networks strengthens and facilitates their shared identity and goals, or
- A social phenomenon dealing with establishing and working with meaningful connections between people.

Communities in the context of technology take on a further meaning – that they can communicate and share knowledge across distance using a variety of technologies but in particular the Internet. This leads to different names to describe such communities. Online communities or virtual communities are two kinds of definitions. Howard Rheingold in 1995 in his book *The Virtual Community* (http://www.rheingold.com/vc/book/) defines virtual communities as 'social aggregations that emerge from the Net when enough people carry on public discussions long enough, with sufficient human feeling, to form webs of personal relationships in cyberspace'.

There are many social communities on the Internet based on systems such as Facebook or U-tube. Most of these are still oriented towards presenting a personal presence on the Internet and their role in business is not yet clear. However, there is an exchange of knowledge in many such activities, especially where more than one person participate in one site. This to some extent reinforces Rheingold's definition of a virtual community.

When it comes to business communities, there are such terms as 'product development teams', 'virtual teams', or 'communities of practice'. Being in a business community is not simply exchanging the occasional message. There must be some purpose to such exchanges. Furthermore, conclusion of research is that an Internet-based business community is characterized by more than just being connected to e-mail. One criterion is that it must be persistent. Its members must stay with the community over a significant period of time and carry out the majority of its work using computer-mediated activities of many kinds. This calls for multiple interaction styles and the capability for real-time interaction. As a further requirement it must be multi-user, in the sense that people in different domains must collaborate across any system. Thus marketing people, production people and financial people must be able to complete some business activity through the Internet.

The question is how to organize such groups across distance and make them sustainable over long periods of time. This then calls for networking services that give people separated by distance the feeling that they are together. It also calls for developing computer interfaces that directly support people's work practices. Any supporting computer system must enable the growth of communities and emergence of new communities in light of changing environment. This leads to the next requirement of knowledge-based processes.

> Process design must create social structures that facilitate knowledge sharing.

Typical social structures will be described in Chapter 4.

6.1   Developing social capital

Leadership in forward thinking businesses must therefore focus on using technologies to develop human capital. Further quotes from the literature reinforce this call. They include the following:

- The new currency will not be intellectual capital. It will be social capital – the collective value of whom we know and what we can do for each other.
- When social connections are strong and numerous, there is more trust, reciprocity, information flow, collective action, happiness, and as a result greater wealth.

What is social capital? It is not just a lot of people getting together and discussing their experiences and work practices. It is more than that. It is when people actually trust each other and work together to some common goal. The question then is how do we create the conditions that lead to the benefits of social capital and how can technology assist here. This is not yet a solved question. Organizations cannot just decree it. They cannot achieve it by simply providing technology. Its evolution also requires support from the organization itself. The organization must encourage and reward processes that result in better utilization of knowledge. The experiences in introducing technology into consulting organizations through technology attest to this. Simply providing technology in the form of Lotus Notes in Anderson Consulting did not automatically generate the collaboration expected of consultants. It is only when processes for such collaboration were defined and reward structures put in place that resulted in new business value.

More general research by Nahapiet and Ghoshal (1998) suggest four important conditions for knowledge sharing. They are the following:

1. Provide the opportunity to exchange and share knowledge;
2. Make sure people avail themselves of this opportunity;
3. Provide the resources needed to motivate people to use the opportunities; and
4. Provide the capability to combine knowledge.

Figure 2.10   Development of human social capital

Even so an environment where social capital begins to contribute to a business will not just occur automatically. It will evolve as people begin to understand each other, and trust each other to work together in a productive way. Figure 2.10 illustrates a path to social development. This sees the development of people and their expertise passing through a number of stages. They are the following:

- Working on common ground, that is on the same kind of problems, probably using the same communication tools;
- Becoming communities of practice or using the same techniques perhaps discussing them and maybe learning from each other, but still working as individuals;
- Creating knowledge capital from their joint work, usually through capturing and agreeing on best practices;
- Becoming experts in their particular area of interest and contributing this expertise to the group.

Most organizations start with supporting communities of practice. This is not simply getting people together. Probst and Borzillo (2008), for example, describe what is needed for communities of practice to succeed. They describe the kind of governance structures needed to nurture such communities. These structures include sponsors, leadership and defining community objectives and measurement of success.

Communities of practice often result in the sharing of knowledge and the creation of best practices. As people share ideas, trust begins to develop resulting in more collaboration and ultimately create social capital. Different processes for creating knowledge capital can be found in the literature. Usually development proceeds through sharing knowledge, negotiation about this knowledge, discovery through discussion and carrying out joint tasks. Nahapiet and Ghoshal (1998) identify some dimensions for the formation of social capital. They include the following:

- Structural which define the structure of personal relationships, the way people are connected;
- Relational, which defines the nature of the relationships and people's behavior, which determines the actions they take in the community;
- Cognitive or ways in which joint visions are developed

> Another important requirement of knowledge processes is to form and support relationships that lead to social capital.

There is also a distinction between weak and strong relationships. Weak relationships in this sense are those where people exchange information but not necessarily directly related to a common goal. Communities of practice are often seen as made up of many weak relationships. People working separated across distance often have weaker relationships than those co-located.

6.2   Linking technologies and social communities

The link between technology and community also requires consideration. Experience, however, has shown that technology cannot be used as the driver of the formation of communities of practice. Venters and Wood (2007), for example, describe the difficulties experienced in using technology as a driver in loosely coupled organizations. Similarly consulting organizations have found it necessary to support technology with organizational structures and policies to ensure useful outcomes. Basically in this and other cases once the novelty wears off the technology is abandoned.

One important consideration in defining requirements is that chosen technologies must fit in with least disruption into people's normal work practices. Technology results in social change as it often requires changes to the way people work and how they exchange information and knowledge. Any designs to support knowledge must be carefully evaluated to ensure that any changes are not excessively disruptive as to either not be accepted or eventually abandoned. Hence introduction of new technologies must be as ubiquitous as possible and be easy to use.

It is generally agreed that successful use of technology occurs only when it is aligned to other dimensions of the enterprise. These have to be closely aligned, otherwise problems can arise. Introducing technology can result in gaps in such alignment. Thus it cannot be taken as a given that introducing technology will lead to immediate improvements to the process.

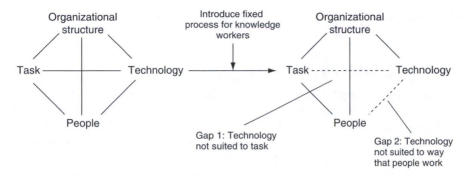

Figure 2.11   Factors in socio-technical design

The term 'socio-technical approach' is often quoted as addressing the introduction of new technologies. This approach looks at ways to minimize disruption to existing processes to determine ways to best introduce new processes. A number of factors are identified and linked to technology.

The effect of an introduction of technology is then examined and any gaps resulting from the introduction of a new technology are identified. The idea is illustrated in Figure 2.11. It draws on the work of Leavitt (1965) and shows links between the factors and then identifies any gaps that arise from introducing technologies. Thus, for example, suppose we add a technology that requires knowledge workers to follow standard procedure. This will immediately result in gaps between technology and task, and technology and people.

These gaps must be addressed and reduced prior to the introduction of technology.

One suggestion is as a first step to introduce those technologies that simplify routine work. This will usually add value to peoples work and not create a gap. An example here is word processing which simplifies work. Those that remember earlier days where document corrections required the use of white outs and considerable retyping will remember the added value provided by word processing. E-mail is another technology that adds value to people's work as it reduces the need for postage and is faster. There is then another requirement here.

Technology and social process

The introduction of a new process or technology should not be disruptive and create no new gaps in the environment – it should add value to people's work.

Socio-technical studies are an area in its own right and could be treated almost as a separate text. This book's objective is the successful introduction of new processes and hence socio-technical considerations are important. The book will continually draw on socio-technical considerations in later chapters that consider the design of new systems.

6.3   Linking technology and process

The important thing to keep in mind is that the space must fit in with your work and in fact make it easier to carry out your work. Computer systems can be seen as providing a workspace. The question is what is needed in the workspace to facilitate work. This as shown in Figure 2.12 requires us to find out what people do and what technology services they will require – a process known as requirements analysis, which is described in detail in Chapter 10. Basically here we:

Determine what the business activities are including communities to be supported;
Select the technologies needed to support these activities; and
Design the user interfaces for the activities.

A related question is how to provide a technical platform to support each person and to enable them to work with teams, which may be distributed. The goal here is to create a space to work in. This is not different from any kind of work – you must always have a space, which may be a room, a workbench or a computer. Ultimately the goal is to create electronic spaces to support work activities and ways to introduce them with minimal disruption. The electronic

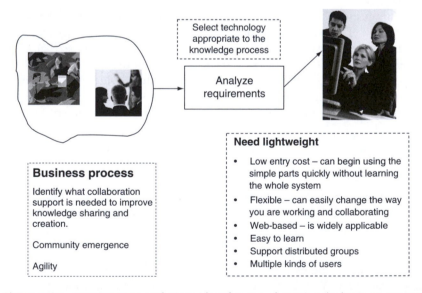

Figure 2.12   Requirements analysis to identify ways of creating the business process

workspace should provide the services needed for people to communicate and interact within the context. Currently many users select often different services for each task. They might communicate by e-mail, keep their reference documents on their personal computer and use a portal to communicate with clients. An electronic workspace should provide all these interactions in the same space to reduce effort of moving between different services and ensuring all actions are taken in full knowledge of the business situation.

There are two options to provide such web services. They are the following:

- Select a different communication service for each business activity. This is often achieved through improvisation, with individuals choosing tools that support some current activity. This can often mean that a person must record information found in each tool and combine it where necessary.
- Provide an integrated platform. Here all services now store information in an integrated platform making it easy to share information found in one business activity with that obtained in another activity. The platform thus provides the notion of maintaining continuity in that everyone in the network including those on mobile devices are continually involved in the process as it emerges rather that simply working on some part of the system. The term 'lightweight' is also often used to describe platforms. This term defines technologies that people can adapt to their own use. They are often relatively inexpensive and can be used on a computer network.

Technology adoption is important. Usually new technologies must be introduced gradually and show early benefits. Again the idea of lightweight is to reduce the social gaps in introducing new technologies for knowledge workers. Their goal is to provide simple ways for knowledge workers to adapt technology to changing work patterns. The goal here is to allow simple changes to services in a workspace – a process sometimes termed as mashing up workspaces. The book will describe lightweight platforms in Chapter 12 onwards.

7 Building communities on the internet

It is of course almost an undeniable fact that much of the sharing of knowledge and the development of social capital in distributed enterprises will benefit from the use of Internet technologies. The way this will happen is still unclear although experience gained in the use of Internet technologies provides many guidelines for potential adoption in business enterprises. The following sections describe some of the ways that technologies have been used up to this time to build communities that facilitate knowledge sharing. Often such communities are based on weak relationships where people see benefits in sharing knowledge for mutual benefit.

7.1   Community networks and networked communities

Internet communities can be seen as a precursor for communities in business. It is important to distinguish here between a community network and a networked community.

A community network is one that is electronically connected and has access to a variety of communication technologies. However, members of this network may not work together. They may use their connection for individual purposes such as, for example, looking up a train timetable. It is only when these communication technologies are used to effectively share and create knowledge that the community becomes a community network. Here people communicate towards some common goal. Hence a community network is one where the community uses their connection to some common purpose. Community networks tend to evolve gradually. One way to classify community networks is by their level of development, in particular:

Accessing and sharing knowledge and information;
Becoming a community of practice; and
Creating social capital that results in the creation of new knowledge.

The creation of such social capital is the ultimate goal of most business communities. The goal of any business is to grow such community networks to create the social capital needed to foster innovation.

7.2   Communities sharing knowledge and information

With the advent of the WWW, there has been extensive growth in bringing communities together using Internet technologies. The term 'community network' in this chapter describes people communicating over a computer network about topics on common interest. In most cases these are usually people who have common ground but are not working to particular goals. The most prevailing view of a community network for a long time has been people sharing knowledge with others through the Internet. Here the person interacts with a community of often distant users about some topic. The interactions are irregular and often focus issues that arise over time. One example here might be someone looking for information about travel in a remote area or finding eating places.

Typical implementations here are Web discussion boards. Information received from one member of the group is recorded in the discussion board and becomes available to all other members thus leading to sharing of information. Such communication also has a role in business and exchange of information using technologies in most organizations is now widespread.

One of the earliest example of developing a community network was the well-known Blacksburg site. It was set up to share and access knowledge with the community in Blacksburg. Although this was an early site there are now many examples of similar community sites. Blacksburg is often quoted as an early community network because of its members' geographic proximity – they are all interested in what is happening in their local community. There are many examples of similar application in practice and the provision of enterprise portals is now common practice. These portals usually implemented on Intranets serve to distribute information throughout the organization.

Progress to a community of practice in such networks is to introduce various interactive tools such as discussion boards or blogs.

7.3   Building personal communities

With the growth of what now is called the dot-com boom the growth of communities on the Web has been staggering. The relationships in these communities are based on some common interest. Many new business models arose to support common interest communities. Sites such as U-tube, MySpace, Facebook or Yahoo now support individual setting up their personal websites. These sites extend the idea of portals to personal spaces. Here participants can set up their personal spaces both to publicize their wares and in many cases seeking new relationships. The value of these sites is that they enable the formation of community networks, which serve very small communities. However, there is some debate on whether experiences gained on such sites will eventually be carried into businesses and lead to the formation of business community networks and consequent growth on social capital.

Yahoo, for example, provides a site for setting up interactive blogs. People post information on sites and the community adds value to it, by posting their comments and interpretations. Collecting comments on what you publish from others adds to your knowledge. You begin to see what other people see in your work and from received comments sometimes see ways to improve what you are doing. The question is how to achieve this in business to get added business value through sharing information between individuals working in similar projects.

The growth of Internet communities has not only resulted in wider networks but also broadened use to virtually everybody and in the type of information distributed. Previously listservers primarily distributed textual information. Now multimedia is increasingly being used. There are now many commercial sites that provide ways to serve personalized or special interests of groups or even individuals through increasingly available blogsites provided by organizations such as Yahoo. People can upload their photographs or artifacts that they have created to bring it to the attention of others. Here, as on many other sites, an individual can buy space to set up their own blogspace for distributing their information and seeking comments on it.

Many sites made available to the general public as well as serving community interests also include marketing information to become financially viable.

Questions are now arising on how such social software technologies can be adapted to business applications. There are numerous opportunities such as, for example, blogs to collect information on clients or to raise project issues. Even more important is how to integrate such software into processes. How, for example, do we ensure that a blog on project issues is used effectively in project management and integrated into other project management tools? Possible ways to integrate social software are described in more detail in Chapter 6.

7.4   Extending to specialized communities of practice

Internet websites can be used to link special interest groups. It has been proposed as a way to link small business enterprises to each other to get the benefits of both networking and exchanging knowledge about their activities.

One recent outcome is to link start-up companies in a technology park or for a city to set up services to support groups working in areas that raise the city profile. Improving the connectivity of groups with a common goal and providing services that support such groups can result in greater and improved performance in the community. It can provide a hub for the sharing of knowledge that helps the whole community.

Many cities or regions are looking at developing strengths in their community and bring business into their community. The interlace program aimed at creating what are called 'living labs Europe' or what are sometimes called 'third-generation technology parks' is an example here. Centered on the Copenhagen Business School it has helped to develop a number of such specialized networks or clusters such as, for example, the Accenture Technology Park in France or a Biotechnology Cluster in Estonia. These are still in their infancy but the goal is to have such communities prosper through the provision of services that foster interaction and provide an interface to the outside world. Such services can include strategy planning, interfaces to clients and support for networking within the cluster.

Such networking is now becoming known as a digital ecosystem. The environment of such a system is a digital infrastructure that contains valuable information for people or businesses in this environment or ecosystem.

New technologies are emerging to support such infrastructures. IBM is now developing an architecture to support a group of enterprises, namely, cloud computing. It has been deployed in both mature and emerging economies. Its primary goal is to allow enterprises access to services provided by the cloud. Recently, for example, such a system was deployed to support the iTricity to serve businesses in the Netherlands and Belgium as well as cloud computing centers in emerging economies in Brazil, India and Korea among others. Although not currently aimed at supporting collaboration it has the potential to support collaboration between businesses served by the system. Again businesses can use these ideas to create communities of practices within business functional area. Global enterprises can set up such ecosystems for people within the enterprise to share knowledge and information. Collecting best practices is an example and is discussed in Chapters 4 and 8.

Emerging nations find considerable value in setting up such clusters with the viewpoint of developing skills to go beyond doing the low-level work in most supply chains. Chaminade and Vang (2008), for example, describe the communities being set up in Bangalore, India, for the software industry. Most work in this area focuses on low-level design and coding of outsourced project. The goal of the community is to evolve the skills to higher levels of the design chain through increased collaboration in businesses in the area to transform the area into a regional innovation systems (RIS) approach. The communities here include Universities, Government, SMEs and technology centers and to strengthen the links between them to add value to each other's activities.

Youtie and Shapira (2008) describe a similar approach by suggesting the development of what are called knowledge hubs. They see an emerging role of universities as facilitators of such hubs that include SME, industry as well as major industry companies and describe creation of one such hub based on Georgia Tech in the United States. Such hubs can also be set up in businesses especially to share knowledge in business networks and supply chains.

7.5 Agricultural developments

Prime examples of digital ecosystems are agricultural communities in emerging economies. These share knowledge and information on better production methods. The result is the formation of large communities of practice developing best practices in food production. Such communities increasingly use mobile technologies where farmers in distant areas can keep track through the community using mobile phones or similar devices. Akram et al. (2008) and others, for example, describe the distribution of knowledge on farming techniques throughout distant Pakistani farms based on mobile technologies. It identifies the benefits made possible through the use of mobile to distribute such knowledge and describes advantages over previous systems based on remote kiosks.

There is obvious benefit in such networks to the participants as they can use this knowledge to raise their levels of food production. These again can be mapped to industry especially to the practice of mass innovation, which is described in Chapter 5.

7.6 Collaborative knowledge networks

The goal of all of these communities is to raise awareness about knowledge relevant to the community and to encourage community participation in using and further developing this knowledge. Communities of practice are often a first step towards the formation of more complex networking structures. There are now enterprises that are global in nature and require awareness to be maintained across all enterprise units. These are characterized by loosely connected that nevertheless must work in unison for some common good. They are characterized by the increasing trend for organizations to be seen as loosely connected communities of practice alongside organizational structures. They can be:

• Large global enterprises that may need to follow common strategies as well as share knowledge across distance;

- Community service networks as, for example, the most quoted one being health networks;
- Loose organizational structures such as global non-profit organizations;
- Start-up firms within a local area.

Design of such networks is proving extremely challenging as here benefits can be achieved through the use of information technology, although the technology must be carefully adapted to user preferences and gradually introduced. They must balance the social actions and goals of individuals with those of the community. Chapter 10 will cover such design and introduction later.

7.7 Trends in business application

Although many of the methods described in these earlier websites are in use in many businesses, they are not often integrated into their business processes. In fact the goal is to develop collaborative knowledge networks within enterprises and use them to support processes that lead to the creation and delivery of innovative products and services. There are, however, trends and initial applications to illustrate such as the strategic planning approaches used by Kodama (2005) and are described later in Chapter 4. It then forms part of the design of Chapters 10, 11 and 12.

8 Summary

This chapter defined processes as made up of a number of linked business activities. It also described the importance of other perspectives, especially social structure, knowledge and technology to business process design. The chapter described a number of additional requirements to be met in process design. These are summarized below:

- Processes must support business networks;
- Knowledge must be captured at each business activity;
- Technology must be chosen to support knowledge capture, creation and utilization across the business;
- Social structures that facilitate knowledge sharing must be created;
- Policies to build and sustain communities that share knowledge through networking must be developed;
- Processes must support the formation of relationships that lead to social capital formation;
- Technology must be introduced into a process not in a disruptive way but add value to peoples work.

The chapter stressed the need to use all of these perspectives in process design and to link them in ways that satisfy broad criteria. It also described the broad relationships between the perspectives. These next few chapters will describe the perspectives in more detail and the way of putting them together to form business processes.

9 Discussion questions

Question 1

Figure 2.5 described activities in business processes as composed of a number of levels. The top-level or the process workflow completes some well-defined goals – like arranging a travel itinerary. How do you understand the lower levels supporting this goal and why is it important to organize these levels to operate as productively as possible.

Question 2

You have now read a lot of books about driving a motor vehicle. Do you think you would have got enough knowledge on driving by reading books and would be very efficient in doing so? If not, what would you get the additional knowledge to improve your skill level.

Question 3

What would you do to use the four conditions proposed by Nahapiet and Ghoshal to improve collaboration in a travel agency? Here the emphasis would be on making travel arrangements for clients. What would you do to provide better services in a hotel? Here the emphasis would be on internal guest services.

Question 4

Designers must avoid socio-technical gaps when matching technology task. What criteria would you use to avoid this gap when providing ways to keep track of a project task, or following up a client query.

Question 5

What is the difference between networked communities and community networks?

Question 6

Find a number of other geographically oriented community sites from councils or government organizations and see what kind of information they provide to their users. Also find some communities and what their common interests are.

Question 7

What do you think characterizes a global enterprise? Is it the location of its offices and people or simply that it sells its products globally?

Case study 1

Data collection

A business, SALES-A, collects information on sales for its clients. A client nominates the products or services to be analyzed. SALES-A collects sales data, identifies purchasers and analyzes it as required by clients, as for example by demographics and regions. In its environment there is the client themselves, there are customers, who need to be identified, and there are SALES-A professionals familiar with ways of collecting sales information and analyzing it.

A business analyst, who is looking at ways to facilitate this process, has used the simple lightweight notation shown in Figure 2.13 to illustrate what is happening. In Figure 2.13:

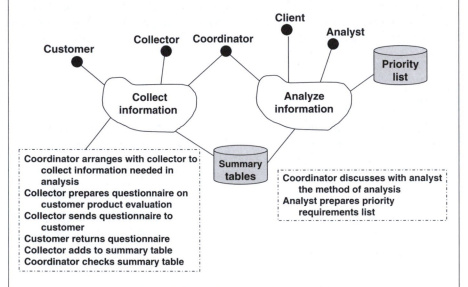

Figure 2.13 A business activity model

- The business activities perspective is shown as business activity model, where each business activity is shown as a clouded shape. In Figure 2.13 these are 'collect information' and 'analyze information'. Scenarios can be attached to each business activity to describe what people do in the activity and the relationships that are important in the activity. These relationships are determined by the roles undertaken by the person.
- The black dots represent roles that make up the social structure. These represent links from social structure to business activities. These links are described later in more detail in Chapter 3, especially in ways that people assigned in these roles interact to create knowledge.
- Information and knowledge is represented as disk shapes.

Figure 2.13 is a lightweight notation that shows the links between the perspectives and is described more formally in Chapter 9. Each business activity has a number of roles. Persons assigned to these roles then take on these responsibilities. Thus the collector is responsible for collecting customer information and creating summary tables. These responsibilities become their roles. Roles define what you do rather than what you are.

However, to practice using the notation, extend the process by creating one or more business activities where the results of analysis are used to suggest changes to products and services. To do this, extend Figure 2.13 to show some additional business activities and the roles.

This is just initial practice to develop an understanding of business activity models. The book will return to activity design in detail in Chapter 10 and then describe modeling in more detail in Chapter 11 that includes guidelines for designing business architectures.

Some further readings

Akram, A., Afzal, M., Zubari, J. (2008) 'Architecture for Extending Agrikiosk Services to Mobile Phones' *Proceedings of the 2008 International Symposium on Collaborative Technologies and Systems*, Irvine, California, May, pp. 144–148.

Leavitt, H.J. (1965) *Applied Organizational Change in Industry: Structural, Technical and Humanistic Approaches* (Handbook of Organization, March, J.G. (ed.), pp. 1144–1170, Rand-MNally, Chicago).

Nahapiet, J., Ghoshal, S. (1998) 'Social Capital, Intellectual Capital, and the Organizational Advantage' *Academy of Management Review*, Vol. 23, No. 2, April, pp. 242–266.

Prahalad, C.K., Krishnan, M.S. (2008) *The New Age of Innovation* (McGraw-Hill).

Tapscott, D., Williams, A.D. (2008) *Wikinomics: How Mass Collaboration Changes Everything* (Penguin Books, London, UK).

Vidgen, R., Wang, X. (2006) 'From Business Process Management to Business Process Ecosystem' *Journal of Information Technology*, Vol. 21, pp. 262–271.

Youtie, J., Shapira, P. (2008) 'Building an Innovation Hub: A Case Study of the Transformation of University Roles in Regional Technological and Economic Development' *Research Policy*, Vol. 37, No. 8, September, pp. 1188–1204.

Connecting People Within Business Activities

3

Developing relationships to help create innovative business processes

Learning objectives
- The importance of communication
- Context and Awareness
- Social Networks and Enterprise Social Networks
- Typical Business Activities
- Defining Roles and responsibilities
- Combining Social Networks and Business Activities.

1 Introduction

This chapter focuses on the social perspective of process design and describes the ways social structures should be chosen to support different kinds of business activities. It thus combines the business activity and social perspective. The emphasis is to provide structures that enable people to share and create knowledge through interactions supported by the social structure. Figure 3.1 also shows three major social dimensions that are now seen as important to achieve an innovative environment. They are the following:

- The vertical dimension is the degree of connectivity between people in the organization shown in the vertical direction. The greater the connectivity, the stronger the ties and the greater the development of new knowledge.
- The horizontal dimension is the amount of interaction or how frequently do connected people exchange information.
- The depth dimension is the amount of sharing of information shown in depth, which often is a personal choice, dictated by the organizational culture that rewards such sharing and is described in detail in Chapter 5.

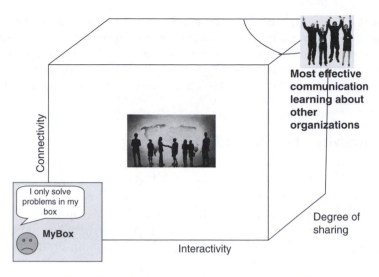

Figure 3.1   The important dimensions of networking

The main focus of Figure 3.1 is to show that communication is becoming increasingly important and that enterprises are placing increasing emphasis on developing policies that support and reward teamwork and knowledge sharing. The goal is to encourage behavior that maximizes the connectivity, interactivity and knowledge sharing in the organization. Businesses are placing more and more importance on people networking in business environments and looking for ways to get business value through networking. The networking goes beyond simply exchanging transactions but includes forming relationships that eventually lead to communities of practice and what was earlier defined as social capital. This environment leads to innovation through the constant discussions, ideas and suggestions that characterize highly interactive groups.

However, at the same time networking can begin to consume more and more time. Continuous exchange of messages and never-ending meetings can become time consuming and impact on productivity. Productivity, especially in an increasingly complex knowledge environment, is an important consideration when organizing ways for people to communicate.

Proper work organization can reduce the time needed to search for information, find people, ask for clarifications, negotiate and support many other interactions. Such productivity increases must now be achieved in the face of increasingly complex relationship structures. Questions that come up are what are the best social structures for connectivity and interactivity. The structure should improve communication relevance and minimize the time spent in communication for a given task.

Socio-technical considerations play an important role here. There are many different kinds of social relationships and these must be matched to the kind of work that people do. It is only by matching the people relationships to the task that socio-technical gaps are reduced and work progresses in a productive way. This applies both to the way that work is organized and to the supporting technology that must match the most appropriate networking structure. This chapter describes ways to classify work activities and structures suitable for the different kinds of activities.

2   Connectivity – Keeping track of everything

Connecting people is not simply providing ways for them to exchange messages. It is also to enable the kind of interactivity that facilitates new ideas, development of new products, or managing projects.

Connectivity also has impacts on the individual who is now in most cases involved in many interactions. In the previous chapter we described today's work environment for an individual. A person usually works in an environment like that shown in Figure 2.9, which was introduced in Chapter 2. It includes the following:

- Formal work with project teams that require keeping track of other people's work and reporting about your own work;
- Social interactions are needed for knowledge sharing and maintaining general awareness about your environment;
- Focused professional interactions in your work situation, for example management meetings;
- Keeping track of mobile workers; and
- Developing your expertise and your own personal information.

Staying connected in this environment can be a very time-consuming process. It requires communication with different people and groups on many topics. In a knowledge-based environment it means that the communication has to be productive in creating and sharing knowledge. This includes your own personal information, information about groups or projects that you are working on and general information about your work environment.

2.1   Improving connectivity – Context and awareness

There are two important considerations in ensuring a person's effective connectivity and interaction. These are context and awareness. Knowledge of context is important as it ensures that any actions you take are consistent with what is happening around you and become more productive in your organization. The context will depend on the kind of work carried out by the person. Expert work will often require a context that is wide and specialized. Strategic work on the other may require a context that is wide and covers a wide scope of areas. Thus designers of systems must consider the kind of work when designing systems to ensure that relevant information is presented to users.

2.2 Context

Context is a generic way to describe the environment in which the individual operates. It is important at all levels of business. For example, it includes the information needed to answer questions like "Are my customers happy with the service I provide?" or "Who can I get to solve this kind of problem?". To do this people require different kinds of information. They require access to documents and people, various manuals and internal reports as well as informal information, even rumors. We often talk about wide and narrow contexts. A wide context is one where information is sought widely and goes beyond a person's individual task. Narrow contexts are those that just focus on a particular task. These differences can be explained by looking at different professions. For example:

Accountants often focus on sets of financial transactions in some activities;
Marketing people usually have a wider context as they need to look beyond current markets and look for opportunities for opening up new markets;
Information technology specialists must keep track of technological developments as well as ways for business to achieve value from technology.

Later we also discuss some cultural implications of context. In particular where there is emphasis on historical aspects when planning their activities. Often these concern maintaining a brand image. Changes to branding need to be careful to ensure that customers happy with the brand continue to purchase the products associated with the brand.

2.3 Awareness

'Awareness' is another term that frequently pops up. It is along similar lines to context and really means knowing what is happening around you and supporting people with the tools to do so. It is also possible to define different kinds of awareness. The two most common are situational and peripheral awareness. The term 'situational awareness' is often used to indicate our awareness of the state of the current situation in which a person works in. Situational awareness is one where we need to be continually monitoring a situation. It usually applies to one business activity. Air navigation controllers or emergency systems are particular examples. In this case the worker must pay constant attention to changes in their environment.

Peripheral awareness is awareness of things that do not directly impact the current activity, but which we need to know. It is often presented as sidebars or ticker tape. Thus, for example, someone trading in shares must know their client requirements and share prices. They must also be aware of any economic announcements or personnel movements in companies. Another example is software developers, who must be aware of the current state of the program and available resources. However, information of potential requirements changes or changes to system software is also important. Furthermore, not all awareness is through information technology. Reading newspapers, for example, is also part of raising ones awareness.

2.4   The common options for keeping track of contexts

We have come a long way from the days of the telephone, FAX and mail as our main means of communication. Context goes beyond technology but includes reading newspaper reports, meetings with people and other titbits obtained in everyday work. Information technology is however one of the main avenues for receiving and organizing work contexts. There are now three fundamental ways to communicate using the technology. They are the following:

- The desktop, which can serve as a platform for keeping track of our personal files and sending them whenever necessary,
- Mobile devices, especially the mobile phone as a means of informal communication, and
- The Internet and Web services provided by it.

It is expected that contexts will be maintained as a combination of all of these with connections maintained between them. Mobile phones, for example, now have Internet functionality enabling them to share information posted on the Internet from desktops. What device is used can often depend on the kind of business activity and the best ways to maintain context within it.

3   Connectivity and interactivity

The most common way of connecting is just talking to each other either face to face or by phone or by e-mail. Information technology presents many other options. They can be simple exchanges of information or they can be longer term collaborations. It presents us with many ways to classify connectivity. One way is to distinguish between:

- Channel-based communication which in general is one-to-one using some medium. Here one or more people communicate directly using technologies such as a mobile phone, e-mail or even videoconferencing, and
- Platform-based communication is where messages are exchanged through a platform. Any message results in a posting on a common platform, usually a Web page or a message board. It can also be a notice board in a prominent office area.

Another popular classification is as *synchronous and asynchronous*. Synchronous is where the interactions are taking place at the same time, asynchronous is where they are taking place at different times.

Table 3.1 The Collaborative Dimensions

	Same time (Synchronous)	Different time (Asynchronous)
Same place	Face to face.	Bulletin boards that describe events.
	Meetings and discussions.	Project rooms for keeping track of
	Negotiations on complex situations.	project progress.
Different place	Video conferencing.	Message boards and blogs.
	Whiteboards	Mobile devices.
		Responses to requests.
		Comments on documents.
		Offers of products.

The type of collaboration chosen in most cases determines the kind of technology to be provided for collaboration. Table 3.1 illustrates a typical classification of collaborative work. It uses the dimension of time and place. Thus:

- Communication at the same time and place is usually face to face such as meetings.
- Communication in a different place but at the same time is often channel based with people discussing some topic by phone, or on a video conference, or perhaps instant messaging.
- Communication at different times is often platform based, with possibly the exception of e-mail. For example, if it is in the same place as often happens in shifts then messages can be left on special boards. If it is in different places, then portals are the most common implementation.

The kind of communication has to fit the goal of collaboration. Negotiation, for example, is often more effective if carried out face to face or at least synchronously, particularly in complex situations that involve many alternatives. However, there is a trend that where collaboration can be structured then asynchronous communication is used. Reviewing a document in most cases is carried out asynchronously. Many negotiations in supply chains are also becoming more structured and asynchronous. For example, negotiations between food manufacturers and supermarkets now use technologies such as message boards for asynchronous negotiation with offers from food suppliers posted for selection by supermarket managers.

3.1 The role of technology in improving productivity

The question then comes up what technologies do people need to maintain awareness in changes in their context. And how can technology improve connectivity and interactivity. Is a mobile phone enough for example? It probably is, if all you are doing is keeping track of the social activities of friends.

It is usually not enough to keep track of what is happening in a complex project. It is definitely not enough if you are involved in a number of complex activities. The question then is how to combine a number of technologies to improve connectivity.

There is no doubt that technology is now an integral part of life. Technology is used for both personal and organizational reasons. Personally we use technology to make appointments, ask questions and keep track of our appointments. We use it to keep in touch with our colleagues and friends and to coordinate work in teams. In all of these activities we use technology. Just look at your own work and ask yourself the question "What would I do if my computer and mobile was taken away from me?" – the answer in many cases of knowledge workers would be "not much".

Although technology has now almost become part of every day life, there are questions on whether businesses are getting full value from technology. Full value in this sense means using technology to optimize a person's productivity in their work.

It also requires the setting up the right social relationships and responsibilities to ensure that communication is productive in the business sense.

4   Social networking and social network diagrams

One way to model social relationships is by using social networking diagrams, which have been widely used for a number of years to graphically show the communications. These show the relationships between people in a chosen community. The most general notation is to show people as nodes and relationships between people as links between the nodes. The idea of the social network diagram is shown in Figure 3.2. Here each node represents a person and the link between two nodes shows that they communicate. Thus, for example, 'p5' communicates with 'p3' but not 'p4'.

Social network diagrams vary in their notation. Often additional information is included on the links, as for example the strength of the relationship depicted by the link. Distinctions are sometimes made between the nodes. Some diagrams like that discussed by Hu and Racherla (2008), for example, include two kinds of nodes, people and organizations, and the relationships

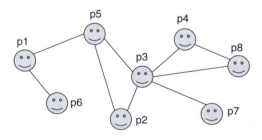

Figure 3.2   A social network diagram

between them. Analysis of social networks can be used for many other purposes, including:

- Finding experts by identifying people whose advice is often sought and who have contributed to organizational activities. Often these people are identified by numerous links with others, who seek their advice, or
- Arranging the location of people within a building by finding people who frequently interact and placing them in adjacent offices where possible.

4.1   Extending social networks to create enterprise social networks

Most writers on social networking refer primarily to informal exchanges between people. The exchanges are shown using social network diagrams like that shown in Figure 3.2. From a business perspective it is useful to extend social network diagrams to distinguish between work and social networking. This book uses an extension called Enterprise Social Networks (ESN).

The ESNs are labeled to show the intensity relevance. Such higher intensity also implies that relationships – the thicker lines indicate stronger relationships. The ESN notation used in this book is shown in Figure 3.3. It is a notation adopted in this book and by no means a standard. In fact there are no standards for such diagrams and this book uses the notation to make a distinction between social and work connectivity and the intensity of this connectivity. It distinguishes between work relationships (solid line) and informal social relationships (dotted lines). Thicker lines indicate more intense interaction, or where relationships are stronger. It is also possible to show the content of such interactions by attaching a description of the link content to the link.

The roles have defined responsibilities and the interactions required of the roles are also included in the ESN. These interactions indicate the kind of

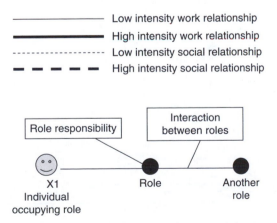

Figure 3.3   Labeling enterprise social networks

knowledge to be shared between the roles. The interactions indicate the kind of communication to be supported between the roles and the communication tools to be provided to support the communication.

It is assumed that business activities include social interactions, as most people in formal relationships also exchange informal information. Hence it is not necessary to draw two lines between them showing both kinds of interaction.

Work networking shows the necessary communication in the business process. It focuses on people's roles. Persons who take particular roles MUST communicate in the way defined by those roles. For example, Figure 3.4 shows the communication between roles in a business process, which responds to client trouble reports. Each role in this diagram is represented by a black node and the role name. The link attached to the role shows its responsibilities. These responsibilities also indicate the kinds of tools and services that must be provided to the role. The links between the roles are labeled by the interactions between the roles.

The links between the boxes show that the way people assigned to the roles interact or exchange information. This may be talking to each other, or exchanging notes or documents. The role responsibility is shown in the box linked to the link. Thus the agent receives the trouble report and sends it to the analyst, who selects the repairer. After repair a report is passed to customer relations to arrange a response. The manager supervises the activities.

People also communicate outside their formal responsibilities. This informal communication is shown by a social network diagram. The combination of social

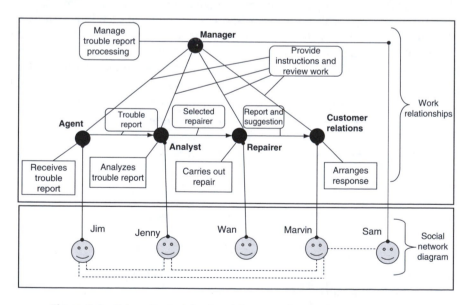

Figure 3.4   Enterprise social network for managing responses to customers

and work diagrams is increasingly called an ESN. It shows all the relationships, both formal and informal, between people in the organization. Figure 3.4 is an ESN as it also shows the informal communication within this system. The bottom part of Figure 3.4 includes the informal communication between them. It shows the people assigned to the roles and all communications between them. It shows people who actually take on the roles. Here Jim is the agent who receives the trouble report and sends it to Jenny, the analyst. Jenny determines the kind of trouble and sends it to Wan and so on. Sam is the manager and communicates with all the others to coordinate their work. In a real system there may be more people than that shown in Figure 3.4. The informal social communication is shown by dotted lines. The work communication is shown by the full lines.

In Figure 3.4, Jenny, Jim and Marvin are probably part of some social circle that regularly exchange informal messages. Wan is seen as excluded from this clique because he may be in a different location.

Social interactions may be totally informal where people exchange information about activities outside the organization or it may involve informally talking about the business process. In either case communication is important to build teamwork. Even informal exchanges build up stronger relationships and raise trust between the team members. Exchanges about the business process itself can improve process by people exchanging their experiences and making suggestions about improving the process.

It is of course possible to further enrich social network diagram with additional labeling. This can include labeling the nodes with their responsibilities and knowledge requirements.

5   Types of business activities

In any enterprise there are many people, each carrying out a different kind of work. It includes many business activities. Each activity often requires different kinds of communication. Furthermore, the kind of communication must suit the kind of activity in which people participate. These in turn will suggest the ways to use technology to support the work activity. The goals here are to arrange processes to minimize flows of information, reorganize work to identify duplicate activities and automate routine activities whenever possible.

Rather than seeing each activity as distinct it is often more convenient to identify the activity type and then use guidelines or templates to choose the best social structure for the activity.

5.1   Kind of work carried out by people

One way to classify business activities is by the kind of work. It mostly applies to knowledge workers. Table 3.2 illustrates a number of categories of work which have been well described by Davenport (2005) that characterize knowledge workers. The boxes also indicate the kind of support usually provided for the kind of work. Here:

Transactive work is routine work usually carried out by individuals responding to a predictable event, such as responding to an invoice or reviewing
a report, or a call center response. The work is usually defined as a set
of standard tasks. Transactive work is often carried asynchronously with
information passed between different users.

Integrative work requires some systematic approach and usually involves a
number of people. Information system development is one example. Here
we are concerned with standard procedures, project phases and monitoring
work progress. This is often asynchronous in nature and uses platform-
based communication. However, often issues have to be resolved using
synchronous communication.

Collaborative work is where there is considerable uncertainty that requires
contribution from a number of workers, such as, for example, resolving
an issue or negotiating a contract. What is needed here is flexibility to
decide on next actions, as for example an evolutionary development of a
report. This work often has a significant synchronous component. Mashed
up workspaces are often proposed for this kind of activity. These allow people to flexibly select from among a number of alternate communication
services.

Expert work is where an individual possesses highly specialized skills and
applies them in their work. Often requires searching for new ideas and
knowledge or reference to earlier cases or discussion with other experts.
Often work is asynchronous when gathering information but synchronous
when discussing its relevance.

Table 3.2   Kind of Work

Integrative	Collaborative
Systematic, repetitive Integration of functions Proformas, process states Standard procedures, process stages	Improvisation Flexible teams Expertise across functions Flexible workspaces
Transactive	**Expert**
Routine work Formal rules Support for one standard task	Requires judgement Individual expertise Earlier cases Cases, databases.

It should be pointed out that the kind of work described in Table 3.2 can be found at all business levels. So an activity can be described by both the kind of work in the activity and its management level. Thus, for example, costing of alternatives can be a task level activity at the strategic level. So can standard procedures for risk evaluation. Irrespective of the kind of work, the strategic level activities generally require a larger context with a wider set of connections than found in transactional work. Such connections may be fairly specific if working in an operational focus but more tacit within a planning focus. Similarly work on a strategic level requires more information than transactive work. Strategic work often requires contact with many people, access to enterprise information, and search support to get information.

6 Combining social networks and business activities

There are a number of commonly found role structures that can be used as templates in design. Such templates provide good design knowledge that is used later in Chapters 10 and 11 to design new business systems. They can then be used in design as standard patterns in design.

6.1 Leadership roles for transactive work

Transactive kind of work generally requires a direct work connection to people in the same task. Work here tends to be asynchronous where people carry out their designated task and occasionally interact with others. The context is usually quite focused in transactional work. Roles are usually classified as task workers or task leaders.

This is possibly the most often quoted role that is found in any business. The leader's responsibility is to define the tasks to be carried out within a team and monitor task progress. It includes maintaining awareness across the team and in facilitating knowledge sharing between the team members. The responsibility also includes motivating people to do the best possible in their work. Figure 3.5 shows alternate leadership structures. It shows the roles by black dots and example participants by faces. A box attached to the roles indicates the role responsibilities, and that attached to the link shows the kind of information exchanged between role participants.

Two alternatives are shown in Figure 3.5. One is where the leader role controls all activities. The person assigned as team leader, in this case 'a1', assigns work to others in the team and maintains strong communication to keep track of the work.

The other is where there is some delegation of responsibility with groups of team members responsible for different parts of the work. Here the communication between the leader and the team exhibits lesser intensity because it focuses on monitoring outcomes and not frequent checks on progress.

The kind of technology support needed by a leader is usually some planning system that enables the leader to keep track of progress of

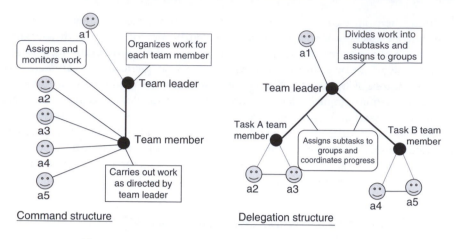

Figure 3.5   Enterprise social network of the leadership role

tasks in the group. The kind of knowledge needed here includes the following:

- Specific task knowledge and the resources and time required by each task;
- Ways to decompose tasks;
- Profiles of people needed to carry out particular tasks; and
- Ways to convey task requirements to team members.

Delegation needs further knowledge on ways to coordinate delegated activities. The reporting is now different as the leader assigns subtasks to groups of team members and focuses on ensuring that subtask outcomes are consistent. Delegation is often preferred with large tasks as responsibility can be allocated to groups. However, it is important for the leader role to ensure that collaboration takes place between the groups.

6.2 Coordination role

Integration work is generally one where awareness and context must be maintained within a specific work context, usually a project. It is a mix of synchronous and asynchronous work.

Here as shown in Figure 3.6, the coordinator ensures that a number of teams work towards the same goal. Figure 3.6 shows three teams each organized in the same way as Figure 3.5. They both look at the outputs of each team and the progress of the team in creating the outputs. The structure shown in Figure 3.6 can also apply to leadership roles where the leader is required to manage a number of teams.

Each team here can be modeled as a separate activity, usually made up of task-oriented work. The coordinator and team leaders together plan the project and agree on resources and completion times. The four roles together can be seen as a separate mostly collaborative activity.

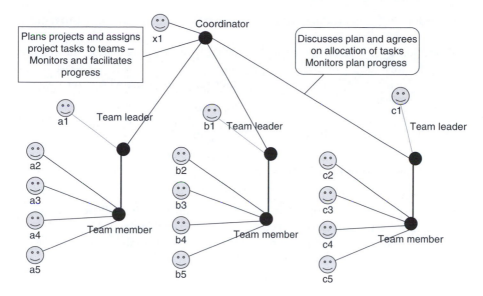

Figure 3.6   Enterprise social network of the coordination role

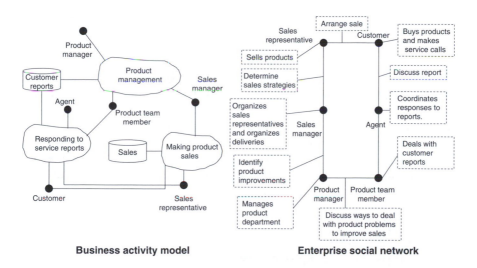

Business activity model	Enterprise social network

Figure 3.7   A combination of coordination structures

Coordination applies not only to teams but take place across teams and the enterprise as a whole. Hence there are many coordination structures in most business arrangements. For example, Figure 3.7 shows three business activities that include some coordination. Here:

- Making product sales by sales representatives that often requires coordination of salespersons;

- Coordinating the product department that includes product improvement using customer report; and
- Responding to customer reports, which requires coordination to resolve reports. Resolution of customer problems commences with a report to an agent which is usually passed to a product team member, who is responsible for its resolution.

These coordination structures are combined into the one ESN.

6.3 Facilitator role in collaboration

Collaborative work has significant synchronous communication and requires the development of shared visions. The context is usually wider in collaborative work as it requires keeping track of a large number of people and activities.

Figure 3.8 shows the facilitator role. This role is commonly found in collaborative work. Here the facilitator mainly observes the work of team members and passes information to them and resolves any conflicts and often brings contextual information to their attention. Common social interactions include discussions, raising ideas, making suggestions, resolving conflicts or helping negotiation between team members.

A facilitator role is quite common in many systems. For example, developing a strategic plan must often be facilitated by someone who can make suggestions on who to consult or bring useful information to the attention of planners. The facilitator often ensures that knowledge is passed between members of the group and also whenever possible to identify new and useful sources of knowledge.

The kinds of technology required must assist the facilitator to keep track of the work of team members.

Here the broker brings people together to carry out some business. Usually the broker has a number of clients, in this case 'c1' and 'c2', who need to develop relationships with others to solve their problems or enter into joint work to realize some opportunity. The broker must know how to solve problems or join with

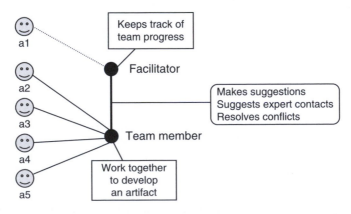

Figure 3.8 Enterprise social network of the facilitator role

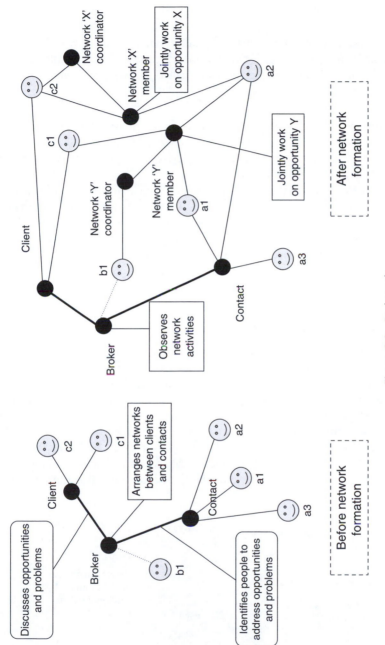

Figure 3.9 Broker role

clients to provide services. Thus a network often changes because of the broker's success in forming networks. For example, in Figure 3.9 two new networks have been created:

- 'c2' and 'a2' have become a network, called network 'X'. There is a network coordinator, in this case 'c2' has undertaken the coordination role, and
- 'a2', 'a1' and 'c1' are another network called network 'Y', which is coordinated by the broker.

Typical interactions between brokers and their clients include negotiation, resolving conflicts and explanations of the benefits of networking.

The most common technical requirement here is to keep track of the different clients and their expertise and goals.

The broker needs knowledge of their client's skills and ways to broker business arrangements between them. They require negotiation skills to bring people together and to arrange contracts between them. They must also have the personal skills to develop their clients' trust, arrange for clients to share knowledge and to develop joint ventures. Typical structures include setting up business networks or taking liaison roles in exchanging knowledge between collaborating groups.

6.4 Advisory or expert roles

The advisory role is one where one person, 'e1' in Figure 3.10, provides expert advice to clients. Often the one adviser has two assistants, 'a1' and 'a2' in Figure 3.10, to carry out some well-defined supporting tasks.

The adviser can be a financial adviser, a doctor or a consultant. Such collaboration structures are most often found in expert activities. The expert or adviser must continually keep abreast about evolving knowledge in their field. They search for knowledge from a variety of sources to build on their expertise. This can include searching through databases as well as attending meeting and conference where such knowledge is discussed. They also learn from their

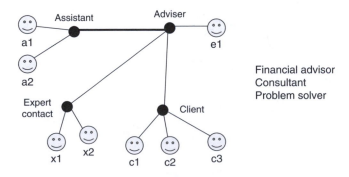

Figure 3.10 Enterprise social network of advisory roles

own experiences and that of their clients. Hence client follow-ups can be useful here.

6.5 Dual roles

One thing to remember is that roles refer to responsibilities and not to positions or individuals. In fact individuals often perform more than one role in an organization. The same person may be a coordinator on a group in a project but at the same time be an advisor to another. Dual roles often become an important factor in knowledge sharing. Passing knowledge from one project to another is one example. Serving a dual role in facilitating interaction between two culturally different groups is another. Here the same person may be a project coordinator in one group but a facilitator in another.

7 Choosing collaboration structures

When organizing activities it is often necessary to choose the right template and assign people to the roles. The choice must fit the kind of activity and also be consistent with the culture of the organization and the way it works.

Organizing to recruit a manager

Figure 2.1 in Chapter 2 outlined a process for recruiting a manager. In describing what people do the most obvious choice is the adviser role. This is the person who will use their expertise to decide how to find candidates and assess their suitability for the position. They will then arrange with assistants to follow a process to find candidates, interview them and provide assessments to the client. The ESN for this process is shown in Figure 3.11 and is based on the adviser template.

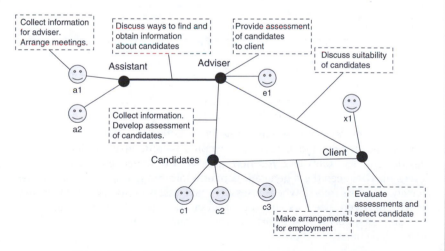

Figure 3.11   Enterprise social network for hiring a manager

It should be noted that in some situations a facilitator role may be more appropriate. This is where the client does most of the interviewing and selection and only needs assistance in finding suitable candidates and arranging meetings with the client.

Another example in business networking the situation may be an opportunity that requires assessment and determining a course of action to be taken by potential business partners externalizing it to their businesses.

Assessing the market

Figure 3.12 illustrates the roles and interactions found when collecting market information, which was introduced in Figure 2.2. It now defines the roles in the process and their responsibilities.

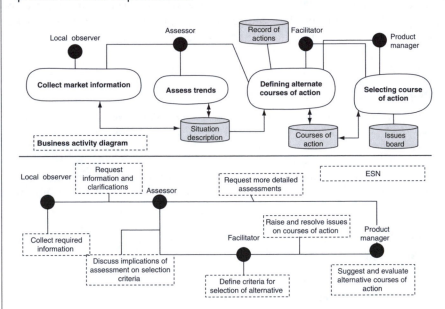

Figure 3.12   Market assessment activities

The business activity diagram shows four activities. One is collecting the market information and placing the records in a database called 'Situation description'. The roles involved here are 'local observer' and 'assessor'. The interaction between them generally concerns information clarification. The next activity is 'assess trends' where assessors make assessments. This is a facilitated activity between assessors and the product manager where issues are raised and discussed between assessors and the product manager. This is followed by selecting a course of action.

8   Using the enterprise social network in process design

One design objective is to identify standard patterns of work that are found in most environments. A design can then proceed at a high level by simply saying 'what we need here is a network that requires coordination between teams'. The alternative is to then start at the detail and allocating detailed work items to people. The higher level alternative presents a professional approach to designing team structures for business processes that require communication in achieving process goals. It also provides a way to identify the best technical platform to support the team structure. The platform chosen will be of the type that most suits the communication pattern commonly found in that type of team.

The ESNs are important for knowledge management. One important aspect of business process design is to define the roles and responsibilities of people and the information and knowledge they need to carry out these responsibilities. The other important aspect is the information and knowledge exchanged between role participants. Later in process design these can be used to define the contents of workspaces provided to role participants.

8.1   Simplifying connectivity

The following can be used to improve the process productivity:

- To simplify connectivity whenever possible to reduce the amount of effort needed to complete a task; and
- To decompose activity into their simplest form so that processes can be easily restructured.

Often productivity gains are made possible simply by rearranging communications. For example, look at Figure 3.13.

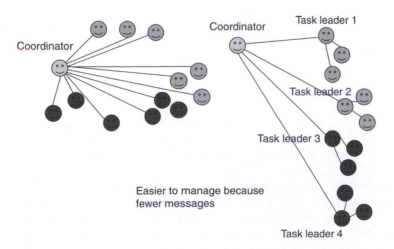

Figure 3.13   Decomposing activities into tasks to reduce connections

Here the coordinator is coordinating the work of 12 other people. The left part of the figure shows that the coordinator supervises 12 people. It means that the coordinator must maintain 12 links and monitor the progress of 12 people. The alternative is shown on the right-hand side. The alternative is to reorganize the 12 people into a number of task groups. In that case the coordinator only needs to communicate with the task leaders, considerably reducing the communication overhead.

8.2 Decomposing activities

Here the goal is to identify the most elementary business activities and then combine them into larger activities. Identifying the basic activity can use the activity classifications described earlier in Table 3.2. The goal is to ensure that each basic activity is of one kind. It is then that we can reduce the socio-technical gap between people and task and choose technology to match the task and in this way support the people carrying out the task. Reorganization requires analysis to see if an activity contains work of more than one kind. One typical example here is where expert work is combined with transactive work – here a highly qualified expert needs to routinely collect information to carry out their expert task, as for example a financial adviser collecting data on financial outcomes of different unit trusts. The usual way is to break this activity into two parts – the routine collection, which is assigned to one person, and the preparation of expert advice or reports. Other design criteria are to that knowledge is shared between activities and to avoid roles through which everything passes. More examples of such design are given later in Chapters 5 and 11.

9 Other classifications of work

Table 3.2 describes a classification of work most appropriate to this book. There are also other classifications.

9.1 Management levels

Traditionally business activities are classified into three management levels as defined by Anthony in 1965 and widely accepted since then. These levels together with the kind of collaboration that takes place are illustrated in Table 3.3.

Many of these activities require services to support them. Generally strategic planning requires services for conferences and meetings, management requires project planning tools and team spaces for team members, and operational groups require special tools for their tasks, such as designing products or organizing manufacture. In general strategic levels are likely to have wider contexts

Table 3.3   Management Levels

Management Level	Description	Outcomes	Collaboration
Strategic	Sets the organizations goals and objectives. It focuses on setting goals and negotiation and tradeoffs between different stakeholders in setting the goals. Joint planning and goal setting produces a strategic plan, where people jointly decide how they will work together.	Community formation Alliance formation Acquisitions Organizational goals	Meetings Issue resolution
Management	Resources are gathered and organized to achieve the organizational goal. Here the focus is on defining tasks, setting schedules, creating teams, assigning them to individuals and tracking progress.	Project plans Resource plans Progress reports	Team coordination Task assignment Designing work processes Progress monitoring
Operational	The tasks are carried out. Generally involves artifact construction, where documents, guidelines or instructions are distributed between responsible operational roles.	Documents prepared Products completed	Task management. Review processes

and require synchronous work, or at least quick exchange of interactions. For example:

Strategic level can include activities with a focus on task execution such as, for example, costing an alternative, or activities with a focus on coordination in arranging the collection of information, or activities with a focus on planning such as developing an acquisition plan.

Management level can include activities with a focus on task execution such as completing a planning document, activities with a focus on coordination such as monitoring progress, or activities focusing on planning such as arranging the execution of tasks.

Often we then look at the difference in the levels by what is produced at each different level. Again categorization may be useful here when we look at detail in work practices followed by people.

10 Summary

At the conclusion of this chapter, which introduced the social perspective, readers will be familiar with the need to choose the right social structures for a business activity. The chapter began by describing the importance of communication and then described different kinds of business activities and social structures that can be used in these activities. The chapter defined the concept of the ESN to model the social structures and provided a notation to model the ESNs for different activities and for the enterprise as a whole.

The chapter also provided a classification of the kind of work and then suggested the kinds of enterprise social structures for the different kinds. This choice of enterprise social structure will be used in later chapters as guidelines in business processes design.

11   Questions and Exercises

Question 1

What kind of work best describes the following?

(a) evaluating the cost of a standard project.
(b) advising a client on financial investment.
(c) arranging a tour for a group of people.

Question 2

How would you classify the following by kind of work and management level?

1. A person, who obtains sales from a salesperson, arranging deliveries to customers;
2. A medical practitioner providing advice to patients;
3. An accountant preparing a tax return;
4. A hotel reservation clerk assigning rooms to arriving guests;
5. Managing an outsourced project;
6. A person arranging the hiring of people;
7. An environmental officer in a city council.

Question 3 – Matching role to activity

You are given the following roles:

(a) coordinator,
(b) Facilitator,
(c) Broker.

You are also given the following business activities:

1. Bringing people together to form a business network.
2. Maintaining a relationship with an outsource partner.
3. Tracking and expediting the delivery of materials from a supplier to a building site.

Match each role to the most suitable activity. Draw the enterprise social network for each activity. For the selected role define its three main responsibilities.

Question 4

A group of six people went into business developing software. Initially they worked informally at one location. As the business grew they both needed to travel further to consult with new clients. They hired a number of junior developers and now have a complement of 30 professionals. Because of constant travel and increased clients they are finding it increasingly difficult to keep aware of what is going on in their projects and consequently their quality and delivery times are losing. As a result they are looking at defining clear roles and formal relationships between them.

They propose to introduce a project-oriented approach. Each project will be divided into a number of tasks and each task will have a team leader. Each team leader will be responsible for a team of about five developers. The developers use software provided by an external vendor. The six partners will focus on client liaison and defining client needs. They will also be the project managers of each project with team leaders reporting to them. Suggest some role structures for the organization. Possible roles are client, project manager, developer and external vendor.

Assume a culture where team leaders report to the project manager, who wants to be constantly aware of all interactions with the client and external vendors.

Question 5 (more difficult example)

Figure 3.14 shows a business activity model.

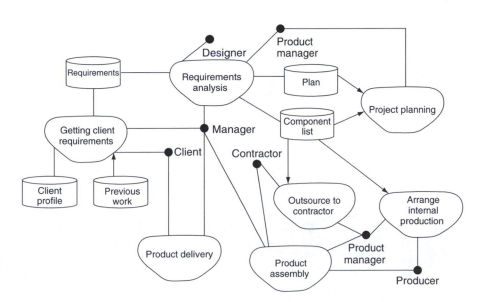

Figure 3.14 Business activity model for question 3

Draw an enterprise social network for Figure 3.14 given the following.

- The manager's name is 'Belinda'.
- There are three product managers – 'Greg'. 'Jie' and 'Mary-Lou'.
- The contractors are 'Gavin', 'Chris' and 'Kerry'.
- The producer is 'p1', 'p2' and 'p3'.
- Furthermore 'Greg' and 'Mary-Lou' are in Sydney whereas 'Jie' is in Melbourne.
- The other Melbourne-based residents are 'p1', 'p2', 'Gavin'.

There is little social contact between people in the different locations.

Question 6

Draw an enterprise social network for the activity diagram shown in Figure 3.15.

Here there are three activities:

Arrange a contract – the client requests the adviser to find an expert, who will work with the client to develop a design for a new product. This includes some negotiation between advisers and experts to find the best expert.

Develop a design – the client works with the expert to produce a design for a new product. This includes discussions on alternative designs.

Make a product – the client instructs their employees on the way to build the product. The client may need to clarify some issues to the employees.

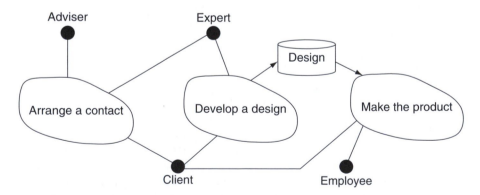

Figure 3.15   Business activity model for question 4

Case study II

Brokering in the sales process

Broker structures are often needed within organizations without them being formally recognized. One example is sales of complex sales arrangements, as for example electrical installations. Enterprise XYZ markets electrical installations for complex engineering projects. Here the sales team negotiates with clients, who are mainly large engineering construction companies. They may be building tunnels, bridges, buildings or other installations. Each construction requires a different electrical configuration, including special wiring and components. A requirement includes the following:

- A construction plan of the engineering project;
- Identification of areas to be lighted and lighting requirements;
- Special power distribution devices, such as transformers.

Sales staff use the plan to identify the special needs of the clients and provide solutions. To do this they continually refer issues raised by clients to internal expert groups to put together a working proposal. They may also need in some exceptional circumstances to include partners in their proposal. The process followed in basically one where:

- Members of the sales team identify the needs of the customer;
- The members of the sales team then refer the customer needs to internal experts for suggestions;
- The internal experts propose solutions and may need to collaborate to do so;
- These solutions are presented to the client, who provides comments;
- These comments are taken back to the experts; and
- The cycle repeats as new requirements and issues arise.

The sales team has a sales team leader and about three salespersons, who act as brokers between the client and experts. They also need to work collaboratively as a team. They also need to liaise with legal and contracts staff in drawing up any contract. There can of course be more than one sale going on concurrently usually to different clients.

Design an ESN to describe the interactions between the roles. Assume there is a set of expert roles in XYZ and sales persons, in the role of brokers, must identify the right expert for the different parts of the solution. You might consider a facilitator role to organize internal experts in responding to an issue. The best approach is to draw business diagrams like those in Figure 3.7, identify the activities and roles for each activity. Then draw an ESN for these activities.

Some further readings

Anthony, R.N. (1965) *Planning and Control Systems: A Framework for Analysis* (Harvard University Press).

Carrol, J.M., Rosson, M.B., Convertino, G., Ganoe, C.H. (2006): 'Awareness and Teamwork in Computer-supported Collaborations' *Interacting with Computers*, 18, 2006, pp. 21–46, Elsevier Press.

Davenport, T. (2005) *Thinking for Living* (Harvard Business Press).

Tapscott, D., Williams, A. (2008) *Wikinomics: How Mass Collaboration Changes Everything* (Penguin Group, New York).

Collaboration, Knowledge and Innovation

4

Bring people to work together in productive ways to the benefit of all

Learning objectives

- Describing knowledge
- Knowledge creation processes
- Managing knowledge creation
- Knowledge in Innovation
- Collaborative structures in knowledge creation.

1 Introduction

Previous chapters introduced business activities and social networking. This chapter continues by describing how knowledge management can be integrated into business activities to create dynamic processes that encourage innovation. This is where collaboration comes in. Collaboration is that property of social structure that enables interactions needed to leverage knowledge for innovation. Evans and Wolf give examples of the value of collaboration in the July 2005 issue of the *Harvard Business Review*. They describe the benefits of collaboration in both informal and formal business environments. Particularly relevant to business is the ability to quickly respond to unanticipated situations. One example of such quick response was the restoring of supply lines to a vehicle manufacturer following a fire in a component supplier site. The collaboration between suppliers and the company resulted in production being restored from an alternate supplier within three days following a major fire using the established social relationships within the supply chain.

This chapter thus sees collaboration not as a goal in its own right but in its role in encouraging knowledge sharing and innovation. It sees collaboration as the underlying framework for helping people to work together, to be innovative and to create new ideas as part of their everyday work. Such new ideas can lead to innovations in products and services that are needed to remain competitive. Innovation, however, just does not happen. Innovation must be part of an organizational culture and requires organizations to create the environment that both encourages and supports people to collaborate and come up with useful new ideas. The role of technology is also often raised here. Sometimes technology is suggested as a driver of collaboration. This is not the case. Technology can facilitate the collaboration needed for innovation. However, it is generally agreed that simply using technology for its own sake does not necessarily lead to either collaboration or innovation. Hansen (2009), for example, describes some experiences of collaboration resulting in no business gains and suggests that it is necessary to identify the business benefits of collaboration and set up collaborative structures to address them. Pisano and Verganti (2008) also agree with choosing the right collaborative structures and describe a number of different modes of collaboration. Again socio-technical factors must be considered to ensure that technology matches the way people work.

2   The role of collaboration in leveraging knowledge management and innovation

Innovation can take many forms. One distinction is shown in Figure 4.1. Here alternative 1 is where an instant response is required due to external pressure. Here, for example, a competitor to an enterprise may introduce a new product

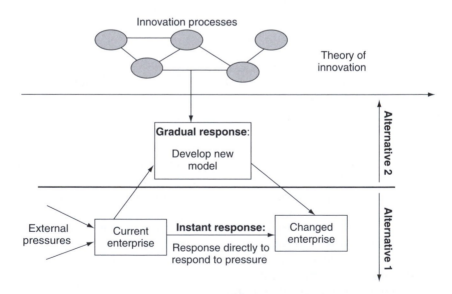

Figure 4.1   Responding to change

or new feature to an existing competitive product. The instant response is for the enterprise to add a competitive feature to their product.

Alternative 2 is a more gradual and planned response that not only looks at immediate changes but looks at projected trends using a process based on innovation theory. This may look at trends in the market place and develop a new strategy or model for doing business. It may use existing theories for organizing innovation and suggesting change. In either case there are many ways that organizations can reorganize their activities to make changes driven by the environment. The more planned change is not to simply respond to any threat in a unique way, but to organize activities in ways that an organization can naturally evolve in their environment, anticipate change and in some ways become a leading organization in their business domain.

2.1 What to change to encourage innovation?

Collaboration should go beyond exchanging information but must lead to people working together to comment on ideas, introduce new knowledge if needed and try out ideas in general. The relationship between collaboration and knowledge is shown in Figure 4.2, which illustrates three important dimensions that can be varied to enable an innovative environment. Figure 4.2 also shows the ways it can provide support to increase an organization's dynamic

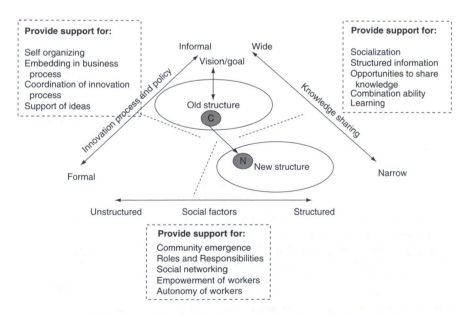

Figure 4.2   The dimensions of an innovative environment

capability. The three dimensions shown in Figure 4.2 that can be varied are the following:

- The social factors and policies that encourage behavior supportive of the creation of new ideas (Nahapiet and Ghoshal, 1998), and the emergence of communities to respond to new opportunities;
- Knowledge sharing by providing both explicit links to stored knowledge and opportunities to socialize with others to exchange and interpret their tacit knowledge; and
- Innovation processes and policies that encourage innovative thinking and its diffusion through the whole organization.

Organizations can provide the necessary support to move to a new structure that is more conducive to innovation. The changes are not only to the way technology is used. They can include social structures that empower teams with responsibility for innovations or providing more opportunities for knowledge sharing through socialization. At the other end there should be some measures of benefits to business value of providing such support. One measure often quoted as a measure of innovation is the proportion of sales of products or services created over the last few years, often three years.

3   What is knowledge and knowledge management?

Knowledge is something that is abstract in reality, it is hard to point to something and say there is knowledge. We can point to a computer and see it, a document and see it, a building, but we cannot point to knowledge. There are many informal ways to describe knowledge in some meaningful way. One common way to discuss knowledge is as in terms of the spectrum shown in Figure 4.3. This shows data at the lowest level. It is often created as a result of local actions or events. It consists of facts that may not be organized with any particular purpose in mind. Typical examples of data are temperature at some location at a given time, or the price of some item. Information is where data is organized in some particular way. Here temperatures may be sorted by time to show trends. Knowledge, however, is more difficult to define – one is to see it as using information to make decisions. Knowledge is more on knowing how to interpret information and providing new insights to some problem at hand. It is often using previous experience to interpret the information and use the interpretation to initiate some action. Thus knowing the temperature influences a person's choice of what to wear based on their earlier experience in similar weather. Knowledge arrives in many forms. It can be someone's experience with a new device. Even an e-mail message received with a comment on an emerging situation can be viewed as knowledge. Wisdom is still not generally defined. It is like having insights on new situations based on earlier experiences to provide expert solutions acceptable to stakeholders.

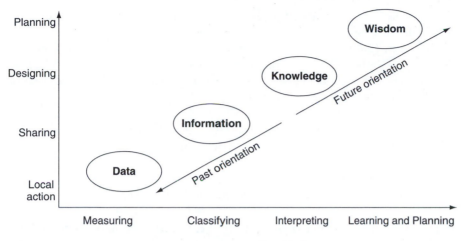

Figure 4.3   A view of knowledge

It is also the ability to transfer knowledge and experience from one context to another.

3.1 Tacit and explicit knowledge

One of the most common terms found in knowledge management is the distinction between tacit and explicit knowledge.

Explicit knowledge is easier to understand. It is knowledge that is codified, stored and easy to access. It can be structured and unstructured. Structured knowledge may be last years' sales, whereas unstructured may be stories about peoples' experiences with clients. This knowledge can be easily made available throughout an organization.

Tacit knowledge, on the other hand, is knowledge that people possess but cannot be easily codified. It is both a combination of physical facts and also the cognitive processes used by people that is not so easy to codify. It is a way that a person approaches and solves a problem. Some do it better than others. Thus two people can come up with a product design, and yet one is deemed better. Tacit knowledge cannot be stored. It can be used in many ways through seeking people's contributions to projects, their opinions or reviews of produced artifacts or in general discussion about some issue that can often provide new insights to others.

3.2 Describing knowledge

The more pragmatic people emphasize knowledge as an object that can be moved, stored and valued. Others emphasize the more amorphous nature as something that gives people the feelings and thoughts that they can use to develop new ideas. It is the difference between explicit and tacit knowledge. Often a balance between the two is found in practice.

Andriessen (2006) has noted this difference in the phrases used to describe knowledge. Rather than the pragmatic approach, they see knowledge as thoughts and feelings may be articulated, elicited, expressed, communicated or verbalized. Some of these are the following:

Knowledge as an object that can be created, stored, transmitted.
Knowledge as a living organism that evolves and grows.
Knowledge as a process.
Knowledge as thoughts and feelings.
Knowledge as a structure that shows relationships between objects.

In fact it is often a combination of all these and more and different people may see as a combination of any of the above – the difference is what we emphasize. The kind of ways that people talk about knowledge also varies and tends to indicate how they see knowledge. Another distinction is between Eastern and Western cultures, with Nonaka (1994) representing the Eastern approach whereas Davenport and Prusak (1998) are seen as typical of the Western approach. These are described later in this chapter.

3.3   Knowledge metaphors

Another way to describe knowledge is to use the idea of a metaphor. One metaphor introduced by Andriessen (2006) is that knowledge is like water. We need to make knowledge flow through the organization to give it life and dynamism. To make this happen we need to build 'knowledge canals' and should make sure that we do not lose knowledge like 'dripping taps'. Thus knowledge should flow like water through an organization bringing life and activity to the different components. Hence any facilitation should improve such flows. The role of knowledge officers can then be to provide these canals by using information technology. Another metaphor is that knowledge is like love. Here we talk about looking for new sources of knowledge, creating quality time, or reframing existing knowledge into new forms through interactions between people to identify new perspectives. Again facilitators should encourage such interactions. We return to the idea of metaphors in the chapters on design, where metaphors are used as design guidelines.

3.4   Knowledge assimilation

The creation and assimilation of knowledge are of primary importance in any strategy. Figure 4.4 shows two major issues in knowledge management. These are shown as two dimensions. The vertical dimension defines the amount of knowledge created in an organization. The horizontal dimension shows the pace of utilization of any created new knowledge. The ideal is to generate as much

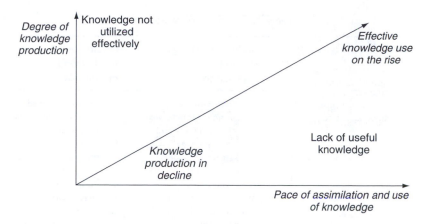

Figure 4.4   The growth of knowledge

knowledge as possible and utilize all the generated knowledge, the top right-hand corner.

Enterprises are thus faced with two goals – one to identify the best ways to create new knowledge and the other to effectively use it. The way this is done varies between enterprises – it is determined often by culture and type of enterprise. Knowledge on new ideas can be gathered from external sources, or alternatively it can be internally generated. Whatever the choice, enterprises must ensure that knowledge flows freely through the enterprise to enable innovation.

4   Activities in developing knowledge

So far this chapter outlined some ways to describe knowledge. The chapter now continues by describing what needs to be done to support knowledge management in organizations.

4.1   Finding knowledge

Apart from defining what knowledge is, another question that often arises is how to find it. This becomes particularly important in multi-national organizations, where people are widely distributed. There are advantages of distributed groups sharing knowledge, as some new idea developed in one group may be of value to others.

Knowledge workers find knowledge in a variety of ways. They do so by using various technical databases as well as personal networks by communicating with others who contribute to their knowledge and problem-solving ability. They have their specific sources that are authoritative in their area but at the same time continually explore other sources to discover new developments that may impact on their work.

Table 4.1   Finding knowledge

Searching for Knowledge	Finding out things known in an organization	Finding out things not known in the organization
What a person doesn't know about an organization.	Socializing within the organization – sometimes through social software.	Tapping into external environments. Messages from external contacts. Personal networks.
What a person knows about the organization	Using search tools and internal personal networks to find out more specific information – for example, how do I apply for leave? Explicit to explicit transformations.	Identify knowledge that is valuable to the organization through external networks that can indicate new perspectives useful to the organization.

Using sources not directly connected to a knowledge worker can improve effective knowledge creation. When the personal networks of knowledge workers evolve they can lead to new perspectives and interpretation on their own knowledge and thus add to their knowledge. Research (Szulanski, 1996), for example, showed that distributed groups are better at using searches to find knowledge from databases than co-located groups. This gets away from the 'group-think' mentality that often characterizes collocated groups and hence constrains their search abilities.

Table 4.1 provides some guidelines for finding knowledge within organizations. Here the rows indicate the state of knowledge of a particular person about an organization. The columns show what is known in the organization. Thus to find out what a person does not know about an organization is best achieved by socializing within the organization. Finding out what is not known in the organization requires tapping into the outside environment.

4.2   Retaining knowledge

Apart from the finding and creating explicit knowledge, it is also necessary to retain it for future use. Experiences are useful later as they provide insights into future actions. Storage of such experiences is often called organizational memory. It often means that previous mistakes are not repeated while good outcomes are made widely known. Storing knowledge has two aspects. Is it to be stored as explicit objects or as the intrinsic ideas and tacit knowledge as people – again the difference in the two approaches?

The first approach of storing and sharing knowledge is to develop a knowledge repository that can be later used throughout the enterprise. It is often referred to as the codification approach. This can include records of experiences and outcomes and interpretation of them. Thus any workspaces should give its participants both access to the repository and the ability for them to contribute to the repository. The knowledge repository is not simply, stored structured information. It also includes relevant experiences, stories and people's comments.

The second approach is often called the personalization approach, where knowledge is mainly held by individuals, who can be called upon to address new situations.

4.3   Transferring and sharing knowledge

At this stage it may be worthwhile to consider knowledge management from the viewpoint of a business process or an enterprise. Businesses emphasize knowledge management for a number of reasons. One is to encourage innovation. Another is to enable people to learn from their own and other experiences and retain what they have learned for future use. Finally transferring knowledge between organizational units also adds value to an organization. This is particularly important in cases where organizations or their supply chains are distributed across a number of locations.

The retained knowledge must be stored both for organizational use and as personalized knowledge. It can be codified or personalized knowledge. Some distinctions are shown in Table 4.2. Many organizations see advantage in codifying information as it can be readily distributed and transferred between units or people. Codified information is also of value to individuals in keeping history about past projects. Personalized knowledge is particularly important to individuals as it includes contacts of people with whom they work, whereas for organizations they provide knowledge of the location of people with expert knowledge as well as the application of the expertise and past experiences.

Table 4.2   Classifying retained knowledge

Context	Codified knowledge for organization-wide use.	Personalized knowledge
Individual needs	Past history of similar projects. Learning about the organizations and its ways of working.	Need to retain contacts about who knows what.
Organizational needs	Keeping track of stages of a supply chain. Development of social capital. Transfer between organizational units.	Knowing the expertise of staff to simplify selection for projects.

From an individual's viewpoint it is necessary to both retain codified and personalized knowledge. This was the approach used in consulting firms described in Hansen et al. (1999).

5 Directions for knowledge management

The next challenge is to propose processes for sharing and creating new knowledge. Two directions have been identified here. One focuses on social structures and interactions, as exemplified by Nonaka (1994), based on research on knowledge management in the manufacturing industry. The other championed by the work of Davenport and Prusak (1998), and focuses on more explicit process steps for finding, codifying and trading knowledge as a resource.

5.1 Nonaka's knowledge creation process

Perhaps the most quoted work on knowledge sharing is that of Nonaka. Nonaka's process is illustrated in Figure 4.5. It includes four phases. The first phase is socialization where people bring together their experiences and share insights in an area. It is basically a transfer or sharing of tacit knowledge. The next step, externalization, is where some of this captured expertise is interpreted into a form that can lead to some actions. The discussions now become more focused with specific issues being addressed and new ideas generated. Generally here tacit knowledge is often used to create explicit knowledge. The ideas are combined where necessary with existing information and then the outcomes of any actions are evaluated. The process then continues by further socialization evaluating experiences and so on. Different tools are needed at each stage. For example, ways are needed to both capture and share knowledge, including developing a common terminology.

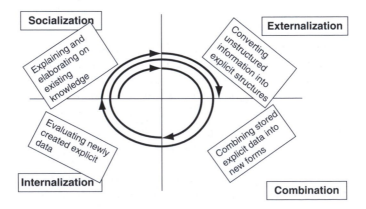

Figure 4.5 Nonaka's spiral process

5.2   Davenport and Prusak

Another often referred to model of knowledge is that proposed by Davenport and Prusak (1998). It is more pragmatic whereas Nonaka's approach is more abstract. The approach focuses on knowledge as an object on trading, codifying knowledge and storing it for further use. It proposes steps that can be easily implemented using information technology. The knowledge process here can be clearly defined and roles are assigned with responsibilities for the process steps. Here knowledge is treated almost as a commodity, something we can buy, sell, store or trade. This differs from Nonaka's approach where knowledge is more based on thoughts and feelings and the process followed in interpreting gathered information.

5.3   Forming perspectives

Boland and Tenkasi (1995) introduce another aspect of sharing knowledge – that of sharing perspectives or how people see things in their environment. Knowledge sharing is easier when people see things from the same perspective or have a common view. Perspective is shaped by culture and one of the goals of managing cross-cultural teams is that of developing a common perspective of any situation. The emphasis then is to form policies that lead to common perspectives in a firm. This again presents choices to managers to form their teams and the roles needed to develop common visions. Later Chapter 6 describes how perspective sharing can be used as a focus in communities of practice with support by social software.

Perspectives are important in the innovation process itself especially in developing metaphors that provide new ways to approach a problem. The example quoted by Boland and Tenkasi (1995) is that of the Wright brothers of seeing planes as flying a kite rather than driving a car in the air as helping them in designing their first plane.

5.4   Enabling knowledge sharing and creation

In the more concrete organizational environment the emphasis is on how to make knowledge sharing happen. How to improve knowledge flows? It looks at the enablers of knowledge management and what the organization must do to make knowledge sharing happen and in this way add to the organization's innovative ability. Again this depends on how we see knowledge – as objects or as abstract processes.

In the more concrete organizational environment the emphasis is on how to make knowledge sharing happen and improve knowledge flows. One way is to identify the kind of enablers that can improve collaboration and knowledge sharing. Figure 4.6 shows typical enablers that determine the extent of knowledge sharing in an enterprise. It focuses people exchanging knowledge, capturing it and reusing it.

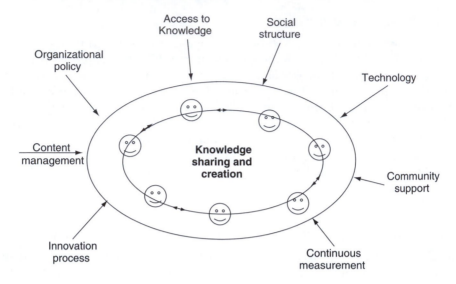

Figure 4.6   Enablers of knowledge

Knowledge enablers

- Organizational policy, especially the support given to management processes, to encourage behavior conducive of innovation;
- Providing access to both internal and external information;
- Content or what knowledge is to be captured and stored or where it can be found;
- Processes that capture and use the knowledge in ways that encourage innovation;
- Continuous measurement often in terms of newly developed products and services and accepted in the marketplace;
- Technology that supports knowledge management and the innovation process; and
- Social structures that define the responsibilities of people in the process.

Again socio-technical factors come into play here as all these enablers have to result in structures with minimal gaps between people, technology, task and organization. If the collaboration can be specified in some structured way, then the technology can be chosen to support this specification. The technology is then aligned at the operational level to the way the business operates. For example, an organization that customizes its products to clients would need different technical and sales support from one that mass markets its products.

5.5 Nonaka's enablers

Nonaka suggests a different set of enablers often described as the middle up and down way. These tend to focus more on the use of tacit knowledge through facilitating interactions between people.

Nonaka's enablers

- A clear definition of organizational intention to focus people's activities;
- Autonomy supported for knowledge workers to work on ways to realize the intention;
- Introduce chaos so that people identify ways to manage the uncertainty that it creates;
- Information redundancy;
- Requisite variety to enable responses to all possible issues that are identified.

---

6 Implementing strategies for knowledge management

Many organizations are now developing strategies for managing and leveraging knowledge. Strategy development for knowledge management is continuing to evolve as the environment becomes more dynamic and competitive. Most organizations use a mix of many of the ideas described earlier in this chapter. Irrespective of whether using the Nonaka or Davenport philosophy, knowledge gathering and assimilation become crucial to an organization. There are other suggestions. Earl (2001), for example, provides a strategy taxonomy that distinguishes between technocratic, economic and behavioral issues. The technocratic focuses on codification, connectivity and capability again closely following the codification stream. The behavioral side focuses on social issues and the economic on getting commercial value. The chosen strategy depends on the way an organization works and not necessarily its industry.

6.1 Codification and personalization

Most strategies aim at reaching a balance of the three dimensions – social, knowledge and process – shown in Figure 4.2. Early work by Hansen, Nohria and Tierney reported in the March–April 1999 issue of the *Harvard Business Review* distinguished between personalized and codified knowledge. This distinction almost corresponds to the difference between the approaches of Nonaka and Davenport. Codified knowledge management is one that focuses on capturing and storing information for later interpretation and use. They describe the development of knowledge management repositories by the consultancy of Ernst and Young, as it was known at the time, that resulted in sales closures of two months instead of the usual six or so as a result of the reuse of stored knowledge and proven procedures. On the other hand, as reported at the time the consulting firm McKinsey adopted a personalized strategy that focused on personal interactions. As reported by Hansen, Nohria and Tierney the approach adopted is not dependent on an industry but more on the type of work, with repetitive incremental work probably best served by a codified approach whereas work that requires unique solutions probably best served by a personalized approach.

6.2   Steps in managing knowledge

How is both organizational and personalized knowledge to be captured and created? The earlier discussion provides guidelines for knowledge management but not the actual process. Irrespective of whether it is codified or personalized there must be some way to capture, reuse and transfer it. In the extreme case it may be something just kept in a person's memory. However, in that case people do keep records of their contacts, client preferences and ideas that worked in the past. This is often stored in personalized databases such as those described in Chapter 3. Organizations are also looking at ways at capturing, recording and reusing organizational knowledge. The term 'organizational memory' is often used to describe such knowledge, which in most cases is of a codified nature. A typical knowledge management process goes through the following steps to create codified knowledge.

Step 1 – Define the kind of knowledge to be captured. Is it knowledge related to business strategy, improving organizational processes, knowledge about customers, technical knowledge or knowledge on delivering services?

Step 2 – Articulation of knowledge, where people's experiences as well as transactions are collected. Articulation can take many forms. It can be collected using technology such as blogs or by meeting or reviews of completed projects. It can be reviews of completed projects.

Step 3 – Filtration to remove unnecessary or irrelevant information, as for example arrangements for meetings. Filtering is used to eliminate that content which has no value and to condense other content. Often it also requires consolidating references to the same object into a single reference.

Step 4 – Codification where the knowledge is categorized using agreed upon categories. This usually requires a commitment or policy to define and maintain a classification scheme and support the classification of articulated knowledge.

Step 5 – Classification, storage and distribution by the kind of work carried out in an enterprise.

One question that arises here is whether management processes aimed at particular industries or businesses can be developed. Hansen and others have described the processes developed within consultancy organizations and the resulting benefits in providing codified databases and support tools used to simplify information retrieval and reduce routine work. Oshiri et al. (2008) have suggested a similar approach and developed a specific process to capture knowledge in software engineering processes especially where information must be shared in outsourcing across distance. In this way the categories are customized to a particular application. In the case of Oshiri, knowledge is classified in terms of the major parts of the software development cycle, requirements, design, construction and release management.

To go beyond capturing, knowledge articulation requires organizations to put in place social structures with people responsible for managing the articulated knowledge. For example, as reported by Hahsen, Nohria and Tierney, the former Ernst and Young established knowledge officer positions to codify, store and disseminate knowledge.

6.3   Knowledge officers

There was also a time early in the field of knowledge management to talk about the position of knowledge officers to manage knowledge. This has not been widely adopted as it is seen that knowledge sharing and management cannot be centralized. It cannot be the province of just some selected people. On the other hand, what is needed is for everybody to use information in creative ways and develop new knowledge throughout the organization. To expect one group headed by a chief knowledge officer (CKO) to develop knowledge for all aspects of the organization's activities is thus unrealistic. The trend is to create knowledge throughout the organization by enabling knowledge creation through appropriate enablers and providing the infrastructure to share the knowledge across the organization. A more important role of knowledge officers in such circumstances is to provide the facilities to support such knowledge flows but not to generate the knowledge itself.

7   The innovation process

The definition of innovation is quite elusive and difficult to describe in precise terms. In everyday terms it is things like finding a better way to do something, or producing something new that others want to use or ways to organize resources better. There are terms like 'process innovation' that imply improvement to existing processes or product innovation to provide products with new features. There is also a distinction between continuous innovation as opposed to one-off innovation, or invention, that generates a completely new device. Similarly, Popadiuk and Choo (2006) also distinguish between radical and incremental innovation. Here, for example, the WWW can be seen as a radical innovation that changed the way business is done. Improving the layout of a website is then seen as an incremental innovation. There is now also an emerging consensus that innovation is not a one-off step separate from ongoing business activities. On the other hand, it should be a continuous activity within any business process. It should be happening all the time. This ensures that products and services continually improve and the business process itself changes to be more productive. Even when innovation creates a new product it is of no great value if there is no interest in the product. Typical examples here are things like gas-opening umbrellas or cheese-flavored cigarettes. Thus innovation is not simply coming up with something new – it is also coming up with something that creates value for the business.

7.1 Innovation metaphors

Sometimes metaphors can help to understand what innovation means. To some it is like growing a pearl from a seed. To others it is like planting a seed and watching the plant grow while watering and fertilizing it. You plant an idea and then nurture it to fruition. The emphasis is on applying additional knowledge and expertise to improve the product or service. To others innovation is a journey through unknown territory like navigating a river in the search of fish. This implies changes in direction if necessary. Going global, for example, can be seen as an innovation for a particular business. All of these are metaphors that in their own ways describe innovation.

7.2 Innovation processes

How does useful innovation happen in an organization? How do you encourage innovation? These are the questions faced by many organizations today. There are no rules that will guarantee innovation outcomes. It is often a matter of encouraging behavior that leads to innovative outcomes and supporting such behavior. Some organizations formalize their structures to give innovation added importance and profile in the organization. They are based on generic processes like those defined by writers such as Dobni (2006). Generally a process is made up of a number of generic activities that are recognized as encouraging innovation. Figure 4.7 illustrates these activities.

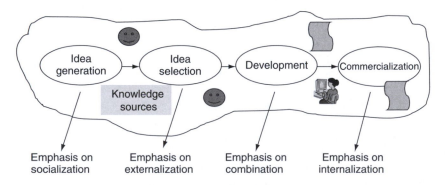

Figure 4.7   Innovation process

The process shown in Figure 4.7 closely follows Nonaka's SECI model. The first process step is the generation of ideas – it is mainly one of socialization. This is often part of a brainstorming initiative but it may also be something in response to client feedback.

This is followed by the evaluation and selection of an idea and its development into a viable product. The emphasis is on externalization or how to convert the idea into a form that can be attractive to customers. Development is then one that focuses on combination of known ways to create a product or service often using known components in different ways. The final part is the commercialization of the products that corresponds to internalization or creating knowledge about the acceptance of created products. In an increasingly networked environment, the activities in Figure 4.7 can include people from more than one organization. For example, it is common to include key clients or business partners as part of the process. They can quickly indicate what will be of value to them and lead to more effective commercialization.

All these steps must take place in an environment that provides continuous access to and sharing of knowledge. This knowledge can come from people, from documents or various searches. It may come from clients, or from people with experience in commercializing products. It must flow through the whole process to ensure good innovative outcomes.

There is also a tendency to classify innovation in many other ways. For example, market innovation is where new ways of distributing and marketing products are introduced. Administrative innovation is where changes are made to administrative structures to improve day-to-day operations. There is also product innovation where products continually evolve as customer needs change. There is also process innovation that looks at delivering products to clients in ways that lead to greater satisfaction through being involved in the delivery process. Irrespective of the kind of innovation, knowledge plays an important part in ensuring that any proposed innovation adds value to the business.

7.3 Adoption of innovation

It is often not the case that a new innovation is taken up quickly. Innovation is not automatically adopted by most people. Initially there are few early adopters. These are often known as champions of the innovation. Then the vast majority of people take up the idea followed by a few later adopters. Early adoption is often the result of knowledge about an innovation, which in turn gives a better understanding of the risk of adopting the innovation. Hence again the importance of knowledge management.

Providing knowledge about an innovation and demonstrating its relevance to potential users can speed up adoption. Such knowledge has the effect of reducing risk perceived by users in adopting an innovation. Often, 'champions' of particular innovations are also needed to speed up adoption. They become the early adopters, who by example illustrate the value and benefit of the innovation to others. They often help others to adopt the innovation and hence should be encouraged and rewarded by organizations.

7.4 Strategic communities in planning

An example of creating planning teams is that of Kodama (2005), who identifies strategic communities in organizational innovation. In this case the innovation was a telemedicine system to support veterinarians. This involved bringing together telecommunications companies, research groups and users to develop strategies for using their combined knowledge to deliver this service. Small strategic groups are set up to study different aspects of innovation. It began with SC-a, called the system innovators, shown in Figure 4.8, where researchers identified the ideal system for veterinarians.

Next SC-b composed of communication service providers was formed with the goal of developing communications system suitable for veterinarians. This was primarily composed of specialist communication system providers driven from inputs from the ideal system and those from SC-c, which were the ultimate users.

The structure can be generalized in the sense that any organization can proceed in its strategic planning through groupings suited to its business strategy. Thus one group may be looking at market opportunities, another identifying ways to develop new product, and yet another looking at marketing strategy. The work of these groups is coordinated to develop an organizational strategy. One suggestion from Kodama is that such groups be composed of

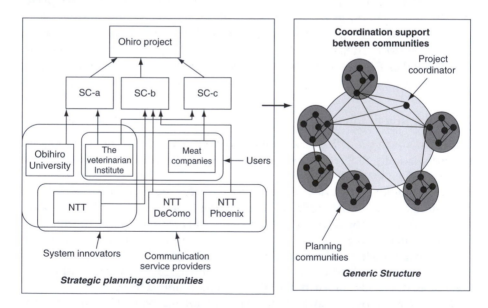

Figure 4.8 Innovation planning

middle-level managers, something that is also part of Nonaka's knowledge enablers.

The idea of strategic communities suggests a generic structure for planning. A possible generic network is shown on the right-hand side of Figure 4.8. This is made up of communities each focusing on a different part of a larger problem. Each community may represent a different professional or cultural group with coordination to exchange information between the groups. Thus one is idea generators, another is communication experts, and the third is users. Each community looks at the problem from their own perspective while coordination is needed to develop interfaces between the groupings.

Figure 4.8 is a typical generic structure of the way innovation can be organized. Figure 4.9 shows typical innovation activities each with a different work type and focus. Idea generation is primarily composed of a collaborative group and so is idea assessment and selection. The important difference is that there is also a coordination activity to ensure that innovation is encouraged and supported and eventually commercialized. Many organizations have ideas but lack the coordination which is now recognized as important in ensuring quick commercialization.

The collaboration network in Figure 4.9 shows the connections between team members in an innovation process. It shows three roles, team member in the 'idea generation' activity; assessor in ideas assessment activity and coordinator who coordinates the activities. The connections in the collaboration network of Figure 4.9 shows the links between the actual team members, who comment on each other's ideas. Here t1, t2, t3 and t4 are team members generating ideas whereas a1, a2 and a3 are assessing the ideas. These assessors can include key clients of the organization. People can also participate in more than one activity. For example, t2 is both a team member and assessor. It should be a continuous process that takes place all the time. The coordinator ensures that the right people are involved in the assessment. This is often essential when team members are distributed. The model can be further

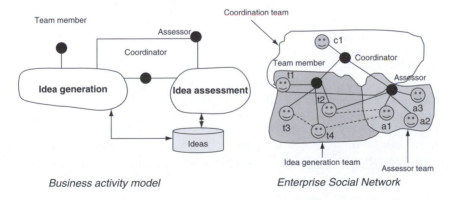

Figure 4.9   The initial part of the innovation process

extended to include groups for assessing commercialization including potential key users.

7.5 Strategies for innovation through open networks

Here organizations use their varied contacts to get ideas. For example, 'who knows how to do something?' The knowledge is seen as existing in the numerous connections that an organization might have. This is common in organizations that are predominantly driven by client needs. It requires contact with clients, partners and various experts. It needs brokers, bridges, gatekeepers, ambassadors to coordinate between the different roles. As a metaphor they are often seen as spaghetti networks with lots of connections between individual entities. For example, manufacturers use the many connections with their clients and distributors to get ideas or even good practices.

One example is that of Procter and Gamble as described in the March 2006 *Harvard Business Review* by Huston and Sakkab. They describe a strategy that goes from Research and Development (R and D) to Connect and Develop (C and D), for getting ideas that provide business value. They describe how Procter and Gamble required a solution for customizing the labelling of Pringle chips. They sent out a technical brief to its global network. A small bakery in Bologna, Italy, responded with a solution. This is seen as often a better approach than going through the usual process of brainstorming, evaluation, commercializing and patenting a solution yourself. Certainly it is much faster than setting up research and developing facilities to develop products internally. The strategy here is to develop a clear description, and a large network of distributors and users. Other examples include the following:

- Goldcorp, who published their geological survey maps on the Web and offered respondents rewards if they identified location of gold deposits from survey maps. They found a large number of responses that enabled them to mine the gold without the expense of setting up their own teams.
- Threadless.com, who seeks ideas on patterns for shirts. Basically anyone can post a pattern on the threadless site. This is evaluated by others in the open market, who give the patterns scores. Designs with high evaluations are then selected for productions with a sum being paid to the designers. Eventually based on such evaluations a number of patterns are chosen and placed in production. The poster of the pattern then receives a monetary payment, which can grow depending on the sales of the pattern.
- InnoCentive that invites people to share ideas and solutions across the Internet.

The 'connect and develop' approach is gaining popularity. The idea is to:

- Get suggestions and ideas for products and services from the open market
- Get reviews of the ideas from the open network
- Select those ideas that get the best open market reviews.

It is something that happens on open markets where stallholders can quickly assess what kinds of goods are selling well except now the open market is the Internet. The term 'mass innovation' is now increasingly used to describe this approach.

Mass innovation substantiates the common tendency for product users to themselves innovate to solve local problems. The pick-up truck is one example here. It is claimed that it was 'invented' by farmers themselves cutting out the back of a sedan car to enable carrying out large objects such as ladders.

7.6 Proactively innovating new strategy

Organizations often look for new directions to expand their activities. The goal here is to see whether their expertise can be applied in new ways – usually by positioning themselves in new markets. There are many frameworks for defining new positions. Bessant (2007) and others provide ideas for frameworks to guide such decisions. Figure 4.10 shows the kind of parameters used in the analysis to use an enterprise expertise to develop a new market position to their best advantage. These include

- New products and services and ways to improve them.
- The process and identifying any potential improvements in delivery to clients.
- Any change of paradigm. For example, if we globalize this means less close contact with clients. Alternatively going to e-learning with most students external is also seen as a new paradigm as we now use our knowledge in teaching but in a different way.
- Repositioning in the market place using the redesigned product and service. The entry of low cost airlines which can provide a core service to a different kind of client. Hence there may be less service but expertise in flying planes is made available in the new market.

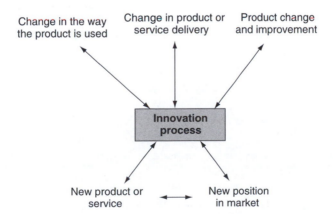

Figure 4.10 Positioning in the market

Irrespective of strategy and ways of gathering it is essential to choose collaboration structures that ensure the flow of knowledge between people in the enterprise.

7.7   A generic model for responding to situations

A generic model of innovation that draws on the earlier ideas is shown in Figure 4.11.

This model is made up of the following activities:

Identifying the situation, where some indications of an opportunity or threat become apparent and require responsible people to be informed. Usually this is indicated through messages from various external contacts, who are aware of an emerging situation. This closely corresponds to Nonaka's socialization phase and usually requires some support from a local analyst.

Assessing situations, which is an activity that is usually carried out by an analyst. It often requires quick interchanges of information between the local and analyst roles to define the scale and nature of the situation. Often the analyst classifies the reports into internal functions that have to internally deal with them. This now includes externalization as external reports are compared to internal status to see their implications.

Defining courses of action, which is an activity to identify any response action and the resource requirements to do so. The activity defines plans and identifies tasks and responsibilities to carry out the actions. It requires continuous consultation between various internal stakeholders. This is now closer to Nonaka's externalization, where knowledge is externalized into the units of the organization. The objective here is to set goals and identify gaps between goals and current situation to suggest actions.

Selecting a course of action, including a plan and assignment of tasks to functional units. The kind of roles envisaged here are coordinator roles as well as task leaders and members.

Execution Planning, where functional units are initiated and task leaders, and team members assigned.

Execution, where the task leaders and members carry out their designated tasks, including coordination between functional units.

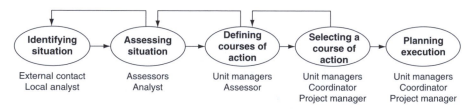

Figure 4.11   Innovation in response to environment change

A particular application is to assessing the market situation introduced in Chapter 2.

8 Some guidelines for matching collaboration to business activities

One goal of design is to choose the collaborative structure that satisfies the business goals.

8.1 Awareness – The simplest form of collaboration

Awareness is perhaps the least difficult way to specify collaboration. It simply requires any change or action within a particular activity group or process to be made known to all its members. Awareness basically means keeping everyone aware of what is happening, which in turn indicates what they are required to do. It is what many meetings are about, where people with similar problems describe their experiences. Usually awareness is maintained through notifications using mailing lists where organizations inform their staff of any new developments within an organization, a project or a group. Notifications can be personalized to reduce the number of notifications sent to individuals. Notifications can be important in global organizations to keep people distributed across the organization aware of what is going on throughout the organization.

9 Guidelines for collaboration in business activities

The way collaboration proceeds often depends on the type of an activity as well as its scope. A good way to proceed is to identify activity type as defined in Chapter 3 and match it to the kind of ESNs identified in Chapter 3. Table 4.3 provides some guidelines for choosing collaboration structures for simple activities. It provides design knowledge that is used later in Chapters 10 and 11.

9.1 Example – Integrative task focused activity – Developing reports

Developing reports is a typical example here. In most cases the work here is carried out at the operation level, is composed of the execution of a task and is primarily integrative in nature. The task execution is often integrative as it can pass through a number of review stages. It requires a facilitator to ensure that the process is systematic. A typical ESN is shown in Figure 4.12. Here there may be a number of authors that must collaborate to produce the document. There is often a facilitator, who ensures consistency and reviewer to ensure quality. On the other hand, if the development was totally collaborative the social structure would be like that for the small team shown in Figure 4.12.

Table 4.3 Task collaboration

Kind of Activity	Process and Knowledge Sharing	Enterprise social network/Technology
Transactive.	Process: Each member carries out a precise task. Emphasis on knowledge related to the task. Knowledge goal: combine different knowledge in an ordered way to complete a task. Created knowledge: better ways to carry out the task.	Social network: Usually a peer structure with coordinators, leaders or facilitators. The leader or facilitator ensures that work flows through the team in the most effective way. **W: Transactional, F: Task Execution** Sequential work · Coordinator · Analyst · Leader · Joint work Technology: Workflow support systems to keep track of job progress.
Collaborative	Process: Facilitating people to jointly develop an artifact. Critiquing rather than reviewing. Knowledge goal: Establishing relationships. Agreed ways of jointly developing artifacts. Defining responsibilities for different parts of the artifact. Improving quality of produced artifacts. Working together on the same task within the task context.	Work structure: Usually self-organized collaboration although a large group may need a facilitator. **W: Collaborative, F: Task Execution** Facilitator · Small team · Large team Technology: Usually a portal together with a blog or discussion system.
Integrative	Knowledge goal: The general goal here is for development of artifacts and improving quality through comment and critique. Created knowledge: Ways to facilitate creation of different kinds of products.	Process: Facilitator to ensure knowledge flows between **W: Integrative, F: Task Execution** Large team · Facilitator · Author · Reviewer Technology: Wikis are being currently suggested as a technology for this purpose. Planning and monitoring system needed for a larger project.

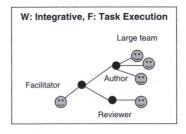

		Collaborative database: Issues board to agree on progress. Shared user views. Responsibilities of different users.
Expert	Knowledge requirement: Specialized service provided to client. Created knowledge: Kind of advice useful for different kinds of clients.	Work structure: Expert is the central element in creating knowledge. May have associates to provide comments.

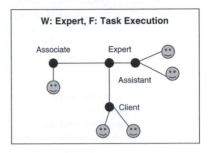

Technology: Case studies, data mining.

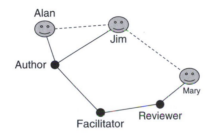

Figure 4.12   Typical enterprise social network in document development

10   Combining activities into larger networks

Most organizations have a large number of activities that must be combined or coordinated to reach a wider goal. Consequently the ESNs become larger. They usually include the roles from each of the combined activities together with roles that coordinate the activities. These are described in Table 4.4.

Typical examples here are team management, which includes outsourcing and coordination of selected activities.

10.1   Emergent large-scale activities – Combining planning, coordination and task execution

Activity coordination can include a large number of activities (see Table 4.4). The outcome can be a large number of overlapping processes. These large-scale interorganizational activities are discussed in more detail in Chapter 14.

Table 4.4 Combining activities

Type of combination	Process/Knowledge Sharing	Enterprise social network/Technology
Combining collaborative tasks	Participants themselves develop local processes. Jointly create and develop artifacts within the wider context of the process across functional units thus speeding up the system. Kind of work: Defining processes and process roles. Definition of relationships between tasks. Explicit definition of work activities and responsibilities. Created knowledge: Location of experts. Previous process experience for reflection and evaluation.	Social Network: Defining and agreeing on roles and assignment of people to roles. Facilitation of progress. Process: Group meetings to resolve issues. A program board to keep track of activities. Often happens in strategic planning or change management. 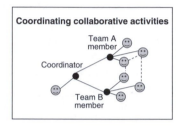
Integrating transactional work	Local teams collaborate to create parts of a larger artifact. The activity of each team can be integrative or collaborative in nature. Created knowledge: Ways to combine tasks into integrative processes.	Social network: A coordinator role ensures progress of each team to a common goal. The coordinator and nominated facilitators of each team can form a coordination group. Typical example is software development teams, where each team is responsible for one part of a larger artifact. 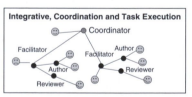
Combining the work of experts.	Putting expert opinions to address a problem. Created knowledge: Ways to combine expert opinions.	Often found in consultancy work. Tender evaluation teams are another example. There may be experts for different parts of the tender. The facilitator ensures that such expert knowledge is located and combined. 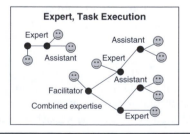

Table 4.5   Emergent large-scale processes

Kind of activity	Process/Knowledge Sharing	Enterprise social network/Technology
Enterprise-wide collaboration	Extending collaboration between activities. Developing shared plans. Devise coordination strategies between organizational units and processes. Develop and agree on enterprise-wide work processes.	Social: Building relationships: Identify new communities. Build on previous plans. Process: Support for group emergence. Understanding of previous experience and activities of external organizations for evaluation.

10.2   Example – Assessing emergency situation

One design approach is to define the activities and their type of work. Then choose the social structure that matches the kind of work using the guidelines.

Activities in responding to emergency situations

Typical activities to determine a quick response to an emergency situation are shown in Figure 4.13 and include:

- Reporting the emergency situation and collecting details about it, a transaction activity composed of a number of transactions made by observers;
- Assessing the situation to determine what kind of response is needed. This is often a combination of expert and integrative work. The roles chosen are assessors, who are usually expert at their work, and a coordinator or facilitator to integrate their work.

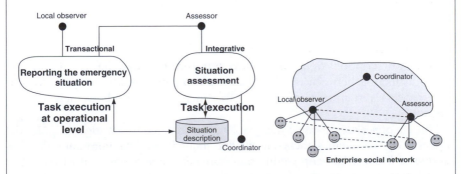

Figure 4.13   Initial parts of situation assessment

The next two stages are shown in Figure 4.14. These are to define and select courses of action using the assessment. There is now collaboration between the emergency team and the service providers to respond to the situation. Once agreed upon the service providers will carry out the actions they agreed to. Task execution becomes the responsibility of the service providers.

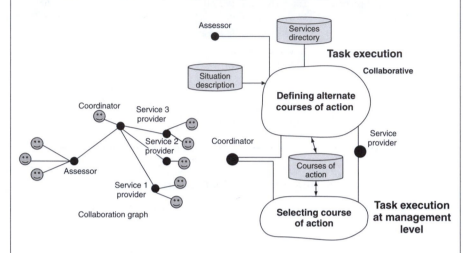

Figure 4.14   Creating and choosing a course of action

The selected courses can include the following:

- Determination of whether there is a need to keep track of effected individuals and find shelter for them;
- Arranging the deployment of a response team;
- Identify the type of equipment needed and its sources;
- Ensure equipment delivery to the emergency site.

11 Summary

This chapter focused on knowledge management. 'Knowledge management' is a term that is difficult to define and yet plays an increasingly important role in the design of business systems. The chapter introduced a number of definitions or at least descriptions of knowledge management. Perhaps the most important is the distinction between tacit and explicit knowledge. It then defined knowledge processes in an abstract rather than concrete way and how they facilitate innovation.

This chapter also identified the enablers for knowledge sharing and potential organizational strategies and policies. The focus is on collaboration and forming teams that can develop common goals to effectively share knowledge. The emphasis is on groups that have common cultures and ways to integrate the different groups through organizational structures. The next chapter continues this by describing the influence of culture on knowledge sharing.

12 Questions and exercises

Question 1

What is the difference between Nonaka's and Davenport's approaches to knowledge management and their implication for organizing teams?

Question 2

Use the idea of Kodama's strategic communities to develop a plan for promoting a city as a tourist destination. Use the ideas of strategic communities in Figure 4.8 and identify the kind of strategic communities that would be involved in formulating a strategy. Describe the kind of collaboration needed in your strategic communities and develop enterprise social networks for them.

Question 3

Evaluate the usefulness of the generic structure in Figure 4.11 to respond to developments in a business environment. As an example, consider responses where a new competitor arrives in the market place, or a change in government policy that favors your business.

Question 4

You should note the difference in Questions 2 and 3 with reference to Figure 4.1. Question 2 focuses on a gradual planned response (alternative 2 in Figure 4.1) while Question 3 focuses on a quick response (alternative 1 in Figure 4.1). Which do you think is easier to implement and what is the difference in the social structures between the two alternatives.

Case study III

Installing and managing back-up power installations

Corporation PowerGen sets up power back-up systems for its clients. These can include major hotels, telecommunications providers, health establishment whose goal is to minimize disruption given a major power breakdown. Back-up systems can include power-generating equipment or battery systems. Such installation usually requires PowerGen to carry out some analysis of the building to determine the right power-generation configuration. They also require PowerGen to maintain and monitor its equipment to ensure continuous readiness. There are also increasing enquiries on using solar power where battery back-ups are proposed.

Case study III

Continued

Usually PowerGen nominates a manager for an installation. The manager then maintains the relationship with each of their clients to initially install the back-up system and then provide services to carry out any extensions or repairs. This does not mean being responsive to client needs by reactively responding to their requirements but also proactively suggest new directions. Development managers are continually faced with devising ways to suggest new ideas for power generation. They must also respond to new requirements from existing clients.

The growing base and distribution of increasing PowerGen clients is creating difficulties for managers to maintain relationships and develop the expertise needed to provide the ever-increasing variety of services requested by clients at numerous locations. PowerGen has been looking at ways to support the global nature of its business especially in ways to provide services following initial installation to maintain a continuing and productive relationship with the client. The range of installations and their distribution is making it difficult to maintain expertise at its different locations.

In line with the more service-oriented approach to solution delivery PowerGen is creating solution teams for clients as suggested by Cova and Salle (2008). They find potential providers in different locations and set up relationships for their clients. This especially applies to solving failures in the equipment that requires setting up a team. The teams can be dynamic in nature and depend on the service to be provided with a different team for a particular service.

Elaborate on ways for PowerGen to maintain productive service arrangements with the clients. To do this:

- Define a strategy using the alternatives discussed in Section 7.5.
- Propose a way of organizing PowerGen activities on the assumption that supports virtual teams that may require coordination across different regions.
- Define the enterprise social network for your chosen alternative. First define the structure to service each installation and then how to coordinate the installations.

In doing so, look at the possibility of building up a distributed 'innovation network' or a 'business hub' for PowerGen clients, composed of the client, PowerGen contacts and local experts.

Client requirements could be posted and virtual teams could be established to provide the required solutions, taking into account the need to establish responsibilities for individuals assuming roles in virtual teams (Lee-Kelley and Sankey, 2008). The strategy must provide capabilities to quickly getting expertise and suggestions to respond to problems with the generation equipment and its installation.

Some further readings

Andriessen, D. (2006) 'On the Metaphorical Nature of Intellectual Capital: A Textual Analysis' *Journal of Intellectual Capital*, Vol. 7, No. 1, pp. 93–110.

Boland, R.J., Tenkasi, R.V. (1995): 'Perspective Making and Perspective Taking in Communities of Knowing' *Organizational Science*, Vol. 6, No. 4, July–August, pp. 350–372.

Davenport, T.H., Prusak, L. (1998) *Working Knowledge: How Organizations Manage What They Know* (Harvard Business Press).

Dobni, C.B. (2006) 'The Innovation Blueprint' *Business Horizons*, Vol. 49, No. 4, pp. 329–339. Elsevier Press.

Evans, P., Wolf, B. (2005) 'Collaboration Rules' *Harvard Business Review*, Vol. 83, No. 7/8, July–August, pp. 1–9.

Hansen, M.T., Nohria, N., Tierney, T. (1999) 'Whats Your Strategy for Managing Knowledge' *Harvard Business Review*, Vol. 77, No.2, March–April, pp. 106–116.

Hansen, M.T. (2009) 'When Internal Collaboration is Bad for Yor Company' *Harvard Business Review*, Vol. 84, No.3, April, pp. 83–119.

Kodama, M. (2005): 'New Knowledge Creation Through Leadership-based Strategic Community – A Case of New Product Development in IT and Multimedia Business Fields' *Technovation*, Vol. 25, pp. 895–908. Elsevier Press

Krippendorff, K. (2008) *The Way of Innovation* (Platinum Press, Avon, Massachusetts).

Minzberg, H. (2009) 'Rebuilding Companies as Communities' *Harvard Business Review*, Vol. 84, No. 4, July-August, pp. 140–143.

Nonaka, I. (1994) 'A Dynamic Theory of Organizational Knowledge Creation' *Organization Science*, Vol. 5, No. 1, February, pp. 14–37.

Pisano, G.P., Vergatti, R. (2008) 'Which Kind of Collaboration is Right for You' *Harvard Business Review*, Vol. 83, No. 8, December, pp. 78–86.

Culture and Knowledge Sharing 5

Bringing people to work together and share knowledge

Learning objectives

- The importance of culture
- What is culture?
- Describing culture
- Institutional and professional cultures
- Relationship between culture and communication
- Impact of culture on knowledge sharing
- The influence of socials factors
- The influence of intercommunity factors
- Changing culture to encourage knowledge sharing
- Managing intercommunity work
- Organizational problem solving.

1 Introduction

This chapter examines the relationship between the social structures and knowledge perspectives in process design. It continues from Chapter 4 with a more detailed examination of knowledge sharing from a social perspective. Knowledge sharing is growing in importance in today's businesses with the increasing realization that effective use of knowledge can lead to innovative outcomes. One process design goal is to create the social structures that encourage knowledge sharing that in turn can lead to such innovative outcomes. However, do not assume that knowledge sharing takes place as a given. There are many social and cultural issues that lead to people hesitating to share knowledge, including fear of loss of ownership, time considerations or fear of their knowledge being misused or misinterpreted.

The focus on culture has been increasing because of the global nature of many businesses, which in turn requires people in different countries, or in the same or different organizations to work together and share knowledge to achieve a common goal. Global business takes many forms ranging from outsourcing selected activities to strategic alliances. One obvious example is outsourcing manufacturing, such as, for example, apparel manufacture or software development, often to India or China. Cultural differences in the way people work in different countries or organizations often need to be considered when setting up working relationships across boundaries. This is particularly the case where knowledge must be shared across cultures.

As a result, management is now paying increasing attention to culture. Cultural differences of course do not apply across nations only. They can apply to two organizations in the same country or even different business units in the same organization. Each such organization can work in different ways and again these different ways of working must be coordinated. Figure 5.1 identifies a number of cultural contexts. First there is the national context that follows some common national norms. These are often influenced by national laws, for example industrial laws. Then there is the institutional or organizational context, which in general inherits the national norms but modifies them in line with its needs. Then there are groups and teams within the institutional culture. The structure of these teams is influenced by general institutional norms and its policies and reward structures. Finally, individuals within these groups define their work practices in ways consistent with institutional practices.

Within such environments, management is required to:

- Set institutional policies that encourage an innovation culture in local groups and individuals and sharing of knowledge across institutions. This includes institutional reward structures as well as formal recognition of innovative outcomes.
- Coordinate processes and teams across different cultures.
- Consider culture when introducing technology as the technology must fit in within the cultural norms. Other questions include what are the cultural characteristics to best deal with complexity or alternatively ways to encourage creation of organizations that can easily respond to change.

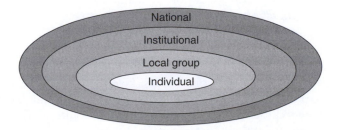

Figure 5.1 Cultural relationships

1.1 Globalization

One driving factor for the greater focus on culture is globalization or the increased propensity of enterprises to span their everyday activities across the globe. Globalization has always been here. The natural curiosity of people has led to exploration and trade across continents ever since time began. Marco Polo travelled to China, and for many years the East India Company brought goods from the east to Europe. Shipping lanes were already well developed before the twentieth century. The difference now is that everything is happening faster and almost all organizations now participate in global or cross-organizational relationships.

One question that arises is how do you describe globalization and use that description to determine how to work in a global environment. A detailed study of globalization can be found on the Princeton University site titled International Network Archive (INA) on http://www.princeton.edu/ina/. It contains a large number of statistics displayed as tables or graphs that describe a number of parameters to show the increase in global activity. These include the following:

- Growth of multinational corporations. For example, the number of McDonalds or Starbucks outlets across the globe;
- The growth of telephone traffic; or
- The tourist traffic or is it the amount of trade.

All of these have been increasing over the last few years. It is also interesting to note that much of the increase has focused on earlier relationships. For example, telephone traffic patterns still focus on previous colonial links. Thus these earlier cultural links still have a large influence on today's global patterns.

From the perspective of business processes, globalization places increasing emphasis on communication and networking across cultures. It especially calls for greater attention to be paid to cultural issues in facilitating knowledge sharing.

This chapter provides some choices that business system designers can make in selecting social structures and human support systems to encourage knowledge sharing. It provides ways to describe culture and the way people work together in different cultural contexts. It then discusses the implication of culture on knowledge sharing. It provides a set of guidelines for designers to select social structures that encourage knowledge sharing.

2   What is culture?

Culture is comprised of assumptions, values, beliefs, norms, behavior patterns, thoughts and actions of its members. Example of beliefs are things like 'Project management is good' or 'Global expansion is good'. Culture effects behavior, as for example those who think 'project management is good' are more likely to work to deadlines and provide progress data than those that do not.

People with different values and beliefs often find it difficult to work together. For example, if one person believes that 'project management is good' and another believes that 'project management is unnecessary', then they will find it difficult to do things like plan or monitor progress together. Changing a culture requires changes to such beliefs, values and behavioral patterns.

Another example of the influence of culture applies on the value placed on relationships with customers. Here values may be things like 'Customer closeness' or 'Doing the right thing'. Conflicts can often arise here. For example, globalization usually results in less 'closeness' to customers. Organizations that have built close relationships with customers may then need to change this culture if they decide to grow and become global.

2.1 Describing culture

One of the more widely referred frameworks for describing culture is that developed by Geert Hofstede to describe and compare cultures. The framework resulted from studies of 100,000+ IBM employees through attitude surveys taken in 1968–69 and 1971–73 within IBM subsidiaries in over 50 countries. He proposed the following five dimensions to explain systematic differences in work values and practices at national level.

Power distance – This dimension is defined as the extent to which the less powerful members of institutions and organizations accept that power is distributed unequally. In high power distance cultures, people are much more comfortable with a larger status differential than low power distance cultures. High power distance cultures construct hierarchies whereas low power distance cultures endorse egalitarianism.

Uncertainty avoidance – This dimension refers to how comfortable people feel towards ambiguity and deal with uncertainty. Uncertainty avoidance is the extent to which a culture feels threatened by unknown or uncertain situations and uses written or unwritten rules to maintain predictability. Cultures which ranked low (compared to other cultures) feel much more comfortable with the unknown. Motivation for work comes from achievement. Cultures which ranked high in uncertainty avoidance prefer formal rules and any uncertainty can express itself in higher anxiety than those from low uncertainty avoidance cultures. Motivation for work comes from security.

Masculinity and femininity – This dimension refers to expected gender roles.

'Masculine' cultures tend to have distinct expectations of male and female roles in society. They value independence, aggressiveness, dominance and physical strength. Women are subordinated to male leadership.

'Feminine' cultures have a greater ambiguity in what is expected of each gender. They value interdependence, compassion, empathy and emotional openness. They seek consensus, cooperation and sex role equality.

Individualism and collectivism – This dimension is defined by the extent to which individuals' behaviors are influenced and defined by others. Individualists prefer self-sufficiency and to satisfy person needs. Collectivists recognize their interdependent roles and obligations to the group.

Long-term versus short-term orientation (Confucianism and dynamism) Long-term orientation cultures tend to respect thrift, high savings rates and perseverance, status and order in positions, or sense of shame.

Short-term orientation cultures tend to respect social and status obligations regardless of cost ('keeping up with the Joneses') and low levels of savings.

A website (http://www.geert-hofstede.com/) provides parameters for a large number of countries as well as the ability to generate graphs that show the difference between selected nations. For example, using this website raises differences between the United States and China. The major differences are in the long-term orientation and the greater emphasis on collectivism is in the Chinese culture. It in fact reflects a difference between the East and the West.

Hofstede's results have been questioned on a number of factors. The most common critique is on the fact that the study was carried in the context of people working in the information technology industry. Nevertheless the measures introduced by Hofstede are now very commonly referred to and results in emphasizing collectivism and power distance have appeared in many other studies. One of these is that by O'Hara-Deveraux and Johansen (1994) on their implication to globalization.

2.2 Context and time as part of culture

O'Hara-Deveraux and Johansen (1994) in their book focus on cultural differences experienced in trade between US and Japanese businesses. They developed similar descriptors, which are shown in Table 5.1. In this table, context is very similar to the long- versus short-term orientation defined by Hofstede. Distribution of power is similar to power distance. These parameters are consistent with the work of Hofstede while extending aspects to information flows and

Table 5.1   Parameters defined by O'Hara-Deveraux and Johansen

CONTEXT	TIME
National outline	Monochronic vs. polychronic
Meaning of Language	Past/present/future
Historical perspective	
Space	
Peoples standing	
DISTRIBUTION OF POWER	**INFORMATION FLOWS**
Authoritarian	Linked or compartmental
Loosely Coupled	Straight to the point or not
	Developing background

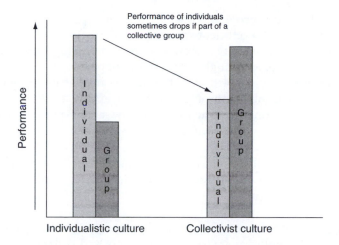

Figure 5.2   Effects of cultural mismatch on individual performance

time orientation. Their studies identified differences between cultures especially in power distance, individualism and in time orientation.

One impact of culture is on decision making. In cultures with a large power distance decisions, even of a minor nature, are often made at the highest organizational levels. Similarly in cultures with a large context, it may take longer time to make decisions, as a wider set of issues have to be considered.

2.3   The relationship of community and individual culture

People's behavior is often a cross-section of their own culture and that of the environment in which they work. People with a predominant culture often feel at ease working within the context of another culture. Figure 5.2 shows one such effect. Here the left part of the graph shows the performance of an individual as compared to the group within an individualistic culture. The performance of the same individual often tends to fall within a collectivist environment, although the performance of the group as a whole can rise. This may be caused by a change of reward structure, where individuals get rewarded on their individual outcomes.

3   Institutional cultures

Much has also been written about institutional culture and its influence of the way teams and processes operate. There are many ways to describe institutional cultures. They include the following:

- Process-oriented versus results-oriented, where, for example, government organizations tend to be process-oriented to illustrate provision of equal service to everyone.

- Job-oriented, where people follow well-defined practices to accomplish processes in the most efficient way, to employee-oriented cultures that emphasize social acceptability of new systems and development of innovative cultures, as for example through communities of practice.
- Tightly versus loosely coupled, which generally implies more independence and decision-making ability throughout the organization.
- Pragmatic versus normative or acting in the most appropriate way in a given situation rather than using agreed standard responses.

Using metaphors is another way to define organizational or project culture. Jeffrey Sonnenfeld (www.managementhelp.org/org_thry/culture/culture.htm) has another categorization.

- Academy – highly skilled employees usually stay in the same organization
- Baseball team – employees are free agents with prized skills
- Club – fitting into the group
- Fortress – employees uncertain about their position in the organization and focus on securing their position.

There are also other categories here, as for example seeing an institution as a:

- Family – where there is mutual support between all members; or
- Neighborhood – where there is emphasis on developing mutually agreeable surroundings.

The influence of institutional culture is particularly important for knowledge sharing and trust. These rely on cultures that build the social capital, which is needed to facilitate innovation within enterprises. Institutional culture can affect work of all kinds, whether it is planning, coordination or task. All of these will be affected by reward structures and policies set by institutions. Leidner and Kayworth (2006) provide a more detailed summary of relationships between the different layers shown in Figure 5.1.

3.1 Professional cultures

Professions also have their own cultures. For example, Figure 5.3 shows the relationship of context to different professions. Hence the suggestion here is that professions characterized by specific tasks such as maintaining accounts or program development work in a narrower focus than, for example, management, marketing or human relationship management that often require a broader view of a given situation. Values also tend to vary between professions. For example, engineers designing critical systems such as airplane controls are more likely to be risk averse as failure can result in disaster. Marketing managers, on the other hand, may be more experimental in choosing media for marketing campaigns, as alternate media can be chosen in case of insufficient response. Terminologies are

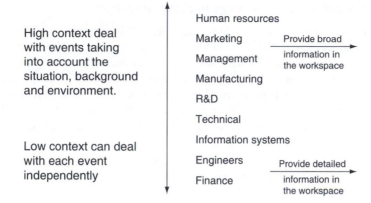

Figure 5.3   Contextual differences between professions

also different in different professions where the same word can mean different things.

Equally, professional cultures can themselves be in conflict with organizational or even national culture. Leidner and Kayworth (2006), for example, describe cultural differences that influence the acceptance of information technology into an organization. One of their results is that where uncertainty avoidance is a strong cultural characteristic, there is more resistance to the introduction of new technologies.

4 Communication and culture

Cultural differences can often act as a brake on working towards common goals, and management should encourage breaking down cultural differences by bringing people together to work towards common goals. Culture has a large impact on the chosen communication structures and in assigning role responsibilities.

Currently there is considerable interest on cultural differences in the growth of business with China. Martinson (2008) notes the strong emphasis on collectivist culture in China. This has resulted in the growth of Guanxi, which are groups with strong relationships in which members can prevail upon each other for help and to develop the trust to share important knowledge and retain this knowledge within the group. They are both cultural but also imposed by the institutional environments, including a tendency to be protective of group knowledge. The Guanxi can become predominant in business dealings as reliance on trust on people and the sharing of knowledge is often confined to the group. Burrows et al. (2005) also report a preference for transfer of knowledge through interpersonal contact rather than formal or written forms. Communication here is often contextual, making it difficult to communicate by electronic means. Contextual communication discourages short messages and in most cases a message must describe the impact of content on all group members.

4.1   The importance of language in communication

Language has a major role in communication within enterprises. If we cannot communicate using a common language we cannot work together. It is, however, not only the structure of sentences that is important but also how different cultures interpret any statements. Hence even using the same language construct can often lead to misinterpretation. Even a simple statement like 'How are you?' can instigate a different response. In some cultures it can invoke a simple 'I'm OK', whereas in others it is seen as a question that requires a detailed description of their current feelings and activities. Of course, such communication is only possible if people use the same language. The English language plays an important role in this communication as more and more people adopt English as their second language.

How prevalent is English? Over one-quarter of world's population has some ability in English (world population = 6 billion). This is especially the case in those involved in professional work in industries such as aviation, business, diplomacy, higher education, mathematics, science and technology. Its role as a second language in most countries has also grown dramatically since 1950. Wikipedia reports that it is the official language in 53 countries as well as in the UN, the European Union and the Commonwealth of Nations. Wikipedia reports that it is the first language for close to 400 million and second language to another 1,400 million, giving a total approaching 1.8 billion. It can thus be considered as a global language for now and in the immediate future.

It is, however, apparent that language plays an important role in cross-border flows when one looks at outsourcing. Most outsourcing occurs between countries that have English as their first language. It illustrates the importance of a common language in global arrangements.

4.2   Language and the Internet

A study of websites has shown the prevalence of English on the Internet although this has dropped recently mainly due to an increase in Chinese language sites. A report by Global Reach (http://www.glreach.com/globstats/index.php3 shows that as at 2004 English has been the predominant language on the Internet with 35.2 per cent of sites based on the English language. Chinese accounted to 13.7 per cent and Spanish 9.4 per cent followed by Japanese (8.4 per cent), German (6.9 per cent) and French (4.2 per cent). It is almost certain that recently the proportion of Chinese language sites has grown.

4.3   The influence of the Internet

The Internet has had considerable influence on culture. It encourages a particular behavior and sense of values. There is now almost an Internet culture evolving with people extensively using the Internet. Most people believe that e-mail is good and are beginning to value the information on the WWW. There are of course negative effects of the Internet, such as the belief that 'everything on the Internet is correct' being held by some people. Relying on all work through the Internet can also lower the value of interpersonal communication and the resulting sharing of tacit knowledge.

4.4 Implication for website design

Internet design is also influenced by culture (Wurtz, 2004). Multinational organizations do not just translate Web pages from one language to another for different countries. They whole page needs to be redesigned to reflect the national culture. For interest, you can look at differences in the sites of selected global organizations. McDonalds is a very good example here. The home page of websites in nations with primarily individual cultures often emphasizes individuals. Home pages of those in nations with primarily collectivist countries often emphasize groups or families. Similarly the choice of colors often depends on culture, with red more likely in Asian websites, green in Arabic and blue in countries with an English background.

5 Culture and knowledge sharing

Culture influences people's approach to knowledge sharing and hence plays an important part in process design and is one of the key elements of good business system design. It leads to benefits that include sharing of experiences, improved quality and innovation in products and services, or reduced delivery time of services through better processes.

Knowledge sharing, however, cannot be taken as a given. There are many issues that arise in knowledge sharing. Some people are reluctant to give away knowledge. As a result, management now places greater emphasis on culture or how to coordinate the work of people with different values and behavioral patterns.

Researchers have suggested that it may be worthwhile to examine the relationship of different cultural parameters on creativity. Research is not conclusive here but there are some early indications. If we refer to Hofstede's measures, which were discussed earlier in this chapter, the general comments here are the following:

- There is some anecdotal evidence that generally collectivism is better for creation of new knowledge than individualism;
- Uncertainty tends to stimulate knowledge sharing and creation;
- Long- or short-term orientation – long-term tends to focus on best practices,
- Power distance, however, does not seem significant in innovation.

Thus culture is not an inhibitor to innovation, but different innovation processes may be followed in different cultural settings.

5.1   The influence of social factors

Knowledge sharing is not a given in any situation. It requires a willingness from people to share their knowledge. Enterprises are in the process of developing ways to encourage knowledge sharing as it is recognized that it can lead to innovation. This, however, requires recognition that there are many reasons for people to be hesitant in sharing knowledge, while at the same time creating the environment that removes these inhibitions. There are many reasons why people may not be so willing. They include the following:

- Why give away my knowledge as it will make more valuable;
- Loss ownership of knowledge where others may use my knowledge to my detriment;
- Should I share my knowledge with a group with which there is some organizational or personal conflict;
- Loss of standing by giving away your expertise;
- Organizational behavior in attributing your knowledge contribution to others;
- Opinions being observed by supervisors with potential adverse effects.

Knowledge sharing can be further influenced by institutional or intercommunity factors.

5.2   The influence of intercommunity factors

Intercommunity work usually involves people who have limited common knowledge and do not frequently work together. As such they often do not have a shared sense of identity and have different values and behavior patterns. Intercommunity factors can be between people in different nations, in different professions or in different parts of the same organization. The differences in the culture of the communities and their embedded knowledge can influence the degree of knowledge sharing.

One common example that has received considerable attention is the cultural differences between information system developers and business users. Here users value the new functionality provided by new systems, whereas developers may value the type of technology used to build the system.

Embedded knowledge is one characteristic that is often ignored. For example, consider professional cultures. There are differences in the knowledge possessed by people in different professions. The embedded knowledge of a user in a financial department is that of accounting systems, whereas the application developer knowledge focuses on computer technologies. Similarly accountants and health professionals may have completely different terminology and objectives. This again results with very little common knowledge and hence reduced common identity.

Another is the lack of identity or purpose between groups. This, for example, often occurs in mergers when people often retain close associations with their former groups rather than forming new relationships.

5.3 The importance of trust in knowledge sharing

Trust is one of the essential conditions for knowledge sharing. It plays a major role within teamwork as people rely on each other to support them in their work and to contribute to the effort and knowledge needed to carry out their tasks. Culture plays a major role here, as trust centers on beliefs that individuals have on the likely behavior of others in honoring their obligations or misusing any shared information.

Often trust can only be developed over a long period of time as people's knowledge of others results from extensive interactions over time. This includes trust in the knowledge provided by the person, their ability to carry out their promised work, and knowing that any knowledge provided to that person is used with respect and acknowledgement. It can also develop from messages received about individuals from others.

5.4 The influence of technology

Technologies are now increasingly used to support communication to share, capture and retain knowledge created through social interactions. Such interactions can generate useful knowledge on the way decisions are made and criteria for such decisions. Generally the kinds of things retained using technology include idea records, rationale for any changes, reasons for decisions, ways problems were solved and other knowledge that may be useful later.

Such views or skills can become records that are widely available and can remain for a long time. Many people in business situations do not like to record their opinions and suggestion for others to see. Making a positive response to an idea that is later rejected could be seen in negative light later. Revealing negotiation skills is also something most people do not like to reveal. As a result social software tends to be used more in the less threatening conversations then in decisions for actions. Designing requires some way to describe such networking structures, their responsibilities and the knowledge they generate.

6 Reducing resistance to knowledge sharing

Organizations who wish to encourage knowledge sharing should establish a belief that 'knowledge sharing is good' and foster this by providing motivation support and reward systems. Two approaches are often identified – changing the culture of the whole organization to encourage knowledge sharing or organizing individual project groups in ways that facilitate knowledge sharing. This is particularly important to project-based organizations, which can benefit from sharing knowledge across projects on best practices, access to expertise or process improvement.

Most projects in project-based organizations do not have the possibility of changing organizational culture but must assume a given culture. However, as suggested by Ajmal and Koskinen (2008) project managers are increasingly relying on capturing knowledge from earlier experiences and earlier projects in the organization. This knowledge includes technical knowledge on specific discipline issues, project management knowledge, or the methods and procedures requiring the management of projects and project-based knowledge concerning clients, rules and evolving market needs.

Much of this knowledge is often possessed by individuals, who take it with them as they move between projects. The capture of this knowledge requires an organizational culture that encourages knowledge through a reward structure as well as providing the tools and methods to simplify knowledge capture. It also requires project-based organizations to coordinate and facilitate the transfer of knowledge between projects.

7 Changing organizational culture

There is a prevalent philosophy that management can change the culture of the organization to reduce resistance to knowledge sharing. There is a debate whether this is achievable or at least how long it takes. This is usually a long and daunting process. McDermott and O'Dell (2001) suggest that any change proceed by first matching current culture and providing networks that support current communication patterns. They suggest motivation can be of a visible nature, as for example linking knowledge sharing to a business problem by having more than one person work on the problem. An alternative is to encourage practices that link knowledge to core business values.

The latter requires the development of a core culture that values knowledge and its sharing. It then identifies the actions that are typical of this culture and fosters and rewards them through human relations policies.

7.1 The role of human relations (HR) policies

HRM policies and business strategy perspectives play an important role in attempting any organizational cultural change. A link from business strategy to knowledge sharing can be effective particularly if linked to reward systems through a HR strategy.

Defining what it is to be a good citizen with the organization and providing support to help people achieve such status is another policy. This may include encouraging autonomy for knowledge workers and providing reward structures as additional ways to encourage knowledge sharing.

7.2 Building trust

Staples and Webster (2008) discuss a number of different organizations and their impact on trust. In particular, their work has considered how group organization can impact trust and knowledge sharing. They noted differences determined by interdependence between tasks. As tasks become more dependent, then knowledge sharing and trust grows between task groups. Such dependence can avoid subgroups developing with possible later conflicts. Often subcultures develop within projects where certain groups find alternate ways to carry out their tasks with resultant conflicts and loss of trust. Their work suggests that subcultures should be avoided in project groups. They are more likely to appear where part of a team is distributed and part local and suggest that such situations should be avoided.

Subcultures can also arise depending on the kind of work in a business unit. Thus design units may follow a different culture, characterized by more collectivist approach whereas the culture in sales departments is more individualistic.

> An important guideline is to avoid the formation of subcultures in the same project activity. Task interdependence is one way – frequently meeting another.

One aspect of management is to choose grouping where trust is likely to be easier to maintain and then coordinate these groupings through boundary roles.

7.3 Organizing communication across the enterprise

The organizational culture can impact on the way knowledge sharing and collaboration takes place. Communities of knowing can be used to distribute knowledge through an organization. Hustad (2004) discusses issues in global organizations and discusses the strategy used in Ericson to create communities of knowing. The communities focus on particular aspects of the business and include interorganizational and intraorganizational focus. At a project level communication methods include the following:

- Committees, which have well-defined roles such as chairperson and secretary. Often they expect certain norms and behavior patterns and as such almost have a culture of their own.
- Peer group, where everyone equally contributes to some activity with members often assigning roles as needs arise.
- Clerical processing that is more often supported with a leader or facilitator structure where people continually meet to improve the process.

7.4 Sharing knowledge across global organizations

Many organizations are now spread across different countries. One issue here is how to develop a common vision to ensure that knowledge is not fragmented but is shared across the global enterprise. Such enterprises often have thousands of workers and may be organizations such as large consulting groups or information technology giants utilizing expertise from many locations. Two broad alternative organizations are possible. One is where the home base of the country provides the main capability and where the majority of decisions are made. Here knowledge flows generally from the home country. This is commonly found in many IT organizations that primarily market similar products across the globe. Dell, for example, has codified its products and markets them globally through local offices that provide product services. The services are defined at the home base. The other alternative is where there are individual businesses each with its own responsibility but a wider common goal.

Zolin et al. (2004) suggest that cultural differences can be overcome by arranging frequent meetings between different parts of the organization. Bellin and Phan (2007) in their study of a large international hotel chain stress the importance of going beyond hard connections and focusing on behavior in different cultures. They describe the idea of developing common mindsets across different locations. One example is to provide standard ways to make decisions across the organization.

Summary – Management options for changing culture

- Developing reward structures that encourage innovation and knowledge sharing;
- Improving communication and increasing the visibility of innovative activities;
- Training to improve teamwork and cohesion;
- Creating communities of practice to share knowledge;
- Choosing work and social structures suitable for the business activity;
- Increasing the autonomy of individuals.

It is also important to note that organizational arrangements of global organizations evolve over time. Initially all knowledge may be centered at head office, with it gradually devolving, as organizations learn better ways to harness local knowledge. Ichijo and Kohlbacher (2008) describe in the case of Toyota. The general evolution here took the following steps.

- Initially Toyota produced cars in Japan only and exported them to other markets.
- In the second stage it moved production facilities closer to the market with most design still carried at Head Office.
- Recently design has also been distributed as local designers better understand local tastes, especially to satisfy the needs of emerging markets.

8 Facilitating intercommunity knowledge sharing

Changing organizational cultures is often a long-term goal. Many managers, however, are faced with achieving goals in a shorter term and need to resolve cultural issues within a limited project. The choice of management technique depends on the situation. Typical situations include managing cross-functional teams often spread across national boundaries or project coordination.

The important issue here is how to develop a relationship between groups where there is sensitivity to the knowledge possessed by the community groups and understanding of the values held by other members of the group. At the same there must be trust that the other members possess the competencies needed to work towards common goals. Culture influences the choice of social structures and the assignment of responsibilities within different community groups. Thus in a high power difference culture, a leader structure is likely to be preferred over a facilitator structure. Brown and Duguid (1998) suggest that specials roles can assist collaboration across different community groups. Introducing roles such as facilitators or brokers has also been suggested by Gherardi and Nicolini (2002). Another suggestion is to define boundary objects that contain shared knowledge that can be passed between communities.

> This leads to an important management consideration – how to develop trust and knowledge sharing in enterprises. One way to do this is by the choice of collaboration structures that include knowledge brokers and facilitators as well as clear definition of boundary objects.

8.1 Project coordination

Project coordination is receiving considerable attention especially as there is increased emphasis on new projects, where teams are often brought together to develop new products in relatively short time periods. One objective here is to define what is meant by performance and what cultural and policy setting are best to achieve it. Performance parameters include task completion times, degree of creativity, sharing of knowledge. Typical team kinds include the following:

- Task teams that often have similar social structures within a given institution.
- Design teams where again facilitation or expert structures are often found.
- Planning groups, which focus on planning some activity to reach an agreed goal.

These teams are often transient where team members work temporarily on one project and then move to other projects. Project teams follow practices dictated by their institution and by the kind of work carried out by the team. In many instances projects can influence organizational culture by suggesting policy settings, as for example reward and leadership structures. Furthermore, team members that have a common culture tend to work together better. They have similar beliefs and behavior patterns and hence can resolve issues and reach joint decisions quicker.

There is also ongoing research into ways to organize project teams to facilitate innovation and product completion. Belassi et al. (2007), for example, have found that in most cases the organizations with strong leadership tend to be more successful in developing new products. Furthermore, environments where leadership encourages employee views and autonomy add further to this success.

One important aspect in projects across different cultural groups is the increase of people working virtually and relying on technology for their communication. Lee-Kelley and Sankey (2008) studied knowledge sharing at a distance that involved projects made up of groups in the United Kingdom, Greece and the Asian region developing a banking application. They identified a number of key issues. One of these was the need to identify clear roles and responsibilities for leadership within the virtual team, as well as cultural differences and trust, especially assessing the reliability of messages between the regions.

> Hence it is increasingly important that cultural aspects must be taken into account in process design, with communications chosen to be consistent with culture.

8.2   Cross-functional teams

Cross-functional and other teams have been attracting attention on research on collaboration across institutions. Zolin et al. (2004), for example, describes the issue of trust in geographically separated cross-functional teams. They noted that cultural differences between professions in such teams have negative influence on trust, as for example between builders and architects, where the emphasis of one is on appearance and that of the other is on building costs and building structure. Zolin suggests that trust in cross-functional teams should be built early in a project through providing opportunity to assess partner groups' abilities, integrity. A management technique such as providing regular meetings and reports is one recommendation. Adenfeld and Lagenstrom (2006) describes some positive outcomes of such meetings. Another research outcome from Staples and Webster (2008) is that task interdependencies that require sharing of knowledge between task teams can lead to the growth of trust between team members.

Is there a general set of criteria to be applied here? The work of Hofstede provides one set of criteria. In addition there are other criteria that have become useful cultural descriptors. Organizations thus have options to create policies that encourage a particular culture. At the same time they must organize their teams to work within the institutional culture while supporting communication across different cultural groups in their partner institutions. For example, where power distances are small power distances facilitators are preferred to leaders. They are also characterized by self-organizing groups. Irrespective of the reason for the cultural difference there are two fundamental approaches to bring such groups together.

Major strategies for coordinating activities

Have a coordinating structure or role to continually translate between the groups, sometimes known as the conduit model of communication, or

- Develop a common language and rules for doing things acceptable to the groups. In this case people play what are sometimes called knowledge games, where different groups have their terminologies and convert between them during communication.

In the first strategy define role structures with the responsibility of translating between cultures. A person qualified for that role, for example, is an expatriate located in a team who acts as a cultural broker.

9   Organizational problem solving

Ultimately most interactions lead to some action. In most cases this is to resolve some issues and decide on future actions. Social interactions in organizational problem solving can range from simple message exchanges to interactions composed of many messages. Figure 5.4 illustrates the kinds of interactions that take place between knowledge workers, who are continually interacting in accessing and creating knowledge to decide on actions. Figure 5.4 describes a sequence of interactions or steps, namely:

- Conversations, whose usual goal is to socialize and share tacit knowledge and come up with ideas. Conversations are usually non-threatening and serve to make people more aware of what is currently happening. These correspond to socialization.
- The next step is usually to look at different possibilities and generate alternatives for actions. This corresponds to externalization.
- Choice of alternatives, especially decisions on the criteria used to select alternatives.
- Decisions on future action, which require the analysis of alternatives and using the interpretations to decide on course of action. It also requires people to state their views and positions in forming the decision.

Some of the steps in Figure 5.4 are cooperative in nature while others involve conflict. For example, idea generation, alternative generation or choosing decision criteria is often cooperative whereas negotiation involves conflict. Each of the steps shown in Figure 5.4 correspond closely to the innovation process discussed earlier in Chapter 4. They can be carried out by different teams if the business is large. Hence there is a possible role for social software in

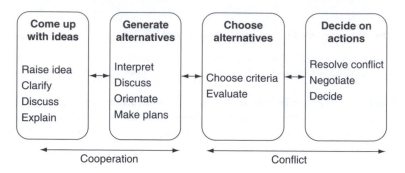

Figure 5.4   Types of interactions

the cooperative steps to collect ideas and alternatives. Where there is conflict synchronous communication is often preferred.

10 Summary

Following this chapter, readers should be aware of the increasing role that culture plays in knowledge-based processes. Culture is not only important because of increasing globalization and its influence on knowledge sharing in organizations. It has meant that management must now deal with cultures that are spread geographically as well as culturally and to create structures that facilitate knowledge sharing. The chapter provided a number of descriptions of culture ranging from national to organizational.

For process design culture is important because it can influence knowledge sharing within processes. The chapter described the influence of both the social and the intercommunity issues on knowledge sharing. It then described methods to reduce the negative effects of cultural differences taking into account the kind of situation. Such reduction often requires changes in human relationship policy settings to create innovative environments, together with support for team structures that work within these policy settings. The chapter suggested some possible management settings.

11 Discussion questions

Discussion 1

What is the culture of your student group in terms of value, behavior and norms?

Discussion 2

Refer back to Figure 4.6 and discuss options for each of the enablers to create an environment that leads to increased sharing of knowledge?

Discussion 3

How do you think Hofstedes cultural descriptors can influence the social issues in knowledge sharing?

Discussion 4

What are the good ways to improve knowledge sharing between two different professional groups? Take, for example, information technology professionals and sales people discussing systems to maintain client profiles.

Discussion 5

Choose a global organization such as MacDonald and examine their home page in different regions. Can you see any influence of national culture on the design of this page?

Case study IV

Global marketing of 'Green' cosmetics

Cosmetic manufacturer Green Cosmetics (GC) is planning to market a new brand of cosmetics (natural cosmetics) globally. They have carried out extensive tests to prove the safety of the products. Reports of these tests have now been published. They have also obtained the services of a well-known green campaigner, JQ, who is prepared to appear in marketing materials on their products. They feel that they will have an advantage in some regions if they focus on the green aspects of their products. However, the presentation itself is important as it must focus on the impact of green issues in particular regions. They have the problem of how to convince the public in a region on whether the product is truly green, and secondly that it is safe. As part of this they also want to portray GC as an environmentally sensitive organization and are considering this as a major feature of their website.

The GC management team, in particular the CEO, CFO and marketing manager, have been looking at their global marketing strategy. The issues in global marketing are now becoming better understood (Young and Javalgi, 2007) and the GC management team is looking at ways to implement them. Apart from language differences the marketing has to focus on cultural differences – a way to think globally but act locally. The marketing must be customized to the cultural norms of particular regions and their environmental issues to evaluate the potential acceptance of their products in the region. Important issues identified by the GC management team are the following:

- Relative importance of green issues in different regions;
- The acceptance of JQ as an authority in the regions; and
- The cultural attitude to cosmetics and to GC in general.

Case study IV

Continued

GC sees the following as important business activities to address these issues:

- Collecting information about current preferences in each regional area, competitors in selected areas;
- Creating a marketing strategy on selected regions;
- Distribution of promotional material through different media and the selection of the media;
- Possible development of links with regional green movements.

Thus although what is to be done is now agreed, the way of organizing the activities can vary between corporations and their particular strengths and business networks. GC is looking at alternative options for managing the introduction of their products into different areas and is aware of the need to address the cultural preferences and sensitivities in the different regions. GC is known for very efficient operations in developing promotion material in their home base in the United Kingdom but as yet have not developed the necessary experience for global marketing in the green area. There appear to be two options for implementing a global marketing strategy in GC, namely:

- Option 1 – Regional development and implementation of marketing strategies with financial approval from central office;
- Option 2 – Central development of marketing strategies and material using the expertise in developing promotional experience with regional verification.

How would you organize GC to process knowledge obtained in the different marketing area to its advantage in the quickest and most efficient way for the two options. In your proposal:

- Define the business activities.
- Define the roles and their responsibilities distinguishing between regional and global responsibilities. Typical roles being considered are local marketing manager, local production manager.
- Describe the kinds of interactions between the roles using ESNs. In doing so, take into account cultural differences especially focusing on power distance.

In doing this note that the GC culture is results oriented, loosely structured and characterized as individualistic with a relatively small power distance. There are some regions some with high power distances.

Some further readings

Ajmal, M.M., Koskinen, K.U. (2008) 'Knowledge Transfer in Project-Based Organizations: An Organizational Culture Perspective' *Project Management Journal*, Vol. 39, No.1, March, pp. 7–15.

Adenfelt, M. Lagenstrom, K. (2006) 'Enabling Knowledge Creation and Sharing in Transnational Projects' *International Journal of Project Management*, Vol. 24, pp. 191–198. Elsevier Press.

Belassi, W., Kondra, A.Z., Tukel, O.I. (2007) 'New Product Development Projects: The Effects of Organizational Culture' *Project Management Journal*, Vol. 38, No.4, December, pp. 12–24.

Bellin, J.W., Phan, C.T. (2007) 'Global Expansion: Balancing a Uniform Performance Culture with Local Conditions' *Strategy and Leadership*, Vol. 35, No. 6, pp. 44–50.

Burrows, G.B., Drummond, D.L., Martinsons, M.G. (2005) 'Knowledge Management in China' Communications of the ACM, Vol. 48, No. 4, April, pp. 73–76.

Hislop, D. (2005) *Knowledge Management in Organizations* (Oxford University press).

Ichijo, K., Kohlbacher, F. (2008) 'Tapping Tacit Local Knowledge in Emerging Markets – The Toyota Way' *Knowledge Management Research and Practice*, Vol. 6, pp. 173–186.

Lee-Kelley, L., Sankey, T. (2008) 'Global Virtual Teams for Value Creation and Project Success: A Case Study' *International Journal of Project Management*, Vol. 26, pp. 51–62.

Martinson, M.G. (2008) 'Relationship-based E-commerce Theory and Evidence from China' *Information Systems Journal*, Vol. 18, No. 4, July, pp. 331–356.

McDermott, R., O'Dell, C. (2001) 'Overcoming Cultural Barriers to Knowledge Sharing' *Journal of Knowledge Management*, Vol. 5, No. 1, pp. 76–85.

O'Hara-Deveraux, M., Johansen, R. (1994) *GlobalWork: Bridging Distance, Culture and Time* (Jossey-Bass, San Francisco).

Staples, D.S., Webster, J. (2008) 'Exploring the Effects of Trust, Task Interdependence and Virtualness on Knowledge Sharing in Teams' *Information Systems Journal*, Vol. 18, November, pp. 617–640.

Wurtz, E. (2004) 'Intercultural Communication Websites' *Proceedings Cultural Attitudes Towards Communication and Technology*, Murdoch University, Australia (edited Sudweeks, F. and Ess, C.) pp. 109–122.

Young, R.B., Javalgi, R.G. (2007) 'International Marketing Research: A Global Project Management Perspective' *Business Horizons*, Vol. 50, pp. 113–122.

Zolin, R., Hiunds, P.J., Fruchter, R., Levitt, R.E. (2004) 'Interpersonal Trust in Cross-functional Geographical Distributed Work: A Longitudinal Study' *Information and Organization*, Vol. 14, pp. 1–26, Elsevier Press.

Social Software

6

Using social software to build working relationships and social capital

Learning objectives

- Recreational use of Social Software
- Social Software in Business
- Potential Benefits of social software in business
- Capturing best practices

- Transferring knowledge
- Managing social software
- Social software – discussion boards, blogs, Wikis
- Services for knowledge management.

1 Introduction

Previous chapters described the importance of social networking in knowledge sharing. Social networking is often the first step in knowledge articulation as it is here that people exchange comments, ideas or general news items. Questions arise as how such knowledge can be shared across distance especially by using computer technology.

Chapter 3 described different kinds of social interactions and social structures found in business processes. It showed ways to model social structures as ESNs. Chapter 4 covered ways to facilitate knowledge sharing through social interactions and the importance of building relationships that result in knowledge sharing and creation. It also introduced knowledge management processes through which articulated knowledge can be converted into forms that can be distributed and shared between individuals and processes. Chapter 5 then described how these interactions can be moderated by cultural environments.

The growing emphasis on collaboration and networking has led to many new innovative technologies, such as blogs, becoming commonly used by people to communicate with each other. One way to describe many of these new technologies is as social software, whose main purpose is to support interaction between people to improve knowledge sharing. Web 2.0 technologies are designed to facilitate the capture of articulated knowledge and there are proposals to combine social software with the idea of the semantic web (Gruber, 2008) to provide ways to distribute this knowledge by codifying it in terms meaningful to its users.

The question now being asked is how to get the benefits from such technologies in business? The solution is not simply to put in the technology but also to match it to the organizational structures and cultural settings of the people involved. The technologies will only be adopted if they do not unnecessarily create cognitive gaps between the people and tasks in the business process. Experience has shown that it is not a matter of simply providing a technology and expecting it to be taken up by users. A conscious effort must also be made to ensure that technology is introduced in ways that lead to perceived benefits and not as intrusive to current arrangements. This is particularly so in the case of social software which can be seen as intrusive in the way people interact with others. Knowledge workers in such environments are often not directed to use particular technologies but adopt them in most cases voluntarily. There is then often a conflict between those who see the use of social software as building social capital and those who see it as something that interferes with their current work practices. Even when the benefits of social software are accepted there is still the issue of how it can be implemented to capture knowledge and put it into forms that can be of benefit to everyone throughout the organization.

Social software supports both synchronous and asynchronous communication. Synchronous communication is one where people exchange messages at the same time. It can be a personal meeting, a video conversation, talking on a mobile phone or working on a shared whiteboard. Instant messaging, or chatrooms as it is sometimes known, is an extension of e-mail, which is asynchronous, to synchronous communication. It is a synchronous communication technique that is not face to face. Here a number of messages are exchanged in real time as shown in Figure 6.1. User 1 asks User 2 about progress on a model, the reply is that there is a hold-up, which User 1 can then begin to explain.

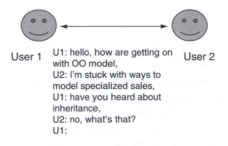

Figure 6.1   Instant messaging

Instant messaging can be quite effective in answering a question that may require some explanation. Instant messaging most often involves two people but earlier chatrooms allowed more than two people to exchange messages at the same time. They also kept track of the message interchange.

E-mail and instant messaging are early examples of social software. There has been a phenomenal growth of social software over the last few years. This chapter introduces a number of social software technologies and describes how the software can encourage collaboration and knowledge sharing within organizations. It compares software in terms of two dimensions – one in its use as a communication tool in creating knowledge and the second in its role in the storage of knowledge for retrieval and use later. One way to classify such technologies is in terms of their use – recreational, professional or organizational.

2   Recreational use – The social networking sites

The last few years have seen the rapid growth of social networking sites. Their main purpose is to get people to make contacts and form relationships over the Internet. Apart from providing the ability to initiate contacts they often include services to collectively share information on some topic or even form small informal groups. The typical social structure is where the site owner manages communication between themselves and their friends and is the only person that can invite others to the site.

2.1   Early blogsites

Blogging became generally available in the early 2000s and its use has spread since then. There are now publicly available websites, or blog hosts, that provide blogging facilities to users. A blog host allows anyone registered at the host to create a blogsite, post entries to the site and invite friends to make comments on the entries. One early example of a blog host is LiveJournal (http://www.livejournal.com), which as reported by Kumar in 2004 had over 1.3 million bloggers. It is perhaps worthwhile to note that the usage of such sites has been almost spontaneous rather than planned in any way. Such spontaneous uptake can perhaps serve to provide guidelines on introducing such technologies into business environments, with greater uptake by its workers.

2.2   Facebook and MySpace

Following the earlier introductions, there has been a phenomenal growth of personal sites using applications provided on the Web. These focus on establishing relationships. Facebook and MySpace are the two best-known ones. Of these, MySpace seems to be more popular in the United States, whereas Facebook is more popular globally. The main focus of these is finding friends throughout the whole world and sharing interesting experiences with them. Worldwide,

Facebook had 132 million visitors in June 2008, whereas MySpace had 117.5 million visitors in the same period (www.internetnews.com). The number of such sites is continually growing, as for example, a new service known as Twitter being introduced during the writing of this book.

The focus of these sites is to enable people to make friends across the Internet. Anyone can set up a personal page including their interests. Others find people with common interests and establish contacts.

There may be some possibility of using similar approaches in business to finding business partners with common interests or with the expertise to solve some problem.

The knowledge in such systems is generally of a personalized nature. People get to know others through the site, their interests and skills and ways to work together with them. Such knowledge can be useful from an organizational perspective, although few organizations provide support for such sites.

2.3   The economies of personal sites

Managing personal websites is not a trivial business. Many such applications have large numbers of servers. Facebook is rumored to have close to 800 servers located in San Francisco, Santa Clara and Virginia. Information maintained on behalf of its users is spread across these sites. Experts are continually required to plan the distribution of information across the sites and find ways to provide quick response times.

Access to social networking sites, however, is free. How then are they funded? The funding comes from advertising revenues. As reported in the *Technology Review* in August 2008, US spending on social networking sites has grown close to over $2 billion in 2008 and is expected to reach $3 billion in 2011. Questions remain whether such levels can continue especially in a less favorable economy. Hence many personal sites are always looking at ways to advertise more effectively and prove this to the advertisers. Personal application site managers are continually working on showing that advertising through their sites does lead to purchases to the advertisers.

2.4   Use of blog hosts

Personal sites go beyond using applications such as Facebook or MySpace. Many focus on sharing photographs or travel experiences. They often start as blogsites on the Internet. A typical blogsite is shown in Figure 6.2. Here a tourist from Taiwan created a blogsite to publish their photos of a recent holiday in Greece, titling this site as "I left my heart in the Aegean". As reported by Lin and Huang (2006) this site raised an immediate and high level of response, in fact 6,000 on the first day, and then about 40,000 daily, with 1 million viewers on the first month. The traffic created problems for the server that hosts the site.

The site was mainly a set of photographs taken by a tourist on a private visit to Greece, who put the photographs on the site so he could share them with

Figure 6.2   A typical blogsite of photographs 'I left my heart in the Aegean'.

his friends on the Web rather than making copies and mailing copies to them. Each such photo is one blog entry. To their surprise the tourist found that many other people, who had been to Greece, began to make comments on the photos, commenting on what they liked and how they enjoyed each location. An analysis of the various comments by Lin and Huang showed most of them favorable and many stating they would visit Greece in the near future.

What makes such sites a success? According to Lin and Huang (2006) there are a number of factors. They include the following:

- The current situation of the viewer. In the case of this site it was a time when SARS was prevalent and the idea of travel provided an escape.
- The identity of the photographer. Here the photographer was an engineer and was seen as sincere.
- The presentation was simple, showing the blue Aegean sea.
- How the site realizes the viewers dreams and simple content, all showing the blue Aegean Sea.

Lin and Huang define the site acceptance by the term "viral" – to imply that access spreads like a virus. This was the case in the Aegean site as the good news and comments posted on the site seemed to encourage word about it to spread.

Sharing photographs as well as travel experiences are now a common social activity. Services provided for these interactions tend to be popular. A service known as Flickr provided by Yahoo allows users to post their photograph on blogsites.

Blogs are typically used as a means of storing local information and advertising or bringing information to blog participants. They generally support small local groups or focused information. It is perhaps fair to say that most blogsites support simple kinds of conversations. They encourage comments on posted pictures or viewpoints but not the creation of relationships or business arrangements or the design of new artifacts. They primarily focus on informal conversations.

Why do people participate in such sites? Little research has taken place here, but it appears that many serve as a focus of common interest. They lead to some weak relationships but there is little evidence that they result in the development of social capital.

2.5 Professional use

Professionals use the Internet and social software to keep aware of developments and good practices in their profession. The most common are sites maintained by professional groups to keep people informed on trends and ideas. These are usually industry based and provide ways for people to enter views and comments to be shared by everyone but not as a rule to support one-to-one exchange of ideas.

LinkedIn is a recent service introduced to facilitate knowledge sharing between personal professional relationships. In summary professional workers invite others into their LinkedIn space and exchange messages about their work in that space. The majority of such interaction involves university researchers or practitioners. There is yet little reported research to evaluate the success of this approach to establishing personal links and few statistics exist on the LinkedIn system.

2.6 Extending to business applications

Personal sites have shown the opportunities made possible by social software for building communities and sharing personal knowledge. This has raised the issue of using such software in business for knowledge sharing and building of communities across distance. It is probably not conceivable, however, that future businesses will simply run on informally organized personal sites, at least not unless there are vast cultural changes. Some formal arrangements and responsibilities will be necessary. The question then becomes what can be learned from the use of such sites to develop what might be called collaborative infrastructures for business.

Blogging is the first technology that comes to mind here. Its impact on tourism as evidenced by the "I left my heart in the Aegean" site can be large.

The question is how to make such interactive sites sufficiently attractive for them to become popular or "viral".

Another area is in marketing. Blogs offer ways to not only market the product but to also provide an associated service. Singh et al. (2006), for example, note that most people respond more favorably to marketing when they can control what they can see. Questions then arise whether social software can be used to provide this experience and in fact create the kind of activity that arose on the Aegean site. Social software does provide this opportunity to stimulate customer activity about a product.

Other possibilities are finding contacts or business partners using services in ways similar to that provided by MySpace or Facebook.

3 Organizing social software for business applications

The potential of social software as a way to share knowledge and innovate is now increasingly recognized. However, although social software has now been available for a number of years, its use in business, except for some organizations, is still sporadic. Yet the advantages that can come about from using social software for sharing of knowledge are possible. There are a number of reasons for slowness of adoption. Some of these include the following:

- Complicated jargon associated with the software and the effort needed to become expert users.
- The context of the business and the general acceptance of recording information for future and general use. For example, people involved in business negotiation often do not want these to be recorded in their entirety.
- The uncertainties of achieving success as the benefits of knowledge sharing are often long-term and hard to measure.
- The danger that people will spend a large amount of time socializing on the sites without any business benefit.

It is likely that increasing use of technology that is occurring now especially in the younger generation will increase familiarity with technology. Much of this familiarity is gained through the use of technology for recreational purposes. Transfer of this experience to business use will require a more systematic approach in order to capture knowledge and avoid subcultures that can result from more informal use.

The question is whether growth is to be ad-hoc and left to individual groups or to be managed by the organization. There are a number of initiatives that organizations can take. The possibilities include the following:

- Maintaining awareness and context by providing people with any events or new policies regarding their work;
- Supporting individual business activities through social software that is specially adopted to the application;

- Supporting communities of practice to enable a number of people to share their experiences and develop their expertise in sharing experiences with others;
- Creating knowledge hubs within supply chains as suggested by Rye, Lee and Choi (2008).

3.1 Maintaining awareness

Most organizations now actively distribute information about important and interesting events to their employees through mailing lists or as postings on intranets. They can also include podcasts that distribute information using audio or video. Again the different kinds of awareness can be used to provide guidelines. A business activity can be seen as a situation and provides a basis for situational awareness. A policy can be established where all roles in the business activity are notified of any changes in the activity. These can be changes to artifacts, or new participants becoming part of the activity.

3.2 Communities of practice and social software

Communities of practice are becoming of increasing interest to business as they are seen as a way of building social capital. They usually have a common activity, some common knowledge with a community identity. They form communities where people find out what others are doing, what their values are, and the knowledge they can transfer. Communities of practice can be spontaneous and open, or they can have specific goals and be managed by organizations. Organizations can have different goals for setting up communities of practice. They include the following:

- A focused community to develop best practices. One example given later is finding best practices for measuring car emissions in alternate designs. This often has to go further than simply capturing articulated knowledge, but must have additional features where such knowledge is codified for further use. They often require some governance to facilitate participation and to make decisions.
- Open discussions where people simply exchange experiences in their professional areas.
- Open communities that are focused to some particular activity with varying and independent goals. An example here might be people preparing travel itineraries.

Boland and Tenkasi (1995) use the terminology 'communities of knowing' rather than communities of practice to illustrate ways to share knowledge. The goal here is for people to use forums to take and share perspectives. They propose different kinds of forums including narrative forums, knowledge representative forums or theory building forums. Each of these requires different technical support. Generally one technology is insufficient to support communities other than those that have limited focus. Alternatively a mix of technologies is needed. These can include ways to share stories, identify and resolve issues, or explain and work on artifacts. Hence ways to bring existing artifacts into communities is essential. All of these must be provided in the one workspace that supports the community of practice.

3.3   Knowledge hubs

Knowledge hubs are similar to communities of practice but focused on some particular activity. They differ as they primarily collect and store knowledge about actions people have taken. A typical example here is responses to customer reports. These form a knowledge base that can be used to find the way to respond given a similar event, in this case report.

Knowledge bases of this kind require what is known as data mining practices to search the knowledge base. The input here is the current situation. Data mining techniques then look through the collected information to find a similar situation, and the actions taken earlier. The business advantage here is that time can be saved in dealing with problems, and the transfer of knowledge between people in a business unit. One example is oil companies where people work on platforms in areas such as the North Sea. Work arrangements on oil rigs often mean that work shifts change quite frequently. Work shifts often have to deal with new problems and knowledge bases provide a way of transferring knowledge on dealing with such problems between shifts. This knowledge is recorded using information technology.

3.4   The issue of governance

Governance can be important to get benefits of social networking. The question as to whether social software can be used in an open manner or it may require governance procedures is still under discussion. To some extent it depends on organizational culture and the technical knowledge of its personnel. Thus blogging in technology organizations such as Microsoft is more common than in others. On the other hand, as to whether any knowledge generated is widely shared or only available to local groups is still to be addressed.

Governance becomes an issue for knowledge management policy. The question under discussion is whether knowledge hubs and communities of practice require some governance. In a best practice environment special people may be designated to facilitate identification of best practices through seeking feedback from users. In a knowledge hub they are custodians of knowledge. Perhaps an up-and-down approach is the best policy. This is to provide open discussions for local groups while at the same time gradually incorporating these into an enterprise-wide social structure.

Research by Probst and Borzillo (2008) indicated some characteristics for the success of communities of practice. They identified successful governance mechanisms that include the following:

- Sticking to strategic objectives;
- Forming governance committees where members review progress and suggest new processes;
- Identifying Community of Practice leaders, who will encourage interaction to promote intra- and interorganizational networks and seek external expertise;
- Defining people abilities in the community. Some communities, for example, distinguish between novice and experts and provide them with different permissions within the community.

Failure, on the other hand, is characterized by lack of one-to-one interaction within communities. Other reasons include lack of a core group, or individualism where members push their own ideas.

One lesson here is to align the use of technology to business processes and objectives. Singh et al. (2008), for example, discuss the use of blogs in marketing. These include blogs focusing on user communities, to differentiate between user kinds. Others may focus on thought leaders.

A further outcome here is that often more than one technology is required to maintain a community of practice. It is not just a matter of putting in one technology and expecting it to create widely distributed knowledge. What is needed is a set of technologies that to some extent follow the knowledge management process described in the previous chapter – articulation, filtering, codifying and distribution. The chapter will describe the role of some commonly available social software in this process.

3.5 Capturing best practices

Communities of practice are now attracting considerable interest in business. Setting up a community of practice is usually the first step in capturing best practices. This is often one if the earliest steps in business to capture knowledge. Practitioners often form communities of practice to share good ways of carrying out some task. It is of an operational nature, mainly task execution but is collaborative in nature. The created artifact is a collection of best practices verified by users. The general idea is illustrated in Figure 6.3. Here practitioners share their experiences in carrying out their work and the success achieved. Other practitioners may comment on these or even use other people's methods and comment on their outcome. This information is collected and posted for use by others. Anyone trying out a suggestion then posts feedback on their experience with it. Good practices then emerge as such feedback begins to identify acceptable practices. The collaboration here is between the practitioners who evaluate each other's activities. Eventually the better practices are increasingly used and become what are generally called best practices. A facilitator is often used here to manage the collected information and keep track of progress. There may also be roles assigned to review the process. Thus in Figure 6.3, Jill records experiences as well as comments on them. Other practitioners such as 'Hung' or 'Grant' can comment on them. 'Andrew' the facilitator can request such comments.

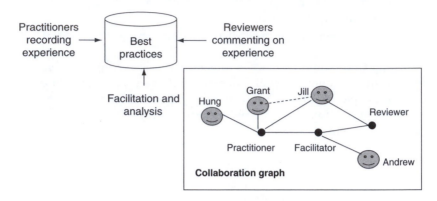

Figure 6.3   Capturing best practices

One example of a community of practice is that discussed by Artail (2006) in capturing ways to analyze emission tests on vehicles. It describes an open community of engineers, who record what are known as configuration files. These describe ways to analyze car emission tests. This system is based on groupware and focuses on the ability to record such configurations on a database and allow changes to them as best practices evolve. The technology is focused on the direct needs of these communities.

3.6   Guidelines for implementation

Adoption of social software is not simply making it available throughout a business unit. It involves both technical knowledge and changing work practices and as such should be introduced in a gradual manner.

An approach to gradual adoption of social software

- Identify communities or workers, who are willing to experiment with social software in some focused activity;
- Identify clear outcomes that can be used as a measure of success and spread the word as success is achieved;
- Identify a growth path;
- Treat the initial trial as an experiment rather than as an organizational change;
- Ensure that growth can be supported;
- Focus on critical issues to make adoption viral.

Communities of practice are one approach often used in organizations, which requires the use of social software.

4 Discussion boards

These are one of the earliest tools providing for socializing on the Internet. Discussion boards are used to exchange information asynchronously and can be part of an extended meeting. These can be used to capture comments in an organized way as illustrated in Figure 6.4. The usual approach is to raise an issue and then others comment on it. Then further comments are obtained and so on. The sequence of such comments becomes known as a discussion thread.

Discussion boards go beyond simple conversations and can focus on pursuing particular issues. It is possible to set up a "thread" that initiates some discussion on an issue. To do this discussion boards must be organized to suit the objective of the discussion. Figure 6.4 also illustrates how discussion structures can be used to capture and discuss issues. Here each top-level statement is an issue. People can make comments on an issue. These comments appear as statements at the next level down. These can be further commented on and appear a further level down. The result is something that is known as a thread in the discussion.

People, who use discussion databases, often need to change their work practices by making entries in the discussion database as a normal course of work. Thus participants must exercise a certain amount of discipline to ensure that important issues are raised and commented on. In most organizations there are usually many discussion boards running concurrently and independently. They take place in many organizational units. The kinds of discussion databases are shown in Table 6.1.

Many people now say that discussion is an essential part of knowledge sharing. Discussion databases capture knowledge articulation but do not in any way distribute beyond the participants or in any way codify the knowledge. To make such knowledge transferable it is necessary to study the discussions and eliminate superfluous comments and focus on the central issues. One way is to go through each discussion and pick out the significant issues.

A discussion system can be invaluable as it often serves to capture issues that arise in a community of practice. For example, discussion with a client can be viewed the next time to reflect on client preferences. However, many people do

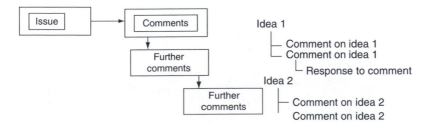

Figure 6.4   Discussion structure

Table 6.1   Using discussion boards

Objective	Possible work practice using discussion databases
After service follow-up	Keep track of customers in separate discussions. There may be one such discussion for each customer. These can become a knowledge base for marketing.
Order customization	Limited use in getting clarifications about an order.
	Possible internal use in collecting information from internal experts once a possible configuration is proposed.
Keep track of issues in developing alliances	Discussion issues to raise collaboration opportunities.
Management planning	Introduce a discussion database for each major issue and then combine at executive level
Support of cross-functional teams in integrative work	The discussions here would also need some supporting discussions such as managing terminologies.

not want to contribute to an electronic discussion as either they do not want to make their knowledge generally available or they do not want their views to be later used under different circumstances, or do not have time to do it.

5 Blogs

The book discussed use of blogs earlier in marketing. Blogging is a rapidly growing idea now used on personal websites but with potential for business use. It is an asynchronous communication method that captures people's comments about topics over a period of time. The idea of blogging is illustrated in Figure 6.5. A person can create what is known as a blogsite. They can then add blogs to the website. A blog in this sense is a piece of text or other artifact that is posted for anyone to see. However, only the blogsite owner can add new

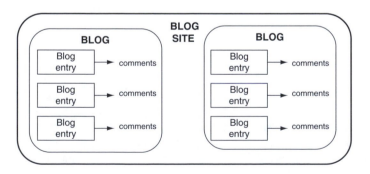

Figure 6.5   Blog structure

blogs to the blogsite. Others can only comment on the blog. There may be any number of blogs on the blogsite.

A blogsite is usually owned by one person, who posts any number of blogs on the site and invites other people to comment on them. Most of the personal sites described earlier are based on blog structures. In a community of practice, however, blogs can serve as repositories of stories and require entries to be initiated by a number of people. Hence some coordination is needed to set up blogs in ways that blogsites owned by different persons can be linked into a single workspace.

5.1 Applications of blogs to business

Most blogs are of a personal nature. These collect information informally. One question that arises is, are there ways to use blogsites in business? There is also potential to collect information and comments within a business. Perhaps the most obvious application is a blogsite about customers. A sales department, for example, can set a blogsite with a blog for every client. People can then make comments about the client's preferences and requirements. Similarly comments can be captured about suppliers or products.

Figure 6.6 is another potential example, in the building industry. Here there are now a number of connected blogsites. Here different roles may create their own blogsite. For example, the architect creates a blogsite as does a contractor and site manager. Each of the roles can comment on blogs in each other's blogsite.

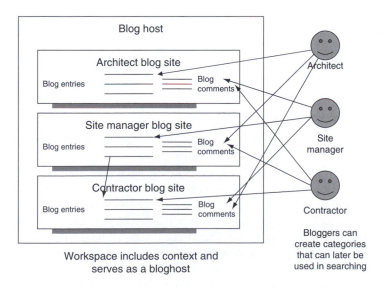

Figure 6.6 Blog structure for construction

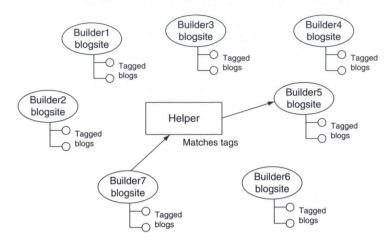

Figure 6.7   Blogs of construction companies

5.2   Sharing knowledge through blogs

Sharing knowledge through blogging is not a simple process. Basically it would require people to read every blog to see if it contains information useful to them. This can be both a long process and sometimes made difficult by people using different terms for the same thing. The problem is that each builder, or any blog user, may use different terms or phrases to mean the same thing. For this reason it is common to tag blogs, with a set of standard terms known as ontology. Tags are terms that in effect classify a blog and are shown in Figure 6.7. They are terms that make up the ontology of the blog domain. However, this requires additional time by anyone entering a blog to properly classify it using some common classification scheme.

The blogs in the blogsite are now tagged with standard terms. This in fact becomes the first step in the codification process.

5.3   What are the standard terms?

Tagging is only effective if it uses terms that mean the same to all the users. A number of industries now have standard terms. Such collections of terms are known as ontologies or sometimes taxonomies. Such ontologies are often quite complex, organize terms into hierarchies and show relationships between the terms. For example, there is an ontology for the construction industry. This means that somebody tagging blogs either has to know the ontology or else refer to the ontology every time they need to tag a blog. This can be quite overwhelming to everyday users who need to refer to the ontology to find the best term for a new entry.

The other alternative is what is known as folksonomies (Morrison, 2008). Here a group of people define their own set of terms as they create new entries.

The alternatives correspond to the conduit versus language game alternatives to communication (Boland and Tenkasi, 1995). Taxonomies define a common language and hence correspond to the conduit approach; folksonomies, on the other hand, support a more open approach where languages are devised as a community evolves. However, folksonomies can create as many problems as it solves. A totally open approach to tagging can result in multiple terms appearing on the same blog with different terms having the same meaning. This may be acceptable in recreational sites but may be detrimental in business situations where misunderstandings of the terminology can result in lack of coordination between people. The website del.icio.us raises many of these issues. Hence tagging can become a governance issue. To some extent the difference between a standard ontology and a folksonomy corresponds to the ways of coordinating activities across cultures – the ontology corresponds to the conduit model, a folksonomy to language games.

5.4   Who does the tagging – A governance issue?

Tagging itself can take some time. The next question is who does the tagging. The options are the following:

- The creator of the blog. This option is often not successful as it imposes considerable overheads on the blog creator. This is particularly the case where blogging is part of somebody's work and cuts into their real work.
- The creator and readers of the blogs.
- Specially designated roles, which may be what are commonly known as knowledge officers.
- Software that analyzes statements in a blog and suggest possible key words.

It should also be noted that tagging is not simply a problem associated with blogs but applies to other social software including discussion boards and Wikis.

5.5   Who does the searching?

Searching for useful blogs can also be time consuming. Again one solution here is an agent that can find blogs given some criteria by a user. Other suggestions are to use data mining techniques to search through collections of blogs, or other kinds of social software databases. Thus in most cases proper use of social software for knowledge sharing requires some investment of management effort to set up collaborative systems.

6   Wikis

Wikis are also a growing new technology. These are ways for people to jointly edit documents thus collectively adding their knowledge to the document. The most well-known is of course the WIKIPEDIA.

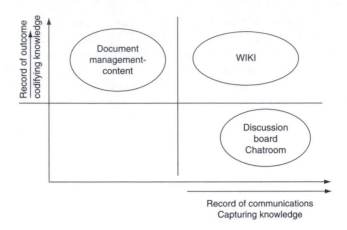

Figure 6.8   Wikis in relation to other software

Another example of the use of Wikis is collecting opinions. Nakata et al. (2005), for example, describe the use of Wikis in assessing a medical result and developing a treatment. It shows scans of part of a person's body and captures interpretations of practitioners of the scans. Practitioners can then put in their comments on potential treatments.

Wikis differ from blogs as a number of people can edit a particular Wiki page. Figure 6.8 indicates a typical positioning of Wiki technology. It principally combines document management and a discussion system. What Figure 6.8 shows is that document management only records the results of an activity. The discussion system is principally communication that is part of the activity. A Wiki system is both. It combines communication while creating the documents that is the result or summary of the discussion. There is then some possibility of a Wiki of its own supporting communities of practice.

Another view is that the horizontal axis is articulated knowledge, whereas the vertical is codified knowledge. In that case documents are primarily codified knowledge; discussion boards are articulated knowledge. Wikis are both.

Table 6.2 compares Wikis with the two main candidates for knowledge sharing – discussion boards, blogs and Wikis.

Table 6.2 shows that Wikis not only capture articulated knowledge but also provide ways for codification and distribution of knowledge. Wiki sites can be made generally available, as evidenced by WIKIPEDIA, although knowledge created here is usually through informal groups. Wikis provide the possibility of developing a local tagging system sometimes known as a folksonomy. Part of a Wiki structure can be the gradual evolution of a set of terms that are gradually built, discussed, clarified and used by Wiki users.

Table 6.2   Comparing discussion boards, blogs and Wikis

Technology	Structure	Who can enter	Who can update	Who can change
Discussion board	A number of entries with responses to each entry	Anyone can make an entry and response	Only owners of entry can update	Only owners of entry can update
Blog	A number of entries with comments about each entry	One person owns each blog entry	Other people can make comments	Entries cannot be changed
Wiki	A number of entries that can be linked	Anyone can make entries (sometimes users are controlled)	Anyone	Anyone can change entry but history is kept

7 Using social software to capture knowledge

Social software can collect knowledge articulated during collaboration and can become a collaborative database. The collaborative databases are set up to preserve continuity of the collaborative process. The general approach is to provide services to support collaborative interactions and to capture information exchanged during these interactions.

Social software primarily captures articulated information and knowledge, the first step of knowledge sharing.

Some services for knowledge capture

e-portfolio – Supports working on a collection of artifacts by a number of people. Different responsibilities are assigned in the e-portfolio to each person. Examples include – education with teacher and student responsibilities. Strategic documents with planning and expert responsibilities or paper preparation with author and reviewer responsibilities. The e-portfolio in this case can be seen as collaboration in the small but carried out within a larger framework. The issues then are how to subdivide a process into e-portfolios while maintaining links to the entire context.

Issues boards – These can contain ideas and suggestions, which are open to comment. It can also include alternatives for taking some actions.

Program board – This contains a list of activities or tasks currently in progress. It provides such a basis ranging from predefined processes to emerging processes that include supporting mobility in the workforce. It can be used as the basis for supporting communication beyond the simple exchange

of messages to supporting more goal-oriented communication that integrates a number of messages into the one interaction. It, however, sees
that support must be provided to manage such interactions and suggests
agents as suitable for this purpose.
Stories – These are descriptions of experiences that may be relevant to others
in a group. Such stories maintained on a story board are the more obvious
examples of sharing experiences with others.
Round table discussion – This is where people address and raise particular issue
in an organized way.

Typical ways of implementing these services include the following:

Program board – implemented as a calendar or blog;
Issues board – the issues raised and how they were resolved usually a blog or
    discussion board;
e-Portfolio – keeps track of documents and changes made to them;
Stories – usually a blog contains one story.

The idea behind a collaborative database is that it facilitates collaboration by
sharing of people's ideas and comments. It ensures that few actions are wasted
and that all actions work towards the agreed upon goal. Any workspaces generated through the knowledge support infrastructure can focus either on activities
or on roles.

8   Ultimate goal – Integration of services to support knowledge communities

Earlier parts of the chapter described some management issues in the introduction of social software. An ultimate goal, however, can be seen as the
gradual trend to knowledge sharing moving from community, to organizational unit and to the whole enterprise – the development of a collaborative
infrastructure for the enterprise. Eventually the technology used in the communities can be integrated in the way shown in Figure 6.9. Here a collaborative infrastructure is used to combine the technologies into one platform.
Usually some middleware technology is used to compose a platform from
available services, including Web 2.0 technologies. These are described later in
Chapters 12 and 13.

8.1   Sharing knowledge across business activities

In this case interactions are shared between business activities. An example is
shown in Figure 6.10. Here the goal is to respond to competitive products.
There are two activities, one is to collect and assess the information about

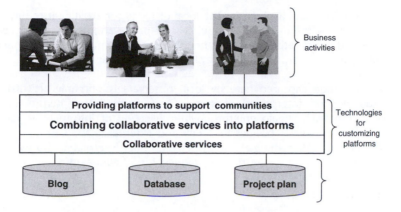

Figure 6.9   Developing a collaborative infrastructure

the products; the other is to plan a response. The information is collected by collectors and assessed by assessors, who may need additional information or clarification. The collected information is stored on a blog whereas the assessment is made on a Wiki.

Collaborative infrastructure for market collection

Figure 2.1 discussed the process used to collect market information. To continue this case we take the ESN and now look at ways to support the interactions.

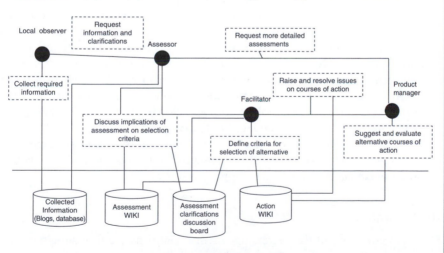

Figure 6.10   A collaborative infrastructure

Here the local observer, who may be a salesperson, collects information that is recorded on blogs. Any assessments made by an assessor are entered on a

Wiki that can be made available to the local observer for additional comment and used later by the product manager. The response and assessment is also available to the facilitator, who then helps the product manager to use and contribute to the interpretations and plan actions to respond to the market trends.

The knowledge captured here by local observers is primarily articulated knowledge which is interpreted by assessors and planners. The interpretations appear in the Wikis. Again enterprise-wide collection of information would require some following activities to codify and externalize the knowledge to a wider audience. Here there are also discussion boards available and used in interactions between the roles to make request for additional information and request clarifications.

9   What of the future?

When looking into the future it may be worthwhile to see what is now attracting research interest. Most of the social software discussed so far support asynchronous communication. Research now is on ways to extend software to include all the kind of interactions in relationships. This particularly concerns synchronous communication that requires spontaneous responses that often characterize knowledge creation and innovation.

Special interfaces – There is ongoing research to design interfaces that reduce the gap between people and technology. Whittaker et al. (2002), for example, describe interfaces that focus on contacts as they see this as an ever-growing area. Erickson and Kellogg (2000) see translucence important. Here users see who is currently active in a particular interface and what they are doing. They then are more likely to participate themselves.

Smart boards – Here electronic boards or smart boards are stationed at different locations but are connected. Changes made at one location appear in the other locations at the same time. The idea is that a draw made at one location is immediately visible at another, allowing someone at that location to immediately comment and add to the diagram.

Virtual workspaces – Russell et al. (2005) describe the idea of disappearing computers. Here computers disappear into the background and displays on walls make people at a distance appear as if they are here.

10   Summary

This chapter described the increasing use of social software in maintaining personal relationships. It then discussed the possibilities of using social software in business processes to share and create knowledge. It outlined approaches such as communities of practice or knowledge hubs and their increasing use in business to share knowledge or capture best practices.

Social software is seen as increasingly important in supporting the knowledge perspective in process design. Almost every activity either uses, creates or shares knowledge through interactions between people in the activity. Social software provides a way to capture this knowledge and make it available throughout the enterprise. This is increasingly important to create innovative enterprises, which should encourage innovation throughout the entire organization. In that case perhaps all business activities should contain elements of communities to gather experiences and analyze them to continually improve its practices. These should be shared through a collaborative infrastructure to share these practices across the enterprise. The design processes described in later chapters will identify possibilities of using social software to capture and share knowledge.

11 Exercises

Question 1

Suppose you are setting up the WWW to provide after-sales service to a client about the software that you developed. One of your goals is to reduce costs of providing after-sales service through a reduction of site visits. Which of the following would be useful? Briefly state how you would do this outlining advantages and disadvantages.

(a) A discussion database;
(b) Electronic mail;
(c) A chatbox or instant messaging;
(d) A combination of the above.

Question 2

How would you use Facebook to develop an idea? Use Figure 4.7 as a guideline here and outline how each of the activities in Figure 4.7 could be carried out using Facebook.

Question 3

How can social software be organized to create communities of practice? The community must keep a shared space to record evolving practices and evaluations and suggested improvements. At the same time it must support entry of new ideas for practices and ways to identify and record best practices.

Question 4

Go back to Case II and suggest ways to support brokering in the sales process using social software? Use the ESN developed earlier to develop a collaborative infrastructure like that shown in Figure 6.9.

Some further readings

Barton, M.D. (2005) 'The Future of Rational-critical Debate in Online Public Spheres' *Computers and Composition*, Vol. 22, pp. 177–190, Elsevier Press.

Boland, R.J. Tenkasi, R.V. (1995) 'Perspective Making and Perspective Taking in Communities of Knowing' *Organizational Science*, Vol. 6, No. 4, July–August, pp. 350–372.

Erickson, T., Kellogg, W. (2000) 'Social Translucence: An Approach to Designing Systems that Support Social Processes' *ACM Transactions on Computer-Human Interaction*, Vol. 7, No. 1, March, pp. 59–83.

Gruber, T. (2008) 'Collective Knowledge Systems: Where the Social Web Meets the Semantic Web' *Web semantics: Science, Services and Agents on the World Wide Web*, Vol. 6, pp. 4–13.

Kumar, R., Novak, J., Raghavan, P., Tomkins, A. (2004) 'The Structure and Evolution of Blogspace' *Communications of the ACM*, Vol. 47, No.12, December, pp. 35–39.

Lin, Y-S., Huang, J-Y. (2006) 'Internet Blogs as a Tourism Marketing Medium: A Case Study' *Journal of Business Research*, Vol. 59, October, pp. 68–81. Elsevier Press.

Majchrzak, A., Wagner, C., Yates, D. (2006) 'Corporate Wiki Users: Results of a Survey' *WikiSym 06*, Odense, Denmark, 21–23 August, pp. 99–104.

Morrison, P.J. (2008) 'Tagging and Searching: Search Retrieval Effectiveness of Folksonomies on the World Wide Web' *Information Processing and Management*, Vol. 44, pp. 1562–1579.

Nakata, N., Fukuda, Y., Fukuda, K., Suzuki, N. (2005) 'DICOM Wiki: Web-based Collaboration and Knowledge Database System for Radiologists' *International Congress Series*, 1281, pp. 980–985. Elsevier Press.

Probst, G., Borzillo, S. (2008) 'Why Communities of Practice Succeed and Why they Fail' *European Management Journal*, Vol. 26, pp. 335–347.

Russell, D., Streitz, N.A., Winograd, T. (2005) 'Building Disappearing Computers' *Communication of the ACM*, Vol. 48, No. 3, March, pp. 42–48.

Singh, T., Veron-Jackson, L., Cullinane, J. (2006) 'Blogging: A New Play in Your Marketing Game Plan' *Business Horizons*, Vol. 31, pp. 281–292.

Whittaker, S., Jones, Q., Nardi, B, Creech, M., Terveen, L., Issacs, E., Hainsworth, J. (2002) 'ContactMap: Organizing Communication in a Social Desktop' ACM *Transactions on Computer-Human Interaction*, Vol. 11, No. 4, December, pp. 445–471.

Whittaker, S., Jones, Q., Terveen, L. (2002) 'Contact Management: Identifying Contacts to Support Long-Term Communication' *CSCW 2002*, pp. 216–225.

Part II
Current Business Systems

Today's Business Applications

7

Providing the opportunity to carry on business anywhere in the world

Learning objectives

- ERP Systems
- e-Business Systems
- How knowledge Management
- Customer Relationship Management

- e-Procurement
- Tendering Processes
- Supply Chains
- Vertical Integration
- Trading Hubs and Portals

1 Introduction

This chapter describes current business systems. It focuses on business activities that follow well-defined processes and ways they have been extended to use knowledge to provide additional services to customers.

Current business systems use a mix of technologies, although some trends can be identified. Perhaps the most prevalent trend over the last few years has been towards ERP (Enterprise Resource Planning) systems, and towards systems based on the WWW, often known as e-business systems. ERP is an approach towards 'enterprise-wide information systems to coordinate all the resources, information, and activities needed to complete business processes'. An ERP solution can be aimed at a subset of business processes and include activities from more than one business unit. For example, a sales process can integrate activities in the sales, invoicing and inventory units. Implementation of ERP systems can proceed in a piecemeal manner by developing business processes in a planned way. Often the first step is to support the flow of financial transactions; the next may be purchasing, then manufacture and so on. ERP systems also provide reports that summarize the business activities. ERP systems primarily support records transfer between the business operations electronically and provide savings through the reduction of human intervention in processes.

e-Business provides further savings through the ability to connect electronically to customers and partners at any time any place. The combination of ERP and the WWW provides the advantage that now a lot of business can take place without human intervention and at any time and place.

This chapter introduces ERP systems and then describes electronic commerce processes. It concludes with supply chains with a comparison between predefined and collaborative processes, which leads to the next chapter that covers collaboration and knowledge sharing in business networking.

2 Traditional business models

The traditional way for describing businesses is the organizational chart shown in Figure 7.1. A business organization is made up of a number of departments, or operational units, each responsible for some part of the business. The chapter uses the term 'business unit' as a generic term for this purpose. Figure 7.1 shows the higher level business units. Typical business units in such organizations usually include the following:

Human resource management, to manage an organization's human resource needs. It includes hiring of people, arranging assignment to different departments.
Financial services such as billing and invoicing;
Inventory management to keep track of the parts stored in the organization;
Customer services, that keep track of customers such as arranging deliveries, taking customer orders, following up with any problems, or finding out about customer needs;
Marketing that raises awareness of the organizations products and services;
Production, that is responsible for the manufacture of products, and keeps track of the tasks and items required to construct the product.

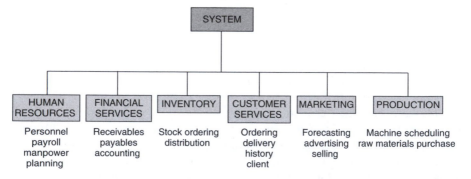

Figure 7.1   Traditional organizational structure chart

Each of the high-level business units is often itself made up of lower level business units that form an organizational hierarchy. Each business unit in turn carries out a number of business activities to meet its goal. For example, the high-level business unit 'human resources' in most cases has a goal of ensuring that the organization has a sufficient number of staff, with the different skills needed in the organization. Two of its sub-units may be payroll, and recruitment. Each such sub-unit may have its activities, or what people actually do. For example, activities in payroll may be to generate payroll transfers, issue yearly earning reports and so on.

A typical business process involves a number of business units. For example, a sale can start in customer services, go through inventory to get the ordered items and then to financial service to invoice the customer.

For a long time each business unit had its own information system, which supported the unit's operations. There were of course interactions between the business units. However, most of these interactions concerned passing transactions. Transactions were often passed (and still are in some cases) between people using paper, as for example, from the delivery department to the invoicing department through input-output trays standing on peoples desks. Similarly a sales transaction was passed to the invoicing unit, which sent out an invoice. The manual exchange of transactions between business units was the usual way of working of the traditional enterprise. There is no reason for human intervention in most of the transaction exchanges. Savings can be achieved by carrying out transaction exchanges electronically rather than by people. Early examples of savings were to interconnect the systems of business units. One of the first was the personnel system where records were passed automatically to the payroll systems, which then update employees' accounts and sends a credit authorization to the employees' bank. Considerable savings are then made through the reduction of handling of paper by human means. The term 'process integration' is sometimes used to describe combining two or more processes into one. Such integration of processes has grown to the extent that now transaction flows are being automated to support most business processes. The term ERP (Enterprise Resource Planning) is now generally used to describe such integration.

ERP systems can be developed either in-house or by customizing software purchased from ERP software vendors such as SAP or Oracle. The choice is often cost-driven, but purchasing software has the advantage of providing best practices captured through use by many customers. An ERP system is made up of a number of modules, with each module supporting a business activity. Typical modules are financial processes, material processes and the manufacturing process. They can pass messages between the different processes. Such integration is achieved through sharing databases between ERP modules.

2.1 Business units in material flow

Many organizations develop new products or services. The general term used here is that businesses add value to their inputs by creating new outputs. For

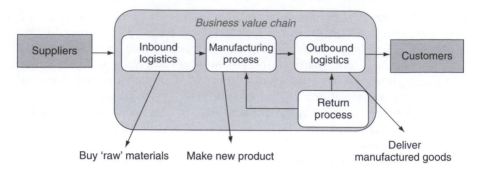

Figure 7.2   Typical production process value chain

example, a business buys a product, say wood, and manufactures furniture, thus adding value to the wood. This is known as adding value to the input. The importance of value adding in organizations is recognized by the well-known and widely quoted Porter (1985) value chain. Figure 7.2 illustrates the basic idea behind the value chain – the business buys some input material and uses their business skills to add value to it, by creating a new product or service and sell it. This process is supported by an infrastructure that includes human relationship management, technology and procurement. The activities here are the following:

- Inbound logistics, which defines how the organization obtains the materials to carry out its business. The process starts with input logistics to acquire a set of input products and process.
- The manufacturing process, which is used to create new outputs adding their knowledge to the products.
- The outbound logistics, which distribute the product to buyers.
- Marketing and after-sales service are the processes that find the buyers and service the product if needed.

Figure 7.2 can also apply to processes other than manufacturing. Product distributors and retail outlets must also plan their input logistics, which in this case are purchasing materials from manufacturers. They add value by developing ways to use these products often by adding to clients experience when purchasing and using products. Often this includes providing additional services, such as finance or after-sales service to add value. Another, for example, may be to create an attractive sales environment. Typical here, for example, may be coffee lounges when buying books. They can also be presentations about potential product uses, as for example preparing meals on a barbecue. Similarly consultants can get client requests, add value to them through their expertise and return reports to their clients.

2.2   Achieving competitive advantage

Porter stressed the importance of firms paying attention to business activities in the value chain and ensuring that all other activities focus on improving the value chain. The focus is often on logistics activities. This is to obtain input materials as cheaply as possible, have an efficient and fast manufacturing process and deliver as quickly as possible to clients. Such focus on achieving quick delivery at minimal cost is essential to achieve the major objective of any organization, which is to survive in the marketplace. To do this a business must increase the number of clients, and then keep clients interested by continually providing new and innovative services. It must achieve a competitive advantage to get and maintain clients and to provide them with better value, either through product quality or through associated services, than competing organizations. There are two well-known ways to obtain competitive advantage, namely:

- cost competitiveness by providing a product in a cheaper way than the competition by continually improving its value chain, or
- service competitiveness by better service especially in quickly responding to new client requirements. Increasingly providing what is known as personalized experiences through services is seen as important. For example, Amazon books provides additional services to marketing books.

Technology of course is one way to improve competitiveness by ensuring smooth flow of processes at each stage of the value chain. Figure 7.2 in fact is an over simplification as each of the boxes may have many steps. The 'inbound logistics' step itself often has many steps. Each of these steps may require different ways to source raw materials and special expertise is needed to convert them to the final product. It is important to get the right people at each of these steps. The specialized nature of many products means that different kinds of expertise will be needed in the 'manufacturing process' step. ERP was proposed as the solution to improving the value chain through the use of technology.

2.3   Adding value

The term 'adding value' is often now used in evaluating business process. Its meaning is still not well-defined but basically its goal is to consider how a process adds value to the business. It usually implies eventually adding value to the organization's clients. Hence improving the logistics process to lower costs of purchased parts adds value to the client as the output produced will now be cheaper if passed on to the customer. The term 'add value' thus focuses all actions of providing value to clients – hence the question asked is always how a proposed change will add value to the client.

Adding value does not always mean reducing cost. Product differentiation, for example, can be another way to add value. Thus a more expensive product can be more acceptable because it provides more options, or even looks better. Choice of vehicles is the most obvious example here. One may buy a slightly more expensive car because of, for example, 'road holding ability' or location of various operating controls.

3 Enterprise resource planning

Although initially most business units developed their own systems, the next step was to get competitive advantage through combining the systems. The objective here was to reduce cost through minimizing human intervention in transactions and reducing response to customer orders. Minimizing human intervention can add value by simply reducing the cost of transaction flows and reducing delivery times to clients. Figure 7.3 illustrates a business that involves a number of business units in a retail business. Each business unit is represented by a rectangle.

The input logistics is where retail businesses estimate the amount of different products that they expect to sell to customers. The input logistics includes demand planning unit, which forecasts demand, and then arranges to purchase these items for suppliers making sure that they obtain sufficient goods to meet customer demand but at the same time not overstock their shelves.

The first unit of output logistics is sales where a purchase is made by a customer and recorded in the 'sales orders' database. Then inventory records are checked and make an entry to retrieve the item from inventory and package it. The 'delivery' unit will arrange delivery with delivery partners and create a delivery record. When the delivery is completed, a delivery record is created and

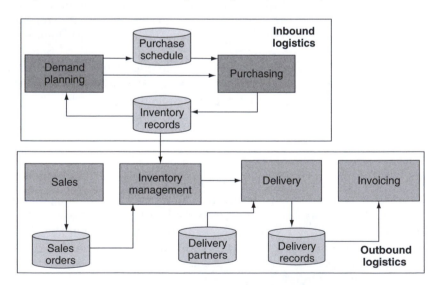

Figure 7.3 An ERP architecture of business units in retail businesses

forwarded to the invoicing unit and an invoice is organized by a person in the 'invoicing' unit.

Each business activity requires a person to take some action. One early step to getting cost advantage is to build interfaces between these business processes and transfer transactions between them without human intervention. Thus a purchase transaction will send a transaction to the inventory system, which will then send a request to a delivery to pick up the item and deliver to the customer. In a normal course of events human intervention is only needed at the point of sale and product delivery.

There are also alternate business models emerging here in the retail industry. Some supermarket chains may provide facility to producers to use their shelves. In that case the producer has to absorb the cost of items that are not sold. It is the producer's responsibility to ensure that they provide the retail facility, such as a supermarket, with the correct amount of product. In that case it is the supplier that must make the demand estimates.

3.1 The impact of ERP systems

ERP defines a strategic approach to developing enterprise systems. One of its main goals is to improve connectivity between business applications. An ERP strategy is used to integrate applications and processes into a unified system that reduces the need for human interaction while at the same time reducing time to process customer requests. ERP is now an established business approach for developing business information systems. It is an architecture for connecting modules to mirror the way the enterprise works and consequently yields cost savings in these processes.

ERP systems have a number of impacts on any business. These can be summarized as follows:

- They can introduce best practices into a business.
- They can be developed in-house or purchased from ERP vendors, such as SAP or Oracle.
- The installation of purchased systems requires some planning to choose the right configuration of ERP modules and to adjust their work practices to follow the processes supported by the purchased modules.
- They are costly to introduce as it includes both the cost of the ERP system and change to current business processes to fit in with the ERP system.
- They limit the amount of flexibility as process change requires substantial program change.

ERP systems are often combinations of smaller modules, some internally developed and some externally purchased. Thus a 'customer purchases' module may itself be made up of a number of smaller modules, one Web-based and another a physical shop. All of these would create the same purchase records to initiate a delivery. Typical modules include the following:

Financial modules, which include accounts payables and receivables, budget reporting, as well as other modules.

Human resources, which can include personnel records, payroll, training, career planning and others.

Customer relationship management (CRM), which can include purchasing and delivery.

Warehouse management including location of different items.

The integration between modules is usually achieved by designing databases that can be read by more than one application.

The goal of ERP goes further than that indicated by Figure 7.3. It includes optimizing material and manufacturing flows. It introduces objectives such as just-in-time delivery, reducing manufacturing cost amongst others.

Thus one class of early systems was known as Materials Requirements Planning (MRP-1), which is characterized by the modules shown in Figure 7.3. The goals here are to ensure that materials are always available when needed in manufacturing, minimize inventory costs and ensure that items are delivered when needed. The following chapter describes the next phase of ERP development. It includes manufacture resource planning (MRP-2), which also includes the scheduling of resources needed to produce the manufactured goods.

Considerable discussion exists on the benefits and constraints imposed by ERP systems. The balance is in the efficiencies brought in by the elimination of unnecessary human intervention and the constraints placed on ability to change and share knowledge in the current dynamic environment. The implementation of an ERP system itself calls for establishing the necessary structures to capture knowledge from different organizational units and to integrate it into one process. Jones, Cline and Ryan (2006) discuss some cultural issues in facilitating such change. They identify barriers to an effective introduction and initiatives to remove such barriers and their effectiveness in four oil companies. The book returns to the introduction of new systems in the next and subsequent chapters.

3.2   ERP systems and knowledge management

ERP systems also do not provide the flexibility needed in knowledge work, which require easy changes to the way information is accessed. ERP system providers are currently looking at ways to provide such flexibility.

4   Framework for electronic commerce

e-Business applications have evolved since the early 1990s following the wide availability of WWW. Initially many traditional business applications were

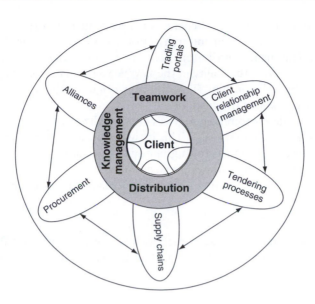

Figure 7.4   e-Business processes

converted to Web-based applications. Many of the ERP modules are now Web-based as ERP transactions often use Internet technologies. The main processes shown in Figure 7.4 are the following:

- CRM, which concerns the ways organizations work with their clients. CRM modules were one of the first provided on the WWW and are now often part of an ERP system and would correspond to the customer purchases module in Figure 7.4.
- Procurement, where one organization arranges purchases from another. This again can be the purchasing module in an ERP system and is part of inbound logistics.
- Tendering processes, which is a special way of CRM where an organization responds to tenders from potential clients and often helps a client to formulate a complex requirement and then provides ways to meet this requirement. They can also be seen as preceding purchases as a customer will make a purchase on accepting the response to their tender.
- Supply chains, where a product or service requires a number of organizations to work together and integrate their activities into a smooth flowing process. Supply chains can be parts of inbound and outbound logistics or part of the manufacturing process.
- Alliances between organizations that are established often as part of supply chains.
- Trading and knowledge sharing portals that provide ways to create initial contacts between trading entities, which can be individuals or organizations.

Electronic commerce provides benefits such as reducing costs of maintaining relationships with clients, reducing transaction costs and reducing delivery times for products. The main contributors here are technologies associated with the Internet, which provide the ability of the WWW to reach customers globally and to facilitate global relationships. This ability is obtained through capturing and storing knowledge about the customers.

They can include customizing services to specialized customer requirements and ways to support these services. This includes bringing together expertise to create new innovative products through knowledge sharing. It also calls for combining existing processes in ways that facilitate new ways of working. There are of course interactions between these processes made to provide business value. They are related in two ways:

- The processes often exchange transactions between themselves. Procurement and selling chains are often related as they are part of input logistics.
- Supply chains often require procurement of parts to be purchased from partners that make up the supply chain.

The processes also have a number of common characteristics that are now becoming important in any e-business process. These include teamwork, working in distributed global environments and increasingly knowledge management. These activities go across all processes, as something learned in one process should be available in other processes.

4.1   Business innovations using knowledge management

One of the potential innovations identified for e-business processes was to use knowledge for competitive advantage. Information collected through customer interactions across the Internet can be easily captured and used later to gain business value by directing specific information to the customers. The steps followed are shown in Figure 7.5 and include the following:

- Identify the general business process, as for example, CRM that will be developed;
- Identify the business innovations possible through knowledge management, such as, for example, cross-selling similar articles to those purchased previously, that will be included in the development in response to the strategic change;
- Identify the business value provided by the innovations focusing on improved business revenue or on value to stakeholders;
- Define typical business processes; and
- Outline some potential technologies to support the activities and in particular the kinds of services that are required to implement the process.

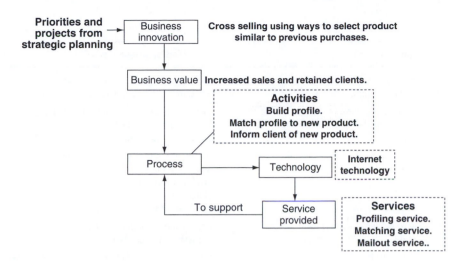

Figure 7.5   Describing e-business processes

It is often useful to use check lists in such processes, especially when looking for innovations. Subsequent sections will include typical innovations and the benefits that they realize. Innovation is a relative term and it suggests new ways that a particular organization can adopt in the way it conducts its business.

The remainder of this chapter describes some of the main processes. It commences with CRM and then describes two important aspects of inbound logistics – procurement and tendering processes. This is followed with supply chains.

5   Customer relationship management

The major objective of maintaining good client relationships is to maintain and even raise the level of service to a client through finding out what the client's current and future requirements will be. The questions are how to attract, work together to mutual advantage with their customers and retain the customers for life. The kinds of innovations that may take place here are shown in Table 7.1. Here business goals can be expressed in terms of the activities. Thus there may be innovative ways to improve field service to clients and thus lead to better retention of clients. Information technology can support innovations and provide the kind of benefits described in Table 7.1. For example, attracting clients using the WWW or building client profiles and identifying products that match these profiles. Ways of doing this will be described in later chapters. The innovations described in Table 7.1 can be used in different ways in different processes.

What is needed to support these innovations is a workspace that includes the latest information about the client to an agent supplying the service. The goal is to use this information to customize services and products to the needs of the client. Clients can use the new systems to follow orders and negotiate changes

Table 7.1   Client relationship management

Business Innovations	Expected Business Value
Direct Marketing by using IT to match customer profiles to new products.	Getting new clients and identifying specific additional services service to existing clients.
Cross-selling by using IT especially data mining to identify products similar to those previously purchased by customers.	Raising the level of activity with clients by identifying potential client services through the use of client profiles.
Service customization to client profile through observing client behavior.	Better retention through meeting specialized needs and making relationships more profitable. Use IT to develop profiles and then match it to services. Personalized information can then be sent to the client.
Responding to enquiries about products and services using IT.	Attract more customers and respond to requests in better ways.
Improving field service to clients by quicker response using IT rather than site visits.	Retention through better service and response.
Event identification – finding things that happened that may call for new services.	Grow the relationships with customers by suggesting what they can do following some major event.

as new information becomes available. The customization and follow up require the maintenance of close and intense relationship with the clients.

> It is perhaps worthwhile to say as a conclusion that the general goal of a CRM system is to provide increasingly specialized services to more clients with fewer people. The ultimate goal is to reduce the cost of maintaining high quality relationships with customers and improve competitiveness of the organization.

5.1   CRM processes

Figure 7.6 illustrates one such CRM process. Each circle in this figure represents a business activity.

Thus the first four activities, 1, 2, 3 and 4, are traditional activities where orders are filled and shipped. They generally make up what is known as B2C (the business to customer link). They allow clients to make purchases from the business. The other activities (5, 6 and 7) are the more knowledge-intensive activities now found in CRM process. Here client profiles are developed and used to provide customized advice and services to the client. They are seen as knowledge-intensive because they keep track of the client behavior and use this to determine future promotions to the client.

Cost savings are achieved by minimizing the time needed to interact with clients. This is achieved by reduced travel to client sites and by making it easy for

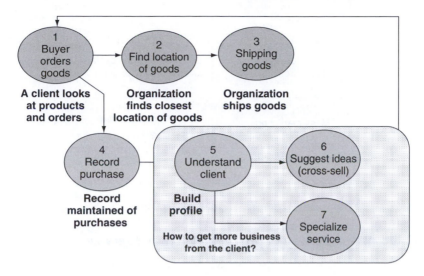

Figure 7.6   A CRM business process

clients themselves to get access to information. Thus often clients can themselves find answers to elementary problems. This enables experts to devote their time to the more complex queries and thus share their expertise with more clients through a richer set of interactions.

5.2   CRM services

The kind of business services provided here are the following:

- A catalog of an organization's products to help customers find products provided by the organization used in step 1 of Figure 7.6;
- A shopping basket to collect a record of purchases by the customer;
- Invoicing service to bill the customer and collect the payment.

The development of 1:1 services is one trend shown in Figure 7.7. This trend is from mass marketing to providing special customized services. This is made possible by many organizations developing customer profiles to focus more on client preferences.

The trend now is to go towards 1:1 service or mass customization. Here each client is provided with a personalized workspace that focuses on the client's particular requirements.

One way of providing personalized services is through call centers. These are now evolving into contact centers with greater emphasis on personalized services. The goal is to reduce the costs of providing personalized services by making personalized information available to call center operators.

Database marketing (Developing of client profiles)	1:1 service (Setting up special arrangements for each client)
Mass marketing (Treating each customer in the same way)	Niche service (Providing a specialized service in the same way to each customer)

Figure 7.7   Evolving directions

6   Call centers as a way of providing customer service

Call centers are usually the first contact of a customer and begin by directing the customer to the most appropriate agent. This agent endeavors to help the customer with their problem. The agent has ready access to any available information about the customer as well as about the problem. The agent service requests or questions about products from clients and quickly finds the best way to answer them. This requires the following:

- Decision support to assist the contact agent to decide on a course of action.
- Ways to keep track of expertise so that the best people can be found that have the tacit knowledge to provide the service or answer a question.
- Ways to support interaction and assist interpretation to minimize the time to respond to a request.

The technology support provided by call centers can be quite varied. Here the initial contact is through the telephone and a system through which the client selects the most appropriate agent through a guided set of questions and responses. Direct connection to the call center software means that the agent has all the information displayed on the screen when answering the call. The call center usually provides the agent with services such as:

All the client details displayed in front of the agent at time of call;
Product details that match the client profile;
Suggested solutions for the client;
Ability to easily initiate a new service;
A script to follow their interaction with the client.

6.1   Call center software and services

Much of the software needed to support call centers can be purchased. A number of vendors provide call center software. They distinguish themselves by providing different sets of services. One early example of such software is Dendrite, initially founded in Australia and then moved to the United States and later became cegedimdendtite (http://www.cegedimdendrite.com). This specializes in support systems in the pharmaceutical areas. Services provided include client information management, building up profiles, scripting services to help agents, client account information and so on. Others include ways of scheduling tasks that follow interaction with agents and other support services.

6.2 Personalized call center services

Customers are increasingly requesting personalized services. Additional technology is required to:

- Maintain client profiles, their history and preferences and any significant events that may effect client behavior;
- Provide better ways for clients to obtain information about the organization;
- Match clients to services and products;
- Notify clients of possible new services.

Such automatic notification can save considerable time while increasing the potential for providing additional services to a client. It is also an example of capturing knowledge during the process.

In more sophisticated centers the assistance can go beyond a single agent. This occurs in those enterprises where the problem may need some additional design or changes to the customer's service. There are two possible extensions where:

- The initial contact agent seeks further assistance from specialized agents in the call center. An example is additional professional help in a consultancy to put the client in touch with experts with specialized knowledge, or
- Where the contact is maintained throughout the process requested by the client. One example of the latter may be extension of communication facilities by a communication company (TELCO). This may require people within the TELCO to extend an existing communication network.

In systems that provide personalized services it is necessary to provide easy access for service providers to information about clients. A client can then log onto the support site and the system can allow the client to do things like following an order through the system, or changing the order as it proceeds through the system.

6.3 Web-based call centers

One important issue here is whether to use Web-based call centers or at least websites that assist in solving customer problems. The services can include searching for solutions. Often they require matching keywords to services that offer potential solutions. Other possibilities here include the following:

- *Predefined menus* that request clients to reply to ever more focused questions. These can be made more sophisticated by using expert systems and client history profiles.
- Examples of *frequently asked questions* are available with many vendor sites. However, others may ask detailed questions of the client and then pass these to experts, who may respond either directly or through the website facilities. Building communities is another way to reduce costs here. Blogs often play a role here.
- Another approach is to *analyze incoming e-mail messages* and provide standard replies. This approach is still in its infancy, as it requires ways to analyze questions within their context.

More sophisticated systems may begin to use customer profiles to customize replies to customers based on their previous history. Possible processes include getting requirements, answering problems and providing advice on ways to use in a given situation.

7 E-procurement

Procurement is an activity in inbound logistics. It concerns purchasing goods that are needed to sustain business activities. These goods may include items such as computers, furniture and so on. It can be part of demand planning in ERP systems. It concerns getting sufficient materials and parts to maintain manufacturing processes in the business or to supply its staff with office equipment. Furthermore, these parts must be acquired at minimal cost.

The term 'procurement' is often used here rather than purchasing as it includes activities additional to purchasing. It follows the process illustrated in Figure 7.8. A common approach is that the process starts with someone identifying a need and making a requisition. Once the requisition is approved a purchase is arranged. The goods are then delivered directed to the original requester and arrangements are made for a payment.

Many procurement processes proceed in a relatively structured ways based on paper ordering, where requisitions are met independently of each other. There are a variety of ways to achieve savings by automating and improving the steps of the procurement process. Some strategic objectives to achieving such savings are given in Table 7.2. These often involve bulk buying of standard products. For example, an enterprise buying personal computers often decide on a standard model and then buy a number of machines from a chosen supplier to get the benefit of bulk discounts. Manufacturing organizations can get the same benefits by regularly buying amounts from a preferred supplier.

The goal of the procurement process is basically to speed up the process and reduce the cost of both the process and the purchases.

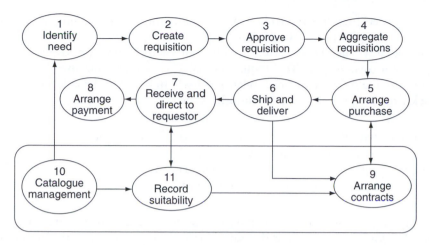

Figure 7.8   Procurement process

Table 7.2   Procurement

Strategic Objective	Expected Business Value
Set up bulk buying with selected suppliers	Reduced cost of purchasing
Automate procurement processes using a workflow system	Speeding up the process. Better integration with ERP systems.
Provide electronic catalogs for selecting purchasing	Identification of preferred parts and suppliers. Quicker selection of preferred parts.
Integrate with back-end systems especially inventory and financial services	Reduced time needed to arrange and reconcile payments.

Computers can be used to manage procurement by supporting a structured process where requisitions can be made electronically and followed through by the requester. These can then be combined with other requests and a bulk order is made. They can also expedite the process by profiling people within the organization and the kinds of goods that they can authorize. Such profiling can automate the approval step and thus speed up the process and achieve savings through bulk buying.

8 Tendering processes

Tendering is another activity in inbound logistics. It is very common with government organizations and in the construction industry. A tender, often known as requests for proposals (RFP), is issued by the tendering organization seeking a service or product. Other organizations respond to tenders, and one of these is selected by the tendering organization.

Managing tender responses is often an important activity in procurement. The response can almost be seen as an extension of CRM. It goes beyond simply

getting orders for standard products and includes the ability to configure specialized and complex orders. Organizations responding to tenders usually require
their sales force members to interact with clients and respond quickly using their
expertise to answer specialized requirements. The strategic objectives here again
emphasize the building of closer relationships with clients to be able to respond
quickly to client needs. These relationships include the following:

Working with the client to configure solutions to their problems;
Developing alternative solutions with the client;
Responding quickly about price and delivery schedules;
Getting commitments for order completion.

Configuring responses to such complex responses is a knowledge-intensive process. It requires support for the sales force to rapidly gather the necessary
information and define a need, and expertise to configure an order in response
to that need. It calls for the ability to quickly evaluate any risks in making a
proposal, including the risk of cost overruns or delivery delays and the conse-
quences of these. Al-Reshaid and Kartam (2005), for example, describe the range
of information that must be covered when responding to construction tenders.

The business innovations in managing responses to tenders are shown in
Table 7.3. The business value results from the ability to better manage 1:1 relationships with clients. This is achieved by developing a better understanding of
particular client needs and providing specialized ways to support these needs.

Table 7.3   Tender response management

Business Innovations	Expected Business Value
Better ways to keep track of knowledge to shorten the time needed to complete tender and improve quality.	Ability to secure orders through quicker and higher quality response to tender.
Customization of products and services to existing client needs by using IT to match client profile and products.	Ability to retain clients by continuously matching products to client needs. Carry out such customization through close interactions with the client. Tracing of individual orders detects problems quicker. Tracing can be implemented through search agents thus reducing cost.
Capturing customer-specific needs that require special expertise. Arranging expertise to meet such requirements	Providing value to clients through specialized services to meet specialized needs. Adding value to responding business through increasing their expertise and knowledge in emerging areas.
Understanding client through interactions using information technology.	Greater value provided to clients through in-depth knowledge of client needs. Greater value provided to responding organization by using technology to maintain and keep records of such interactions.

Collaboration with clients in order formulation.	Providing better service by specifying order configuration taking into account special client needs.
Client participation in order fulfillment through the use of workspaces that allow clients to continuously monitor order creation	Ensuring that delivered products meet customer expectation by closer monitoring orders and responding to feedback.
Costing client services and evaluating risks,	Getting higher quality assessment through easier distribution of documents for comment, thus raising quality of service.
After-sales service.	Use of information technology to provide quick responses at reduced cost. Ability to provide services with reduced site visits thus reducing cost. Ability to respond quicker and more effectively to problems.
Coordinate team selling	Put together complex requests faster across distance and thus improve the chances of getting client orders.

8.1 Business processes for managing responses to tenders

Each of the objectives in Table 7.3 must be met by following some business process. A possible process for customizing responses in request to proposals is shown in Figure 7.9. An example here is someone looking to buy a computer network. They produce a requirement and the requesting business looks at ways of meeting this requirement by following the process shown in Figure 7.9.

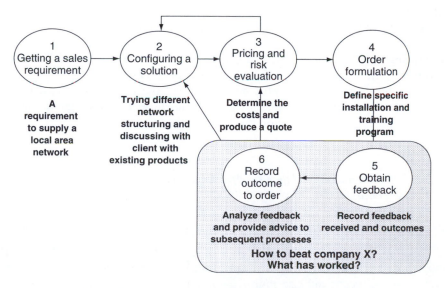

Figure 7.9   A tendering process responding to a proposal

Again there can be a distinction between the standard and knowledge-intensive activities. Activities, 1, 2, 3 and 4 are the usual steps used to configure an order. Activities 5 and 6 are concerned with developing knowledge that can be used in future occasions. Thus any positive or negative feedback, suggestions would first be recorded and then analyzed and classified for use in future processes. Knowledge kept in this way is sometimes known as organizational memory.

Another example may be to design a specific educational program. The first step is to identify what knowledge the customer needs. The second step is to configure a solution – which may be to define a lecture program. This may use existing modules and supplement them with specialized lectures. The third step is to cost the preparation of the educational program and its delivery. Finally the business model can specify here how these steps are actually carried out. One important factor here is the involvement of a client in configuring a solution – that is proposing what are the important issues to the client and suggesting relevant case studies.

Further possibilities here are ways to improve activity 3 in Figure 7.9 through automatic configuration and pricing or by standard proforma. This can also be improved by continual involvement of people with previous experience in developing and delivering similar programs. Al-Reshaid and Kartam (2005) describe the kind of information that must usually be provided when responding to tenders in the construction industry. This includes technical, financial and environmental factors. It also includes describing the capabilities of the responding organizations, its performance to date and a proposed implementation plan. Responses must conform with the evolving evaluation criteria now found in the construction industry and is described in detail by Chen et al. (2008).

There are many variants to this process. One difference is whether:

- Existing products can be used and reconfigured and amended as is often the case with developing specialized educational programs.
- A new product or service must be developed from new. In that case it may be necessary to include external experts or include a step for gathering the information needed to develop the new service.

> Again the overriding goal here may be seen as ensuring that order configurations are best suited to the needs of the client and can be provided at minimum cost and risk to the business.

Technology can be used to assist the order configuration process by keeping track of past configurations to speed up the process and what has worked effectively before. It can also improve communication between the clients and business experts to ensure that client needs are correctly interpreted. Cost savings are achieved by being able to develop a proposal in less time. Services for tendering processes require knowledge of history of similar requests and clients. They can include the following:

- Developing a knowledge base to provide easy access to similar requests;
- Client history and preferences;
- Competitor information;
- Documentation requirements;
- Costing and risk analysis guidelines.

8.2   Economics of supporting tendering processes with collaborative technologies

Tendering processes are usually project based and of a short duration. Consequently supporting each such process with technology is not usually viable as it could absorb a significant amount of the total cost of preparing a proposal.

9   Business networking

There is an increasing trend for processes to go across organizations, the so-called B2B (Business to business) electronic commerce. Organizations exchange transactions in a variety of ways. Figure 7.10 illustrates a typical set of interactions where transactions are exchanged across organizational boundaries. A buyer organization may order something from a supplier organization to sell to a client.

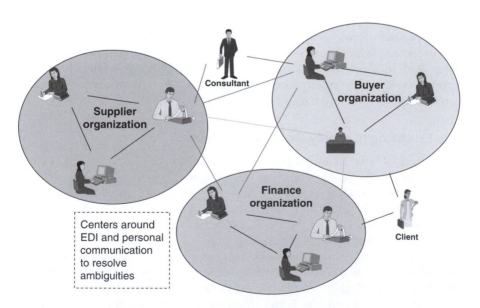

Figure 7.10   Networking between organizations

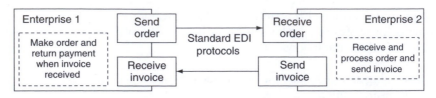

Figure 7.11   EDI – electronic data interchange

It may also arrange for payments to be processed by a finance organization. The finance organization then transfers funds from the buyer to the supplier.

Different people in the collaborating organizations generate the transactions, which are captured electronically and sent to related organizations. Reducing human intervention across organizational boundaries can also result in savings. Exchange of transactions between organizations is usually provided by Electronic Data Interchange (EDI) systems. Thus in Figure 7.11, enterprise 1 makes an order for parts needed in a project. The order is then sent electronically using a 'send order' module to enterprise 2 using a standard EDI protocol. Enterprise 2 has a corresponding 'receive module' to receive this order. Enterprise 2 has a 'send invoice' module to send an invoice, which is received electronically by enterprise 1, which then makes a payment. The order and invoice modules can be part of the ERP system that are linked to the customer purchases and financial systems.

Figure 7.11 describes networking support at the transaction level. Business networking can take place at other levels. These are covered in detail in Chapter 14 but include integration of functions, services or providing a one-stop shop for client support.

One problem often encountered in communication between organizations is that of terminology. Often two organizations use a different name for the same thing. Such inconsistencies must be resolved in any exchange of electronic transactions between the organizations. One approach here is to use a technology known as XML to define transaction transfer.

9.1   Extending to supply chain management

Advantages of networking go beyond simple exchange of transactions between two organizations. There are other advantages. They focus on the ability of organizations to use the expertise of other organizations to add value to their products. Many organizations now focus on the development of a particular expertise sometimes called their core expertise. Other organizations can then access this expertise through networking.

Such networking is now becoming commonplace because it is now virtually impossible for organization to develop expertise in all aspects of their business. Organizations then tend to outsource or form partnerships to get external expertise into their process. Better innovation is achieved through networked communities. The outcome is the growth of what are known as supply chains.

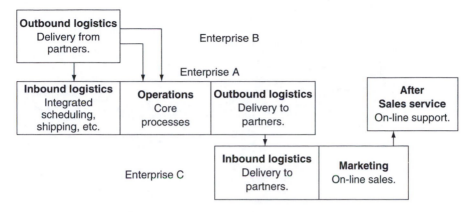

Figure 7.12 Networking for agility

Supply chains can be of the push variety or the pull variety. In a push supply chain an organization is distributing its products and mainly working together with distributors and delivery company. In a pull supply chain it is manufacturing a product and trying to get the raw materials to do so.

There has also been extensive discussion on the applicability of Porter's model in supply chains especially from the perspective of achieving competitive advantage. The trend is for a manufacturing business to disaggregate the manufacturing process and distribute the different parts to other organizations. If these organizations have the expertise to complete that part of the process both quickly and at less cost, then the manufacturing organization can also deliver its products quickly and at reduced cost. The idea is illustrated in Figure 7.12. Here Enterprise A works together with Enterprise B to obtain materials through its logistics process – an example of a pull operation. Its outbound logistics is to ship the material to Enterprise C for sales.

To obtain competitive advantage, the primary goal is to optimize the flow of goods through the production process that includes suppliers and clients. A supply chain can include a number of businesses. The businesses in a supply chain are the following:

- The business that supplies a product or service;
- Any partners involved in producing that product and service;
- The suppliers of any parts needed to produce the product and service; and
- The business clients who buy the product or service.

The fundamental operation of a supply chain is illustrated in Figure 7.13. Here there are three organizations in the supply chain. They depend on each other for the supply of parts. Thus Enterprise A is a client business, which may require parts from enterprise B. Thus Enterprise A sends a request A to Enterprise B, the supplier business. Enterprise B in turn requires a part from Enterprise C, its partner, before supplying the part requested by Enterprise A. Once Enterprise C

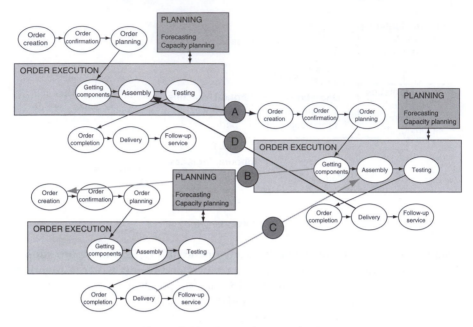

Figure 7.13   Connecting organizations

completes the part it notifies Enterprise B using transaction C. Enterprise B then completes the part requested by Enterprise A and Enterprise B sends transaction D to Enterprise A. Enterprise A can now complete the customer order.

The follow-up service may require more than one supplier. Information technology can be used here to keep track of orders, send out reminders where necessary to ensure that resources are available on time, provide easy access to data and quickly notify people whenever situations that require unexpected action arise (see Table 7.4).

Supply chains are most effective when they can be implemented electronically using electronic transactions like those illustrated in Figure 7.11. In that case the system can work almost automatically with minimal human intervention, resulting in large cost reductions. Hence they are most commonly found in relatively stable businesses, like retail or vehicle and other manufacturing processes, where there are many similar parts exchanged on a regular basis. Here the logistics processes are thus more stable and cost advantage can be obtained through the use of technology-supported supply chains. Businesses that do not have such regularity in their logistics processes often find it difficult to adopt supply chains. Akintoye et al. (2000), for example, describe the role of supply chains in the construction industry in the United Kingdom. Here there is considerable resistance to adopting standard supply chains for building sites, in particular for smaller firms. There are, however, possible advantages in larger firms that can gain advantage through bulk purchases of items that can then be used in different projects.

Table 7.4   Supply chain management

Business Innovations	Expected Business Value
Just-in-time delivery of parts or retail needed in production by using IT to track progress and initiate orders.	Reduced inventory costs.
Maintaining client liaison during production through keeping track of the progress of orders through the supply chain using workflow technologies.	Improved relationship with client through awareness that allows client to match their activities to production and often results in reducing client costs.
Keeping track of production schedules.	Ability to keep track of orders and ensure on-time delivery. Reducing delivery costs by combining deliveries.
Production planning to minimize inventory holdings and improve lead times.	Making sure that the capacity is always there to meet orders. Reduction of delays.
Reducing logistics costs by integrating invoicing and payments with ordering process.	More effective ways to resolve queries.
Maintaining liaison with business partners.	Partners know exactly what is needed thus reducing the time needed to putting components together.

On the other hand, one might argue that what is needed are more collaborative supply chains that can tolerate some flexibility.

9.2   Extending collaboration to supply chains

So far the book described supply chains that are relatively smooth flowing and can be supported by ERP software. Many of the evolving supply chains now go further and must support the exchange of planning and operational data between partners. This is necessary to support coordinated change as customer needs evolve. The proposal here is to integrate the businesses of different industries to flexibly change their supply chains. The entities involved in a supply chain and processes must bring people in these entities together. Often they must integrate transaction systems with planning and ordering so that people can keep track of what is going on.

The kind of change is shown in Figure 7.14. The left-hand side shows the current approach of maintaining a number of separate 1:1 relationships. Thus in Figure 7.14 there are four such separate relationships. The producer will have to maintain all of them. Thus, for example, if there are partners that share an order then the supplier would often need to keep separate relationships with each partner. Furthermore, they will have to pass information between the different participants. For example, putting clients in touch with business partners where necessary. A collaborative alternative is to have the network view shown in the

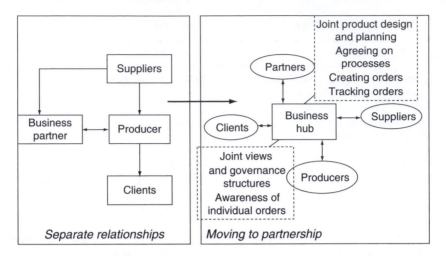

Figure 7.14 Collaborating entities in supply chains

right-hand side of Figure 7.14. Here there is a business hub, which supports businesses to make networking arrangements. Typical services here can include the following:

- Catalogs of items available from suppliers;
- Arrangements for making contracts;
- Suggestions for changes to products or services;
- Ability to create short-term supply chains;
- Providing training in the use of the business hub;
- Support for auctions;
- Getting actively involved in partnerships to design the new products and services.

9.3   Disaggregation and vertical integration

One effect of the trend to supply chains is in the disaggregation of existing businesses into specialized markets. For example, vehicle manufacturers originally made all the component parts. However, now most of the parts are produced by associated business partners, who specialize in manufacturing different components. There may, for example, be specialized business making tires, or transmissions. These component manufacturers have core competencies in producing such components – for example the transmission system and their businesses focus on continually improving these components. The vehicle manufacturers purchase these components and assemble the components. They can select the best components from the component manufacturers. The term 'vertical integration' is often used to describe putting together parts produced by different business into an integrated product and is illustrated in Figure 7.15.

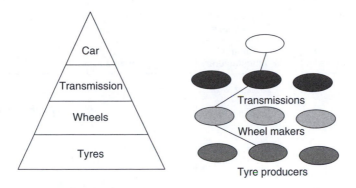

Figure 7.15 Disaggregation in the automobile industry

The supply chains of the different organizations are integrated to ensure a smooth manufacturing process. It is perhaps interesting to note that this is the way Japanese firms achieved competitive advantage over US vehicle manufacturers in the early 1960s. The purchase of components is supported by supply chains, in most cases using information technology in the way shown in Figure 7.13. The relatively stable nature of the manufacturing process provides substantive benefits using information technology to support the supply chain.

There are many suggestions of ways to get additional benefits from supply chains. One is to get away from standard suppliers and adopt a more flexible approach where suppliers can be chosen dynamically. Howard et al. (2006) describe the approach of using business hubs that include producers and consumers of auto parts and illustrate two alternatives, one using a system known as 'Covisint' supported by Ford and 'eVEREST' used by Volvo. The systems differ in their operation. The former is based on an auction system, with a perceived goal to reduce cost. The latter focuses on greater integration with suppliers with a goal of process improvement. The use of business hubs, however, requires negotiation of contracts rather than simple purchases as stability is required over long periods of time and hence as described by Howard not adopted. This may not apply to all industries.

9.4 Example in telecommunications

Figure 7.16 describes the product aggregation in the telecommunications industry. Here the basic components or chips are produced by organizations with the skills needed to manufacture small chips that deliver substantive power. These are then assembled by hardware manufacturers into products such as computers.

All the organizations in this supply chain must collaborate to ensure that products acceptable to customers are constructed. Thus the service provider learns what services are expected by the consumers. This knowledge is passed to the equipment provider who designs the required systems to deliver the services. The equipment provider in turn specifies the components needed to construct the equipment.

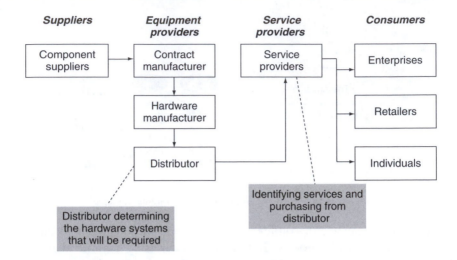

Figure 7.16   Telecommunications

Telecommunication supply chains have changed over time. Heikkila (2002) describes such changes and their impact on the Nokia organization. They also describe the dynamic nature of the supply chain which changes as technology evolves. Thus Figure 7.16 describes the supply chain for retail to customers whereas other supply chains focus more on building the telecommunications infrastructure. For example, Heikkila identifies telecommunications technology vendors, who provide switching equipment to base transceiver stations, which are managed by telecommunication operators, who focus on end-user services.

The significant difference here from some more stable industries is that the chain is driven by customers and in fact becomes a demand chain.

9.5   Example in electric power generation

Separation of electric power systems into generation companies, transmission companies and deliverers has led to greater efficiencies. Here different enterprises run generators, whereas others transmit the electricity, and still a third is responsible for direct sales. Large organizations can benefit from such arrangements as they can buy their power from the cheapest supplier and switch suppliers very quickly. In fact it is common for power to be purchased by larger manufacturers in intervals of a few minutes given the current technology. On the other hand, people who have solar devices that generate more power than they need can feed it back into the grid.

10   Trading hubs and portals

There is an increasing trend to virtual environments that match the needs of consumers with goods and services provided by producers. These like eBay

Table 7.5   Trading portals

Strategic Objective	Expected Business Value
Finding experts with skills	Improved service quality
Finding matching services	Access to a wider range of providers
Putting teams together	Teams have the necessary skills to carry out projects

provide the facilities for customers to trade goods. There is of course nothing to stop a hub from trading knowledge and skills. How to develop trust in a portal in a virtual organization such as hubs often requires an authentication service. One way is to use trusted authentication services. Here a consumer uses a trusted service to review and report on producers within a portal. This is similar to what happens now in practice – many people use reviews in magazines to decide on their purchases.

Usually portals provide improved access to consumers of services with access to a wider range of service providers. Thus consumers can register their needs while suppliers register their products and services. The portal then matches consumers to suppliers (see Table 7.5).

10.1   Extending hubs to the tendering process

Electronic trading has gained popularity through individuals using sites such as eBay. There are, however, many other possibilities for using trading hubs in business. Procurement through trading portals is one example. Responding to tenders is an often quoted example. Earlier the chapter described tendering assuming that organizations receive tenders by direct correspondence. It is also possible to envisage a situation like that shown in Figure 7.17. Here an enterprise, A, which requires some item posts its requirement on a portal. Other

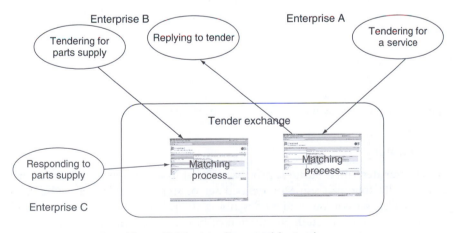

Figure 7.17   A trading portal for tenders

organizations are automatically alerted of the arrival of the new tender and can examine it and if interested commence their tendering process to formulate a tender response. Enterprise B may itself tender a third enterprise to provide the required input materials.

11   Integrating services into business processes

So far this chapter described ways to achieve cost reduction through process integration and distribution through the WWW. The next step is to provide services with innovative products to clients. Hence we are looking at new ways of doing business where clients and suppliers work together to co-create the product and its associated services. The services themselves are now almost becoming the main consideration of sale rather than the product, where the services are seen as adding value by enhancing the client's experience.

Such co-creation is made possible by Internet technologies. Simply converting a legacy application to a Web application is not the best way. It may achieve some cost competitive advantage for a while but competitors will soon do the same. A more effective way is to provide better and innovative services together with the product. The question is how to do this? This is where innovation through collaboration comes in. It is necessary to find new ways to delivering services. Some alternatives include the following:

- Improve a process through better interfacing with clients and using client feedback. Sometimes a better Web interface can in fact improve client retention.
- Combine or integrate processes to provide better interaction with clients. Such combination ensures that any request by the customer can be easily traced through the different applications.
- Respond quickly to changing requirements through collaboration and networking with clients and potential partners. This also requires support for collaboration between people in the organization to tune predefined workflows when needed.

Managing such joint co-creation is becoming more and more important. Cova and Salle (2008), for example, describe the gradual move to what they call S-D (service-dominant logic) of marketing and the transition from the G-D (goods-dominant) logic. These will be covered in more detail in the next chapter.

12   Summary

This chapter described business processes found in today's industry. These processes usually followed some predefined set of steps to achieve a well-defined goal. The chapter commenced by describing the role of ERP systems in providing cost advantages through elimination of human intervention in processes. It then described the extension to businesses processes to the WWW and further advantages achieved through better connectivity to clients and partners and use of knowledge to provide more customized service to clients.

The chapter then described typical processes on the WWW and continued with a description of supply chains. It differentiated between supply chains that support a predetermined set of business units and those that support more flexible arrangements. These flexible arrangements allow partners to change more flexibly. This heralds the trend to business hubs which support collaboration in arranging business arrangements. The next chapter builds further on this trend in describing the developments in business networking and the ability to achieve business value through facilitating greater flexibility in forming supply chains.

13   Questions and exercises

Question 1

Referring to Figure 7.4, why are teamwork and knowledge management important in e-business processes. What kind of knowledge can be shared between the kinds of processes shown in Figure 7.4?

Question 2

Identify some ways in which organizations use mobile phones to provide added value to their processes. Compare their application in CRM systems, supply chains, procurement and tendering.

Question 3

What are the characteristics of industries that can benefit from using ERP systems in their supply chains? Identify some such industries.

Question 4

What are the characteristics of industries that can benefit from knowledge hubs?

Exercise 1

Electronic mail has been proposed as a way to maintain contact with your clients. Do you think it would be useful for the following?

(a) Direct marketing where you target clients with specific products and send them information about these products;
(b) Cross-selling to your clients where you suggest to clients products very similar to those that they have purchased previously;
(c) Arranging meetings with clients;
(d) Following up after service requests.

Assume that you can have a large number of clients. Describe briefly how you would use e-mail in each case.

What other software, in particular social software, would you suggest to provide a better service?

Case study V

Building teams for responding to tenders

Team formation, especially in dynamic environments, places many challenges because teams must be assembled quickly but at the same time a solution must be created at an acceptable cost. This is especially so when responding to tenders where there is almost an expectation that each request will require a new product in the sense that the building will be different from those previously built.

Responding to tenders in construction is an important activity in any large construction business. Responses to tenders require expertise in a number of areas and the ability of experts in different domains to address increasingly complex requirements and to resolve conflicts and provide a successful outcome. Tender responses have now become more formalized and structured with considerable detail required on a number of issues. These include the following:

- The technical design that must meet technical evaluations;
- Economic factors including the financial status of the organization;
- Environmental factors such as local council requirements; and
- Implementation plan including access to resources and personnel needed to complete the work in the stipulated time.

Often tender responses are made by transient teams chosen because of their availability and expertise. Tendering organizations must create a team to analyze the tender situation. In choosing the team the organization must pay attention to the cultural and language skills of the team members to ensure that they can complete a satisfactory response in often limited time.

The CEO of BCC (Building Construction Conglomerate) following decreases in successful tendering decided to look at possible causes and perhaps instituting new processes for responding to tenders.

The BCC business model operates as a set of projects, with a project manager assigned to each project. The project manager is the person, who followed a tender right through from conception to implementation. Currently when BCC identifies a potential tender, a project manager most likely to undertake the work is assigned to make a tender response. The project leader then assembles a team which mostly operates in virtual mode. Often team members are chosen based on availability rather than required skill. The leader assigns particular tasks to different members, who may be available at the time.

There is a suspicion at BCC that the culture of assigning tender responses to project managers available at the time may not be the best approach. A project manager is required to run an existing project, often in its final stages, while at the same time managing a virtual team in responding to a tender. Often people chosen by the project manager responsible for the project may not have the complete set of skills needed in the response.

BCC is considering setting up a special tender response group. One responsibility of the group is to develop standards of some aspects of the process to identify routine components and automate them. The other responsibility is to respond to tenders. Two alternative ways are proposed for such responses.

One alternative is to set up a team for each tender response. The team would be made up of experts chosen for the specialized skills needed for a particular tender response. This team would include experts in these areas. The other alternative is to establish a flexible structure with a full-time coordinator with administrative assistance. Project managers would be consulted in an advisory capacity as would experts as needed.

Develop a proposal for one of these alternatives illustrating with an ESN. These teams would have a range of specialized skills and only use external experts in exceptional circumstances.

In your response, examine the tendering process shown in Figure 7.9. This already assumes that a team has been assembled to compile a tender response. Look at each activity in Figure 7.9 and suggest:

- What roles are required in each activity, the knowledge they need, and how these roles will interact with roles in other activities;
- Define the skills needed by people assigned to these roles;
- Ways to assign roles to more than one tender evaluation team;
- Extend to include an activity that assigns people to different evaluation teams, distinguishing between two possibilities. One is a team assembled for the duration of an evaluation. The second is where there is a coordinator who calls on experts as required.

Some further readings

Akintoye, A. McIntosh, G., Fitzgerald, E. (2000) 'A Survey of Supply Chain Collaboration and Management in the UK Construction Industry' *European Journal of Purchasing and Supply Chain Management*, Vol. 6, pp. 159–168.

Al-Reshaid, K., Kartam, N. (2005) 'Design-build Pre-Qualification and Tendering Approach for Public Projects' *International Journal of Project Management*, Vol. 23, pp. 309–320.

Chen, Z., Li, H., A. Ross, A., Khalfan, M., Wong, S.C.W. (2008) 'Knowledge-Driven ANP approach to Vendors Evaluation for Sustainable Construction' *Journal of Construction Engineering and Management*, Vol. 134, No. 12, December, pp. 928–941.

Jacobs, F.R., Weston, F. (2007) 'Enterprise Resource Planning' *Journal of Operations Management*, Vol. 25, pp. 357–363.

Jones, M.C., Cline, M., Ryan, S. (2006) 'Exploring Knowledge Sharing in ERP Implementation: An Organizational Culture Framework' *Decision Support Systems*, Vol. 41, pp. 411–434.

Howard, M., Vidgen. R., Powell, P. (2006) 'Automotive E-hubs: Exploring Motivations and Barriers to Collaboration and Interaction' *Journal of Strategic Information Systems*, Vol. 15, pp. 51–75.

Lorincz, P. (2007) 'Evolution of Enterprise Systems' *LINDI 2007, International Symposium on Logistics and Industrial Economics*, 13–15 September, Wildau, Germany.

Porter, M.E., Millar, V.E. (1985) 'How Information Gives You Competitive Advantage' *Harvard Business Review*, Vol. 79, No. 7, July–August.

Achieving Dynamic Capability Through Business Networking

8

Not only carrying out business globally but being innovative on a global scale

Learning objectives

- Agility in business systems
- Business value chains as a way of achieving agility
- Greater emphasis on the social perspective to achieve agility
- Project management and outsourcing
- Product development
- Collaboration to achieve agility in business networks
- Collaboration Services.

1 Introduction

This chapter continues from the previous chapter by describing business processes where collaboration and innovation are essential to adapt to changing environments. At the conclusion of the chapter, readers will be aware of the additional requirements of these more dynamic systems from a number of perspectives, especially the social perspective when compared to the ERP systems described in the previous chapter.

Today's processes go beyond the early re-engineered Web-based applications that reduced costs and provided better connectivity to clients, as for example, Amazon books or Web-based businesses that arrange accommodations for travelers. These require no human intervention in the process of placing an order or making a reservation. Similarly, ATM machines allow people to make cash withdrawals without going to the bank.

The current business environment is becoming more dynamic and requires businesses to quickly adapt to changing customer demands, and adjust their processes to changes in the business environment. Such dynamic capability is needed to respond to a new competitor, new opportunities provided by technology, government policy or many others. It is also needed to respond to changing demands from customers. It impacts both on business activities and business culture and on all the perspectives of process design. Thus there may be changes to the business activities, the social structure or knowledge requirements. The organization structure perspective also comes into play here.

Response to such changes is often hard to accomplish when working through an organization's hierarchy. Agility requires ways alternate to those used by organizational hierarchies to respond to change, in particular a more team- or community-based approach, greater process integration and the ability to change processes as the business context changes.

1.1   Business characteristics and trends

Business characteristics in this new environment have been described as part of a broad vision, known as Enterprise 2.0 as defined by McAfee (2006) in his article in the Sloan Management Review. Enterprise 2.0 is a natural trend towards obtaining additional competitive advantage by using the new technologies such as those currently emerging through Web 2.0. The Enterprise 2.0 vision describes in relatively abstract terms what new businesses will look like. It sees a business environment where collaboration extends from groups and individuals to organizational units and whole enterprises. The emphasis on collaboration is also expounded in research such as that of Evans and Wolf, who in their 2005 article to the *Harvard Business Review* describe the kinds of results that can be achieved by teams working together on focused goals. One case quoted as an example was where a supplier could quickly respond by supplying valves to a car manufacturer. When a Toyota plant supplying components burnt down, arrangements were quickly made with their suppliers to supply the parts and restore operations within four days of the fire.

Although not commonly found in business, the idea of bringing people together quickly to address problems is gaining attention. It sees evolving collaboration between organizational units that were sometimes seen as silos to collaboration across firms to form a business web. It is perhaps fair to say that Enterprise 2.0 sets a direction rather than a concrete structure.

The characteristics of Enterprise 2.0 are illustrated in Figure 8.1. They focus on innovation and the ability to create and protect new ideas. They also emphasize knowledge sharing, which in turn requires support for relationships and networking that encourage such sharing. The other dimension is client value and how enterprises can add value to clients. This includes developing new products that are of value to clients, as well as the ability to deliver them, reduce costs and provide services around products that lead to raised client satisfaction. In this way, the business maintains a posture that is perceived as forward looking while

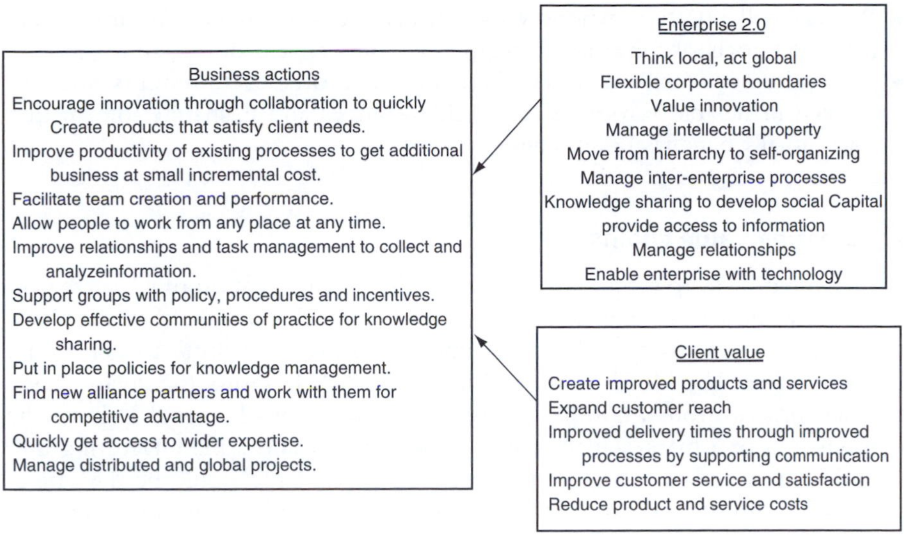

Figure 8.1

Business actions

Encourage innovation through collaboration to quickly
   Create products that satisfy client needs.
Improve productivity of existing processes to get additional
   business at small incremental cost.
Facilitate team creation and performance.
Allow people to work from any place at any time.
Improve relationships and task management to collect and
   analyzeinformation.
Support groups with policy, procedures and incentives.
Develop effective communities of practice for knowledge
   sharing.
Put in place policies for knowledge management.
Find new alliance partners and work with them for
   competitive advantage.
Quickly get access to wider expertise.
Manage distributed and global projects.

Enterprise 2.0

Think local, act global
Flexible corporate boundaries
Value innovation
Manage intellectual property
Move from hierarchy to self-organizing
Manage inter-enterprise processes
Knowledge sharing to develop social Capital
   provide access to information
Manage relationships
Enable enterprise with technology

Client value

Create improved products and services
Expand customer reach
Improved delivery times through improved
   processes by supporting communication
Improve customer service and satisfaction
Reduce product and service costs

Figure 8.1   Characteristics of Enterprise 2.0

at the same time taking actions within that posture that create value for clients. Often people speak of a vision when looking at ways to change a business.

Figure 8.1 then identifies the kind of business actions that are necessary given the enterprise characteristics and client value. These business actions focus on developing flexible organizational structures. The actions include the facilitation of social relationships, support for team structures and developing relationships that lead to new ideas and innovative products and services. The role of technology is to support these business activities and integrate them into a business process. Social software that is now become increasingly important on the Web is expected to play an important role in providing such support.

1.2   Greater emphasis on collaboration

Dynamic capabilities require continuous changes to the way that enterprises work to encourage people to work together to find better ways to do things. There are now many industries where new products are almost a necessity. Telecommunications is one where new mobile phones are almost a daily occurrence. But such dynamism is found in many others. The apparel industry is one example where networking includes retailers, apparel designers and manufacturers working in an environment of quickly changing fashions. One trend in this change is to facilitate and encourage collaboration. This chapter addresses this trend to collaboration in three levels, namely:

- Local task collaboration which was primarily described earlier when we discussed social software with a limited goal like preparing a joint report;

- Process collaboration where value chains are coordinated to implement particular goals, as for example creating an innovative product; and
- Enterprise-wide collaboration where different organization units are networked in flexible ways to share their resources and exchange information for mutually beneficial outcomes.

2 Creating value chains

One common way to achieve dynamic capability is the creation of what are now commonly known as value chains. The idea behind this term is that a business constructs its process from business units that most contribute to generating business value. The idea is illustrated in Figure 8.2. It shows the creation of a business process from a number of operating units. Thus Figure 8.2 shows the combination of a market analysis unit, a design unit and a manufacturing unit to quickly respond to emerging trends. This, for example, could be the case in the apparel industry where fashions change quickly and require capabilities to quickly respond to these changes. At the same time interfaces must be established between these business units. Usually the interfaces require collaboration between people to negotiate new work arrangements. For example, some negotiation is needed to decide what design to follow given outputs from the market analysis unit. Value chains like that shown in Figure 8.1 can include units from different organizations, some in different countries, as well as different kinds of work. One goal of creating such value chains is to select the best available units to create the best business outcome. In many cases business networks are formed from business units, which come from different enterprises.

In this context agility is characterized by the ability to quickly change the network by adding, deleting or replacing operating units. Such ability requires

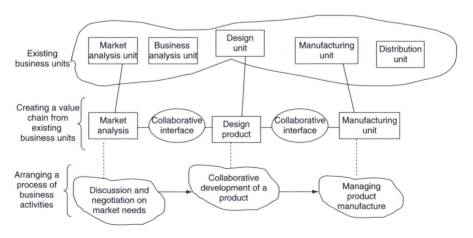

Figure 8.2 Creating a value chain

a clear definition of interfaces between the units and following best practices across the interfaces. There are some common practices that can assist such value chain creation. One, for example, is outsourcing, which is common in many industries. Software development or apparel manufactures are another two businesses where outsourcing is common. Outsourcing is where one business gets another business to carry out some activity. This may be writing a piece of software, manufacturing an item of clothing from a pattern, or finding a suitable person for a position.

2.1 Collaboration and knowledge sharing in value networks

Each business unit in a value chain process carries out some business activity. Some of the activities may be simple, others may be more complex. All these activities must be integrated into a unified process. Figure 8.2 also shows the activities found in designing products for emerging market needs. It begins with analyzing the market needs, which primarily requires discussion and negotiation to agree on market needs. This is followed by collaboratively producing a product specification and manufacturing the product. Agility requires enterprises to quickly put these kinds of activities together in flexible ways and furthermore to change such arrangements as needed. Hence the interface between these activities is most often collaborative.

In a collaborative networked environment each of these activities may be carried out at a different location but they must be orchestrated into a complete process. The interface between the activities must be smooth and seamless. This presents a challenge to design components that can flexibly fit into a variety of value chains. It requires seamless transitions between different kinds of processes, as for example, collaborative and predefined processes. These often use different technologies or work practices and putting them together into seamless processes often presents difficulties. Thus highly skilled negotiation is supported by face-to-face video communication, whereas specification development will need joint document editing, and project management some of which can use asynchronous means. The question often is how to combine the different technologies so that fewer manual transfers of information are required between activities.

2.2 General business process requirements

To realize Enterprise 2.0 vision requires enterprises to focus on setting up new relationships with people who are good at what they do and creating processes that combine their knowledge to develop new directions. This in turn places generic requirements on enterprises such as:

- Supporting teams that themselves are agile, well-coordinated and knowledgeable and can quickly make decisions in complex global situations.
- Negotiations to form new teams quickly as well as to create value chains.

- Ways to integrate or evolve ERP and e-business processes, described in the previous chapter, to provide such flexibility. Processes such as sales, or billing, or payroll or some other function are generally prescriptive in nature, and often cannot provide flexible connectivity across processes to respond collectively to changes in competitive environments. Innovation often requires changes to more than one function and rigidities in structure restrict innovation.

3 Process-oriented collaboration

Collaboration in processes focuses on achieving some well-defined goal. Figure 8.3 shows the kinds of processes now found in the business environment and their dependence on knowledge sharing and consequently on collaboration. The diagram in Figure 8.3 ranges in two dimensions. The vertical dimension is the complexity of a process, ranging from predefined to emergent. Melville and Ramirez (2008) suggest that process complexity is determined by factors such as product variety, production variety and the degree or speed of change. It also depends on the degree of connectivity and interactivity, which often depends on the type of process. Generally the connectivity in transaction-based processes is at the level of exchange of transactions between one or two individuals. The horizontal dimension defines the complexity of knowledge needed in the process. Knowledge that is relatively stable is seen as less complex than where there it is rapidly changing.

In Figure 8.3 the lower left-hand corner shows the transaction-based systems where process are comparatively structured and can be predefined. The

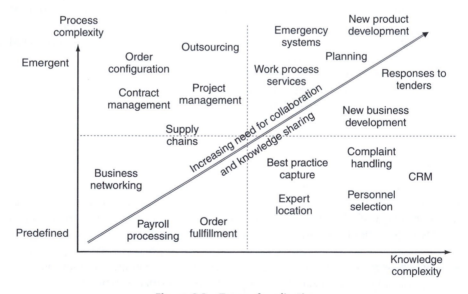

Figure 8.3 Types of application

knowledge needed at each step is also well structured and shows little structural change. Thus, for example, salary scales do not change frequently. Figure 8.3 shows where the best potential benefits lie in getting most benefits from agility and networking. These are in the top right-hand corner and include new product development, developing marketing strategies or product innovation. Here benefits of networking can be realized by experts distributed across the globe contributing their expert knowledge to the design of a product. Or, there can be arrangements made to manufacture products in different parts of the globe.

The processes in the top right-hand column are complex processes and hence require alternate design methods to those used in structured processes. These are the processes that are flexible and are composed of networked business units. At the top right-hand corners processes such as tender evaluation require continual exchange between a number of individuals to quickly bring their expertise on how to respond to a tender. The processes found in the top right-hand corner of Figure 8.3 are often found in distributed environments and require collaboration across distance. They must be more agile and be designed to both deliver products in a quick manner and to respond to changes required from its client or imposed by its environment. These include the following:

- Bringing creative design teams into a business network to create new products and services;
- Finding the best manufacturing processes to develop the new product designs;
- Outsource business functions, where the benefits often center on reducing cost through having non-core business functions carried out by a third party;
- Getting access quickly to new expertise and providing the agility to create new services quickly; and
- Sharing value through sharing best practices.

3.1 Where is the complexity?

It is not often the case that all the activities in a business process are all at the same level of complexity. Complexity is often confined to only parts of a particular enterprise or even industry, or some parts of a process. As an example, Figure 8.4 shows that complexity can happen at different parts of a given industry. It shows the difference in complexity in two industries – the wine and wood products industry. It is based on research by Melville and Ramirez (2008).

Figure 8.4 illustrates the difference between the two industries especially showing that complexity may exist in different parts of the value chain. Thus, for example, the actual production of wine follows relatively standard processes developed over many years. The marketing and distribution can however be quite complex as it must take into account changing tastes and distribution channels. Similarly inbound logistics can be complex as they must find quality grapes, which can be seasonal in nature. With wood products production can be complex as it can depend on the quality of the timber. Inbound logistics are straightforward as they usually focus on a well-defined forest area.

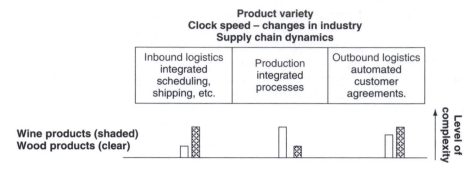

Figure 8.4   Complexity in the business

4   Project-based organizations

One kind of process achieving attention is the project management process in project-based organizations. Ajmal et al. (2008) outline the advantages that can be obtained by paying greater attention to the social and knowledge perspectives in project management. They see project management as a complex process that increasingly needs to adapt and use knowledge from previous experience in their everyday work. This particularly applies to projects learning from each other in a multi-project organization. Potential benefits include the following:

- Reduced time for the preparation of designs and proposals by using agreed upon proformas and knowledge;
- Capturing and transferring project management knowledge about procedures used to improve performance in terms of time and cost in related projects;
- Learning from similar other projects about potential customers.

They describe the need to develop a culture across all levels of the organization that encourages creation of social processes that is conducive to knowledge sharing within the organization. In many cases this now extends to forming partnerships and other arrangements with other organizations.

4.1   Extending to partnerships

Business arrangements can grow further and develop into partnerships from which all partners get value. In partnerships organizations collaborate on ways to combine their expert skills to create products that could not be created by one organization simply asking another to carry out some tasks. This requires much closer collaboration than found in outsourcing. It requires both partners to collaborate on creating new designs and jointly producing them. The collaboration goes from coordination of two teams to one of facilitation of experts sharing their knowledge.

4.2 The importance of trust in business relationships

Trust plays an important role in any business network. A business relies heavily on its partners and requires them to be both timely in the delivery of any products and services and to maintain high quality. Business partners must rely on each other to both produce what is needed on time and also help each other overcome their problems. This is where the collectivist culture provides the guideline for building businesses on strong trust relationships where all partners understand their role and place strong emphasis on achieving their broader goals.

What to do if trust is lost? Sabherwal (1999) discusses trust in some detail and the impact of trust on managing relationships in software outsourcing projects. He makes a distinction between a virtual cycle, where a high level of trust reduces the need for tight coordination as the outsourced partner is trusted to deliver on time, and the alternate vicious cycle, where tight coordination is needed to ensure correct delivery. Here intermediate check or progress points must be defined and monitored. Such loss of trust with the consequent additional work can only be seen as a negative effect on a process.

5 Outsourcing

One of the most common business relationships found in project management is outsourcing. Outsourcing results from businesses concentrating on activities where they possess the greatest expertise or their core business. Instead of doing everything yourself, the trend is for businesses to concentrate on what they are best at and to outsource their non-core activities to external parties. These are often called the organization's *core competencies*. The process that uses these competencies to provide a product or service is the organization's *business core process*. The trend is to focus on core competencies and outsource other activities to external parties. The goal of such outsourcing is to find organizations with core competencies in the outsourced functions. Outsourcing activities enable an organization to be more agile as they can now concentrate on developing new directions in their area of expertise while networking with other businesses to support their core processes. They can also now become more agile as they can quickly change their process by changing their business partners instead of restructuring their business. The most typical outsourcing discussed in the information technology community is that of software development. However, many other functions can also be outsourced. Typical outsourced functions include the following:

- Software application development where part of software development is outsourced to a software developer.
- IS management and infrastructure where entire processes are outsourced together with the equipment infrastructure required to run them.
- Call centers that are managed external to the organization.

- Human resource management which includes the hiring of staff and can also include staff training.
- Travel management to achieve discounts through obtaining favorable treatment from travel providers through block purchases.
- Marketing and distribution of an organization's products especially in distant locations.
- Voice and Data Communication Systems.
- Security of the organization's premises.
- Vehicle fleet maintenance.
- Provision of cleaning services.

For outsourcing to be successful, it must be seamlessly integrated with other enterprise operations. The outsourced service must be delivered at precisely defined times, it must be of acceptable quality and must be delivered to the right people. A typical high-level outsourcing process follows the following steps:

- Decide what to outsource. Apart from focusing on core business there are many other factors that come up in the outsourcing decision. Milligan and Hutcheson (2006) identify such additional factors such as staff reduction, lack of internal expertise and the cost of outsourcing. The benefits and risks of outsourcing must be clearly identified.
- Choose a provider that matches the organization's requirements and that can work together well with the organization.
- Make an agreement that includes an integration plan and an agreed upon process. Ensure that there is seamless integration with internal processes.
- Arrange contacts.
- Initiate and manage the outsource activity.

5.1   Deciding what and whether to outsource

Organizations are now deciding on the potential benefits of outsourcing and forming networked arrangements. The fundamental choices are on what to outsource. One approach in making this decision is to focus on the enterprise core business and outsource functions in which the organization has no particular competitive advantages. Factors in making this decision include the following:

- Ability to hire staff in a non-core area. This can impact on costs as special management structures would need to be created to manage such staff.
- Evaluating the costs of outsourcing and comparing to current costs.
- Evaluating any risks associated with outsourcing including potential loss of commercial information.

Many organizations, for example, now outsource their call centers. Call center management often includes special skills and operations and many organizations may not wish to invest their funds in developing such skills. It is often better to use such investment to develop better competitive advantage in their core business rather that duplicating what already exists in industry.

5.2 Choosing a vendor or provider

This will often mean looking at a number of alternate providers and alternate functions to outsource. Then an agreement is made and a contract is signed. The contract defines how the process is to be carried out and how the parties interact. The most common form of outsourcing in information technology is that of application development. Another common function that is outsourced is call center management.

5.3 Reducing risk

Outsourcing presents risks to organizations. These include quality of delivered products, loss of control of delivery services, loss confidentiality and intellectual property, Rottam (2006) suggests diversity of suppliers to maintain competition, and breaking into segments to protect against loss of intellectual property.

5.4 Arranging the contract

Any contractual arrangements must not only specify financial considerations but must clearly define the processes to be followed in any outsource arrangements. They must create a service-level agreement and identify roles and responsibilities of these roles and their expected interactions.

Outsourcing arrangements often specify different arrangements to be followed during different parts of the business process. The contract must then identify the different kinds of work to be undertaken, the way collaboration is to take place for each kind of work, and the artifacts produced. It should define the roles and responsibilities of people in the outsourcing interface. For example, the vendor Mastek, who provides a software development service, requires that any original specifications or any changes must be carried out face to face. The coordination of program development can be carried out across distance.

5.5 Maintaining the relationship

Maintaining the working relationship between parties is often a matter of establishing trust though continual exchange of information. Frequent exchanges of messages and explanations about each other's activities are important here in sharing knowledge. Carrying out mutually beneficial tasks also helps in establishing trust.

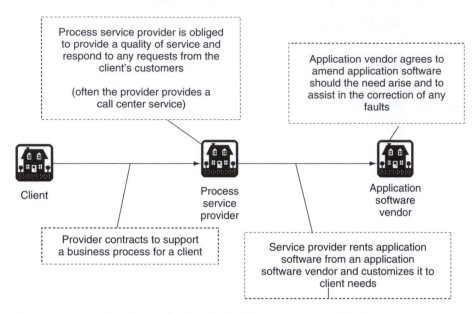

Figure 8.5 Typical relationships in process outsourcing

5.6 Outsourcing business processes

Most people in information technology usually infer that outsourcing means the outsourcing of software development. It is possible to outsource other processes and to outsource the running of entire processes or parts of processes. Decisions here are often made from an organizational perspective. For example, an organization might outsource delivery of products and collection of payments but not their production. Figure 8.5 is a model from the organizational perspective that illustrates the business arrangement where the service provider must support the entire application. The notation used in the diagram is that the house-like icons indicate different organizations. The links between them describe what is expected of the relationships between them. The outsourced application can be invoicing, payroll or any other application. Here there can be a number of participating parties and contracts between the parties. Thus the provider has a contract with a client to support the outsourced process. The provider also has a contract with the vendors of the applications. Figure 8.5 the process service provider supports a process for a client. The provider purchases application software from application vendor and customizes them to client requirements. Both contracts include quality of service requirements.

The process service provider must:

Provide the requested service to the client;
Obtain resources from vendors needed to provide the service;

Provide service support to the clients customers in answering customer queries;

Engage with vendor managers in any modifications to their services.

5.7 Managing outsourcing

Figure 8.6 is the business activity model for managing an outsourced process for a client. The application being outsourced, in this case, is billing. Here the provider manages a call center to collect any customer requests or problems from the client's customers. The role 'operations manager' is responsible for managing the outsourced operation.

The major business activities are the following:

- 'Customer report management', usually through a call center;
- 'Outsourcing management', which includes the contracts between the client the operator and the vendor;
- The outsourced activity to manage everyday operations, in this case is 'billing operation'.

Figure 8.6 also illustrates the roles that are part of the agreement. They include an 'operations manager' who coordinates all the service provider activities and leads the outsourcing teams in the billing operation activity. The operations manager also liaises with application vendor and the client. This is the role that is part of the interface between the provider and other parties.

The process can be even more complex than shown in Figure 8.6. There may be, for example, many clients, or many more applications or even many countries in a global environment.

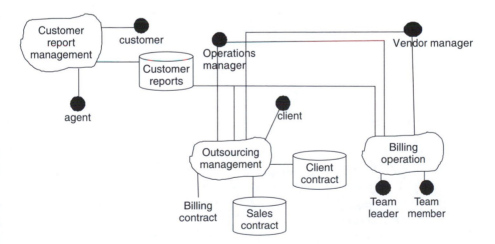

Figure 8.6   Activities in process outsourcing

Dynamic capability for the service provider is achieved by developing ways that lead to expanding the provision of services to new clients with marginal costs. What one is after is to build the value network further. It should be possible to "plug-in" new services for the same client, or new clients for the same service. How easy it is to achieve this depends on the interfaces between the different network components.

Such dynamic value network creation again often requires platforms that simplify the management of collaborative relationships through the use of technology. In this case the dynamic capability is where it is possible to quickly add a new client for the same kind of service or add a new service for a client. The important criterion of dynamic capability is whether this can be done quickly with small incremental cost.

Thus dynamic capability here focuses on the ability to expand without necessarily incurring a proportional increase of resources. The goal is to put in place collaborative systems, which can reduce the time spent in managing the outsourcing processes. In that case new clients can be added or new processes can be supported with minimal increases of staff.

5.8 Collaboration in outsourcing

A well-established practice is for organizations to outsource the software development, or any other manufacturing process, often to countries that offer such services at lower cost. As shown in Figure 8.7, this involves identifying tasks to be carried out, who carries out the tasks and how interactions between the client

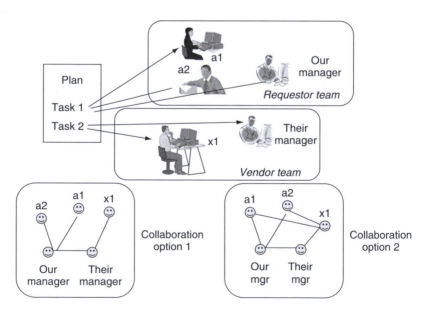

Figure 8.7   Carrying out a software development project

and the provider organizations are to be managed and supported. Often there is one team in the client organization and another in the provider organization. Processes must be set up to coordinate the activities of these two teams and to support such coordination with appropriate tools.

Figure 8.7 illustrates that the requester team carries out task 1, usually the system specification. The vendor team carries out task 2, usually the development. Two alternatives collaboration patterns are shown in Figure 8.7. They are the following:

- Collaboration option 1, where all communication between organizations take place between managers; or
- Collaboration option 2, where formal exchanges between members in the two teams will be allowed.

The outsourcing process often separates the design aspects and the development aspects. The collaboration can be different at each of those activities. Figure 8.8 distinguishes between local collaboration and interorganizational collaboration. It shows that in general:

- Requirements specification and design carried out mainly through the collaboration of the internal team with some minimal interaction with the supplier on their capabilities.
- The contract is developed through the collaboration between the vendor and the client team. The outsourcing agreement defines how the initial requirements must be specified by the developer team and delivered to the vendor team. Such specification is often discussed face to face to clarify issues.
- The development is carried out by the vendor's team with minimal communication between the teams.

Another question that comes up is whether the collaboration is synchronous or asynchronous. The general consensus is in most cases it must be synchronous, as for example contract negotiation. This is recognized by many organizations that provide outsourcing services. Mastek (www.mastek.com), for example, preferred

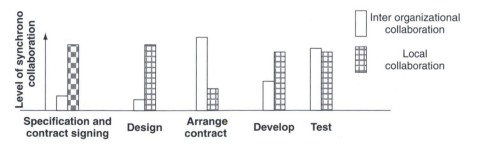

Figure 8.8   The changing nature of collaboration

initial requirements and changes to be carried out synchronously whereas the development is carried out in-house. Anyone designing such systems must determine the best way to support such collaboration with technology.

Impact on business process requirements

Designers of business must place greater emphasis on the social perspective in supporting relationships between business partners. This must include ways to build and maintain trust to support collaboration.

Negotiation is playing an increasing role in business with the continuous need to form new alliances and renegotiate existing arrangements.

---

6 Product development

Product development more often than not involves a business network. Most products are complex in nature and require a large number of sources of knowledge. It can be a motor vehicle, or a computer, clothing or a mobile phone. Any product requires designers to construct a specification, which defines the product structure. It usually defines different parts that must be put together to make the complete product. Parts have to be purchased, work schedules arranged, machines scheduled and deliveries made. All of this puts product development in the general category of collaborative network of many different people. The goal of any support system is to reduce the cost and time from conception to delivery and encourage innovation through collaboration. The supporting system in product development requires the following:

- Maintaining awareness between all stages of product design;
- Setting up the teams to create the product and ways for team members to communicate; and
- Maintaining documents between the team members.

6.1 The apparel industry – An example of dynamic capability

The apparel industry is perhaps a prime example of business networking in product development. It is characterized by continuous change in product as dictated by fashion trends. A good description of this industry is given by Sen (2008), who outlines the industry as a supply chain of five major segments shown in Figure 8.9, namely:

- The fiber producers;
- The material manufacturers;
- The designers;
- The garment manufacturers; and
- The retailers.

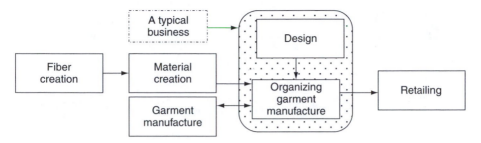

Figure 8.9   Businesses in the apparel industry

The typical supply chain is that fibers, such as cotton, are used to create materials which are then sewn into apparel items. The designs of apparel are determined by consultation between retailers, who often monitor fashion trends. The designs determine the material cuts that are sewn into clothing items.

A particular business can include any of the five segments. The most common are fashion designers who in discussion with retailers create designs for sale through retailers, thus creating a value chain. Another, which is shown on Figure 8.9, illustrates a business that designs and produces the garments, but organizes ways to outsource that actual garment manufacture. The design creates patterns which are used to create pieces of apparel. Design itself is a complex process with the goal of minimizing material wastage with suitable patterns. The fashion designer business then outsources the garment manufacture. Such outsourcing often is to low-cost countries such as China. The apparel trade is very competitive and often retailers go past the manufacturer directly to the outsource partner to create retailer labels.

Seamless interfaces between the different business units often rely on standard practices within an industry. For example, patterns form an interface to manufacturers. They define ways to cut and sew material pieces together to form garments.

Collaboration occurs at most of the interfaces shown in Figure 8.9. Retailers talk to manufacturers to see what designs might sell. Designers negotiate manufacturing costs with manufacturers. The whole process is dynamic. Relationships can easily change with a retailer finding a new designer or even doing some designs themselves. Designers are always searching for manufacturers that can produce products at lower cost.

6.2   Product development activities and processes

Product development can of course be managed by one organization. There are a large number of activities in product development. Each of these activities may require a different supporting service. The main activities are shown in Figure 8.10. They assume that it is for a particular client or for a given class of customers.

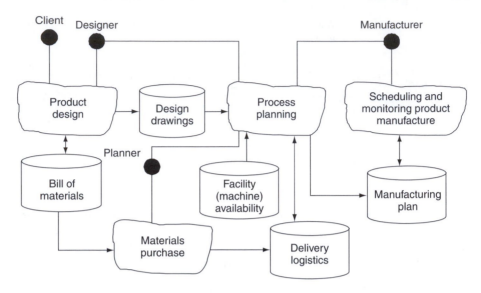

Figure 8.10   Product development activities

The typical activities are described by Ming et al. (2008), who developed their CAPP (computer-aided process planning) which includes the following:

- Product design from the client specifications. Special tools are often needed to do this. Engineering design often calls on CAD (Computer-aided design tools).
- Materials planning that includes identifying the components needed to build the product, what is often called bills of material, and arranging the purchase of the materials. These is usually an ERP system.
- Process planning to define the sequence in which the different components will be constructed. Again there are tools available to assist scheduling.
- Arranging the delivery of parts.
- Scheduling and monitoring the manufacture of the product.

The simple approach is to carry out these activities in sequence. One way is to start with design, then create the manufacturing process, and then manufacture the product. However, pressures to speed up production times often call for what is currently called concurrent engineering. Thus instead of waiting for the whole design to be completed, parts of the design may be scheduled for manufacture. The manufacturer may give feedback to the designers with new ideas that may improve the whole design.

6.3   ERP systems – Manufacturing resource planning

Manufacturing resource planning or MRP-2 provides software support to manage the manufacturing process. This now has additional goals of ensuring flows

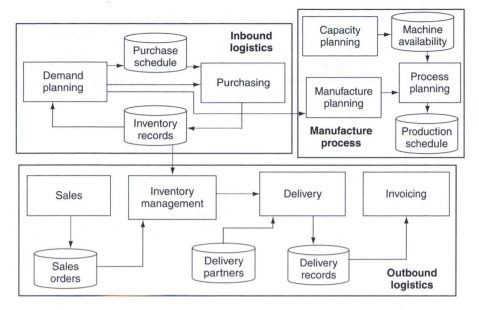

Figure 8.11   An ERP manufacturing architecture

through the manufacturing process. It includes optimizing the utilization of resources such as machines, batching similar items together to reduce setting times and the timely arrival of parts. Figure 8.11 shows a configuration of possible ERP modules to integrate the production process. It extends Figure 7.3 by including modules for manufacturing process. It includes the following kinds of modules:

- Demand planning, which estimates the expected demand for the enterprise products;
- Manufacture planning that determines the schedule of the items to be manufactured to meet customer demand;
- Capacity planning to determine the resources need by the production prices and schedule them into the process plan; and
- Process planning that defines the schedules for each resource, as for example machine tooling and person availability.

There are also the collaborative activities that center around this process. These include arranging customer purchases, and the purchase and delivery of parts required to manufacture the products.

They also include discussions on ways to improve processes. Unexpected changes in customer demand, changes to designs and potential improvements to machinery all require collection of information and its interpretation to identify potential improvements to the processes. These are usually carried out outside the automated process that is usually predefined.

Mold preparation is one quoted example here. Ni and others in 2007, for example, describe a system that integrates all the activities that surround mold production. The manufacturing process here has to be sufficiently dynamic to support changes in mold specification from customers. Previous customers here often require slight product modifications and hence the product design database becomes very valuable. The activities include the following:

- Responding to requests for quotes, where often reference is made to a client's earlier requests, and requires a quotation preparation;
- Customer order processing once a customer order is received;
- Layout design that involves customer review;
- Detailed design that must often be reviewed by the customer and finally released by the project manager to production;
- Material purchasing that includes preparing purchase orders, and managing inventory levels;
- Production planning and management.

Ni and others defined a process model that shows the relationship between all the process activities. They also designed a database that includes all the information needed in the business process activities. They report that such integration of the activities and information resulted in 20 percent saving in design, 20–30 percent in labor and materials and 10–30 percent in setting up tools.

6.4   Collaboration in product development

Manufacturing and product development processes are going through a period of rapid change. There is some agreement that greater client participation in the process may be desirable. This puts more emphasis on collaboration. Research work in Korea has demonstrated some of the capabilities that must be provided to achieve customization. The idea here is to go beyond e-manufacturing to i-manufacturing where 'i' stands for intelligent or innovative.

The focus here is on integrating collaborative software into the manufacturing processes to allow stakeholders to input and share knowledge at all points of the manufacturing process. Rye et al. (2008) describe the structures developed for this purpose and its application in a number of enterprises in the molding industry. He and his co-workers propose that knowledge hubs be set up at different parts of the process where people can contribute knowledge to that part of the process. Hubs are ways to organize collaboration in ways that complements the manufacturing process. For example, there is a design hub, a production hub, an engineering hub.

The activities here are the same as in Figure 8.11 but the services to support the activities are organized in ways that encourage collaboration. The hubs include the relevant files for the particular activity as well as support for interaction between people involved in each hub and the tools needed to carry out their tasks.

7 Extending product development to services

Customers are now increasingly demanding services as part of any purchase. Vargo and Lusch (2008) see this is a marketing trend from G-D (goods dominant) to S-D (service dominant) marketing.

Cova and Salle (2008) see an emerging trend to co-design where the producer works together with customers and service providers to create a product. The increasing emphasis on 'service science' is one outcome here. It is a study of personal preferences.

Service orientation applies both to relationships with clients and within a business.

7.1 Services to clients

Collaboration is now becoming more common in most business processes. Some that are increasingly more common are capturing best practices reported by some clients and notifying other clients about them, responding to personalized client requests and tracing problems reported by clients in supply chains. In dynamic environments systems must be responsive and as such quickly developed. There is now growing opinion that business systems should be composed from services that can somehow be put together to meet emerging client needs.

7.2 Delivering dynamic capability to business services

The service-oriented approach is found increasingly useful in domain where technology is deeply integrated into everyday work processes. A service approach gives a more flexible approach to dynamic capability. What you often need to do is add a new service or improve an existing service rather than changing the whole organization. Typical examples here include most health services and many services concerned with managing complex tasks, such as contract management. The idea of services within a business is shown in Figure 8.12.

Figure 8.12 distinguishes between business process services and Web services. Here Web services are provided by information technology. They may be a document management repository, a discussion system or a blog. Business process services are what are needed to run a process. This may be placing an order, sending a report for advice, getting results from a test and so on. A designer of a service must then identify what is needed, then find a Web service to support the business process service and then assemble the Web services into a platform. This platform may be a Web portal or a workspace. The platform must place the

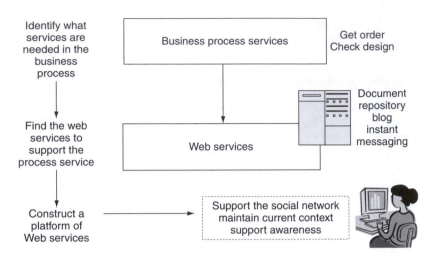

Figure 8.12 Business process services

Web services in the work context to support work activities. What are the business services to be supported? There are services needed for specific application areas or those that are general.

Possible general services are capturing best practices, finding experts, repairing supply chain problems, tendering or contract management.

7.3 Finding experts or people to work with

One important part of setting up new networks is to find the right partners. The two most obvious alternatives are to contact someone you have worked with before or find partners that fit a particular profile. These can be partners, individuals, consultancies, or specialist contractors. Maybury et al. (2001) suggest that the best way to find experts is through examining their experience rather than published CVs.

Another example of partnership formation can be in getting design expertise. This especially applies to smaller companies in networked environments. Small manufacturing firms, for example, cannot afford to get experts in many areas and may rely on getting external advice. The goal here is to allow external experts to examine proposals and comment on them, suggesting possible improvements. Table 8.1 describes some benefits of working with external experts.

7.4 Services for fault tracing

Fault repair often is not simply a straightforward activity in fixing some local problem. Many faults or customer problems arise in supply chains where it is not entirely obvious where the problem arises. Often these supply chains

Table 8.1   Value from external design expertise

Business Innovation	Benefit
Providing better access to knowledge outside the enterprise.	Quicker and more accurate problem identification
Finding and focusing available staff and experts on a problem or idea.	Development higher quality solutions through easier access to experts
Delivery of specialized services to clients.	More clients can be supported by the same number of experts
Retaining and capturing information for later use.	Solutions can be quickly found using earlier experiences.

cover more than one organization and requires collaboration to locate the source of the problem. There is a large variety of faults and they can appear unannounced. It requires interaction between many participants and has tight time constraints. Yet in many cases e-mail is the only medium used in communication.

Fault Tracing

Fault tracing in supply chains must first identify where the fault is and then repair the fault. Even in a simple supply chain like the one in Figure 8.13 the problems can include the following:

- Order not filled, which could mean an omission at any of the stages at any of the involved businesses;
- Wrong items delivered, which could result in failure in the ordering process, errors in supplier order or delivery arrangements.

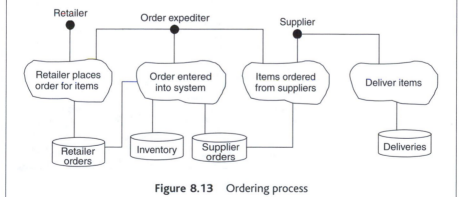

Figure 8.13   Ordering process

To find the reason for failure all parts of the supply chain must be investigated. There is still a tendency to use e-mail for this purpose. However, with the growing complexity of supply chains the kinds of communication problems described in Chapter 2 can occur. The result is that often some problems require considerable collaborative effort from a number of people. As a result the problem reports can get lost in the system. Better support for the collaboration needed includes the following:

- A space for maintaining the context for reported problem with all participants regularly kept aware of progress in fault correction;
- Ability to quickly assemble teams to both identify and correct the problem.

7.5 Technical services

The challenge is to provide the technology needed to bring all the activities together. Often each activity uses its own technology, and integration can become difficult because of the difficulty of transferring information from one technology to another. Figure 8.14 indicates some of the technologies that can support the different kinds of activities found in business processes. For example, customer support systems need portals for distributing information about its products and services and allow customers to make orders. It then needs a call center to resolve any queries.

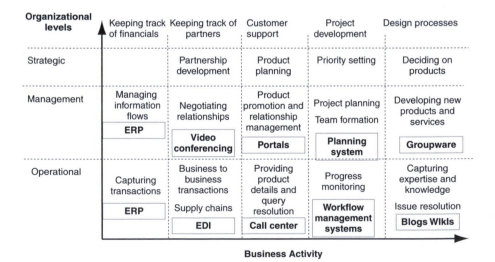

Figure 8.14   Matching technology to activity

8 Summary

This chapter focused on business networking and described a variety of applications focusing on their requirements for knowledge management and social arrangements. It illustrated the new kinds of requirements that must be met by processes in networked business environments. These particularly emphasized greater support for negotiation, and ways to encourage the formation of trust between partners in different organizations. Both of these emphasize the social perspective using the methods described earlier in Chapters 4 and 5.

The chapter emphasized project-based work and product development and then later identified the trend to providing services together with products. There are of course many other application kinds that have similar characteristics. The creative industries now emerging are one example where people with expertise in different aspects of digital services work together in forming business value chains.

9 Discussion Questions

Question 1

Identify the kinds of business activities for an enterprise that distributes specialized products to different locations. It arranges for local distributors to distribute the product and provide specialized advice to clients. One important aspect here is to provide feedback to the enterprise on the acceptance of its products and suggested changes.

Question 2

Choose the enterprise social network for collaboration in a supply chain. You might approach this problem in a number of steps. First develop an enterprise social network for a supply chain as a sequence like that shown in Figure 7.13. Then consider what happens when a hub is set up between each pair in the supply chain to share knowledge at how to make that pair work better. Then suppose all of the hubs are combined into a collaborative group from all enterprises involved in a supply chain to develop ways to make the whole process work better,

Question 3

Suggest the kind of business services you would need for the following:

- Keeping track of maintenance requests.
- Finding business partners.
- Monitoring outsourced work.

Case study VI

Responding to trouble reports in supply chains

One well-known supplier of sound and entertainment systems, CONNECTION-ENTERPRISES (CE) installs sound systems throughout a home or business such as a restaurant. The installation is made up of components sourced from other component distributors. Components may be an amplifier, recorder, TV display and any number of other parts that make up a sound system. Each component may be purchased from a different distributor. Clients place orders with CE salespersons. An order from a client is made up of a number of order lines. Each line in an order identifies the component and the supplying distributor. It may also include the provision of an installation service. The sale may include the offer of an installation either by a service organized by CE or by one of the component providers. In a large order there may be a number of different installers for the different components. For example, the supplier of speakers may include installation of the speakers as part of the offer or CE may organize the installation service. Each line is monitored and updated once the components are received and installed.

The order may be sent electronically or often by FAX or mail to the CE delivery unit. FAXed orders are entered manually into the SALES-SUPPORT system. Orders can also be entered by salespersons. CE delivery unit then initiates the purchase of the components and makes arrangements for their installation.

CE has undertaken to provide a SALES-SUPPORT service to ensure a high quality standard of delivery. Customers can address queries as to the status of their order, or report troubles in either what is delivered or its performance. This service will be provided through a call center to collect and trouble reports from customers or salespersons and to respond to these as quickly as possible. Two other business relationships have been createded to provide the call center service. These are with:

- ALPHA, which is an organization that provides the hardware and network infrastructure needed to provide the service; and
- BETA, which is a supplier of ERP software that is used to program the sales system. The ERP software will be customized to run the client software.

The SALES-SUPPORT service is managed by an operations manager, who is employed by CE and manages a team responsible for the operation of the system. The operations manager liaises with designated managers in ALPHA and BETA. This liaison covers the day-to-day issues of keeping the system running as well as responding to trouble reports. Trouble reports can originate from sales persons, who are attempting to enter complex orders, or by customers enquiring about delivery times, installations or incorrect deliveries.

The trouble reports are collected by a call center agent. Simple reports are answered by the call center agent, whereas the more complex trouble reports are passed to the operations team.

Trouble reports received at the call center ultimately become the responsibility of the operations manager. A trouble report can be from a client, who received a wrong configuration, or in delays in the provision of components or in the installation of services.It can even be a query from a component distributor or installer.

Develop a business activity model like that in Figure 8.13 to show the kinds of the interactions expected of the operations manager in resolving those trouble reports that cannot be handled at the call center. Assume that both ALPHA and BETA have managers that are consulted in finding the cause of a problem. Potential problems include an order being incorrectly placed by a customer, a fault in the software supplied by BETA, a network problem with ALPHA or errors in customization by CE. It is possible that a transient team may need to be set up to solve more difficult problems.

In your solution consider the possibility of creating a knowledge base of trouble reports and the way these were solved. This knowledge base may be used to quickly identify solution for newly reported problems that have similarities to previously solved problems.

One way to proceed is to extend or replace Figure 8.5 with the organizational relationships in this case study. Then use Figure 8.13 as a basis for developing the ESN focusing on the CE operations manager of.

Some further readings

Artto, K., Wikstorm, K., Hellstrom, M., Kujala, J. (2008) 'Impact of Services on Project Business' *International Journal of Project Management*, Vol. 26, pp. 497–508, Elsevier Press.

Cova, B., Salle, R. (2008) 'Marketing Solutions in Accordance with S-D Logic: Co-creating Value with Customer Network Actors' *Industrial Marketing Management*, Vol. 37, pp. 270–277.

Gumm, D.C. (2006) 'Distribution Dimensions in Software Development Projects' *IEEE Software*, Vol. 23, No.5, September/October, pp. 45–51.

Lings, B. Lundell, B. Agerfalk, P. Fitzgerald, B. (1996) 'Ten Strategies for Successful Distributed Development' *Proceedings of the IFIP TC8 WG 8.6 International Working Conference*, Galway, Ireland, Springer, pp. 119–137.

Maybury, M., D'Amore, R., House, D. (2001) 'Expert Finding for Collaborative Virtual Environments' *Communication of the ACM*, Vol. 44, No. 12, December, pp. 55–56.

Milligan, P., Hutcheson, D. (2006) 'Analysis of Outsourcing and the Impact on Business Resilience' *Proceedings of the IFIP TC8 WG 8.6 International Working Conference*, Galway, Ireland, Springer, pp. 199–208.

Ming, X.G., Yan, J.Q., Wang, X.H., Li, S.N., Lu, W.F., Peng, Q.J., Ma, Y.S. (2008) 'Collaborative Process Planning and Manufacturing in Product Lifecycle Management' *Computers in Industry*, Vol. 59, pp. 154–166.

McAfee, A.P. (2006) 'Enterprise 2.0: The Dawn of Emergent Collaboration' *MIT Sloan Management Review*, Vol. 47, No.3, Spring, pp. 21–28.

Ni, Q., Lu, W.F., Yarlagadda, K.D.V., Ming, X. (2007) 'Business Information Modeling for Process Integration in the Mold Making Industry' *Robotics and Computer-Integrated Manufacturing*, Vol. 23, pp. 195–205.

Rottam, J.W. (2006) 'Proven Practices for Effective Offshoring IT Work' *Sloan Management Review*, Vol. 47, No.3, Spring, pp. 56–63.

Rye, K., Lee, S., Choi, H. (2008) 'Modularization of Web-based Collaboration Systems for Manufacturing Innovation' *Proceedings of the Tenth International Conference on Enterprise Information systems*, Barcelona, 12–16 June, pp. 174–177.

Sabherwal, R. (1999) 'The Role of Trust in Outsourced IS Development Projects' *Communications of the ACM*, Vol. 42, No.2, February, pp. 8–86.

Sen, A. (2008) 'The US Fashion Industry: A Supply Chain Review' *International Journal of Production Economics*, Vol. 114, pp. 571–593.

Part III
Organizing for Knowledge Management

Modeling Business Activities

9

Understanding what is happening in the process

Learning objectives

- Modeling as a communication tool
- Modeling different perspectives
- Combining models of processes perspectives
- Business activity models
- Knowledge requirements models
- Design processes

1 Introduction

Previous chapters described the perspectives to be considered in business system design. They also introduced various lightweight modeling tools to model business systems from these perspectives. This chapter consolidates the lightweight modeling methods used in the book to develop a complete model of a business system. It develops ways for modeling business systems from all perspectives. It then combines the perspectives into one model that can be used as a tool to create a new business architecture and organize its business processes.

To create a model of any perspective, it is necessary to collect information through interviews, questionnaires and simply observing how business is carried out. Data collected should look at the explicit information in the system as well as how people get access to the kind of knowledge they need in their work. This information is used to construct the model of the process.

One important criterion is that models use precise terms that mean the same thing to everyone. In that case there are no misunderstandings in any discussions about the system. Modeling is thus used for two main reasons, namely:

- As a communication tool to describe processes in precise terms usually to define the requirements of the system;
- As a design tool, where the models are used to organize the business system including the technical designs of computer support systems by information technology professionals.

This chapter focuses on the former so that readers can clearly discuss business objectives and requirements from a number of perspectives. The social perspective has been described in detail in previous chapters, especially in Chapter 3 where ESNs were used to describe the relationships between roles in the business process. This chapter elaborates on the business activity model, the knowledge perspective and the process perspective and combines them in business system design.

Readers should also note the difference in the terms business systems design and system development method (SDM) used in information systems development. The former refers to the design of the business systems whereas SDM refers to information system design. Increasingly these two go together and the SDM becomes part of business process design. In fact with information technology now so closely integrated into many business processes the two almost go together and modeling in most cases considers all of these perspectives. The chapter describes a number of modeling methods some coming from SDM processes and their integration into business process design.

2   Revision of business activity model

The business activity model (BAM) describes the business activity perspective. The terms used in the BAM are given below:

Role – defines responsibilities in system
Artifact – data objects such as documents
Activity – produces well-defined outputs and usually requires many actions and interactions to do so (e.g. Produce a planning document)
Participant – a specific person assigned to a role
Group – a set of participants.

Figure 9.1 illustrates a BAM using a simple example. Here roles are represented by black dots, activities are represented as clouded shapes, and artifacts are represented as disk storage devices.

There are two activities in Figure 9.1 – 'Searching for information' and 'Preparing report'. Searching for information produces an artifact called 'Collected information', which is used as input to the 'Preparing report' activity.

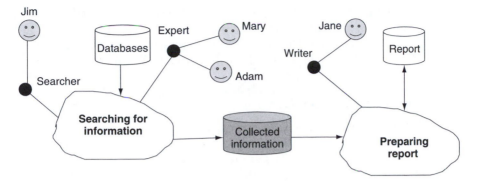

Figure 9.1   Representing business activities

Any business process can contain any number of activities. Thus in Figure 9.1, activity 'Searching for information' has two roles, 'Searcher' and 'Expert'. 'Jim' is a 'Searcher', and 'Mary' and 'Adam' are 'Experts' in searching for information. Some BAM rules include the following:

- Participants assigned to roles in business activities produce artifacts.
- Links between roles and the activity show the roles that are necessary in the activity. There is no arrow on the link between the role and the activity. The link just shows that the roles in the activity.
- Links between artifacts and the activities show the artifacts used in the activity. An arrow to the activity indicates that the activity only reads the artifact. An arrow to the artifact states that the activity can change the artifact.
- There are no links between artifacts and roles, as a role can only access an artifact by taking some actions.

It should however be noted that BAMs are seen as a communication tool. Hence there is some freedom in choosing the ways to represent the concepts.

2.1 The importance of roles

The concept of role is central to any business activity. People are assigned to roles. In most cases more than one person can be assigned to the same role. For example, a number of people can be assigned to the role 'team-member' in a team. Roles model the responsibilities and rights of the people assigned to the role in the collaboration. The ESNs described in Chapter 3 provided ways of modeling roles and their responsibilities. As a result they often determine the behavior of people.

Sometimes role is confused with a person's position in an organization. Role and position, however, are not the same. A person occupying a position can have many roles. A manager may, for example, have a role in a planning committee, as well as leading their team or take on the role of arranging a workshop. Roles in collaboration have more flexibility than positions. It is possible to change, add and delete roles fairly easily. The same does not apply to positions. Hence roles provide the flexibility needed to model collaboration within emergent processes.

2.2 Some examples of BAMs

Figure 9.2 is a BAM that describes the business process of getting experts to carry out consulting studies. They develop a project plan on ways to carry out these studies for clients. Here roles are represented by figures. It also includes a symbol for groups, as for example the 'legal team'. The model in Figure 9.2 shows two major activities, namely:

- 'getting client requirements' where the manager finds out client needs. The outcomes of this activity is a proposal, which describes what the client requires, and
- 'developing project plan,' activity to create a project plan for carrying out the study. Three teams, legal, budget and technical, participate to create this plan.

The business activity diagram in Figure 9.2 also shows that information about previous projects can be used to formulate a proposal. It also shows that the PROJECT PLAN is also used in the 'Getting client requirements' activity. This

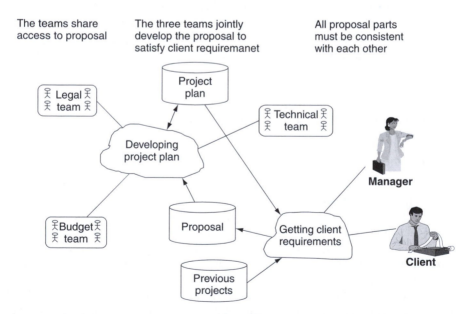

Figure 9.2   A conceptual model describing responses to client requests

is possible as the proposal may need to be amended should the plan identify problems in meeting a proposal.

At this stage it may be worthwhile to ask questions relevant to knowledge management. For example, what are the sources of information used in developing the project plan? These may be previous similar plans, they may be consultations with people who have carried out similar work or worked with the client. One source of knowledge here are PREVIOUS PROJECTS, which can be used to identify similar projects and what methods were used to ensure their success. Other sources may be outside experts. These sources should also be shown on the BAM, or alternatively shown on a document that is eventually used to define the knowledge repository for this application.

2.3 Going into more detail

A BAM can be expanded into detail. In a top-down approach, there is a top-level BAM that describes the entire system. A top-level model can be expanded to show some of its activities into more detail. Expanding an activity creates a new model. Thus if we expanded every activity in a BAM, we would create a new model for each expanded activity. The result is a set of diagrams each showing an increasing level of detail of how the business works, as shown in Figure 9.3. All of these parts can be given names. In Figure 9.3, the top level BAM is decomposed into three lower level BAMs, A, B and C.

As an example, the BAM for the activity 'getting client requirements' is shown in Figure 9.4. Here we see that first there are some client requirements defined which are then formulated into a project proposal. You should also note that the expanded BAM of a higher level activity must include the roles and artifacts in that activity. It also shows that client requirements may be amended in light of problems identified in the project plan.

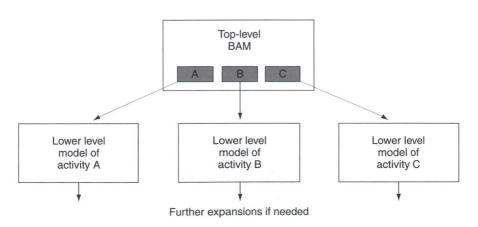

Figure 9.3   Decomposing business activity models

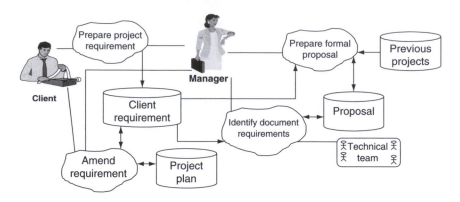

Figure 9.4   A detailed expansion of activity 'Getting Client Requirements'

Each activity in Figure 9.4 can be expanded into more detail. The question is how far to continue such expansion. Sometimes people will expand to the level of a work-item, showing any smaller work-items or actions. However, you SHOULD NOT expand to the level of detailed action – that is do not model an action, like 'send a message' or interaction as an activity, instead describe the work-item by a scenario. Scenarios are described in Chapter 11.

3   Modeling the process perspective

So far we have shown business activities as running independently with no sequencing order. The process perspective defines the sequence of operations across business activities. Business processes can be classified by the variability in the services they provide to customers (Hall and Johnson, 2009) and often require to be designed in different ways. Figures 9.5 and 9.6. illustrate one way to compare different kinds of processes. They range from predefined to emergent processes as shown in Figure 9.5.

Many early business processes, such as those described in Chapter 7, were structured with a well-defined set of steps to achieve a well-defined objective. They were predefined in the sense that each transaction was carried out the same way and provided a standard service to clients. Examples are bank transactions, invoicing procedures, payroll system or an inventory system that keeps track of warehouse contents. The goal was to improve performance of business

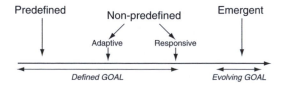

Figure 9.5   A range of process kinds

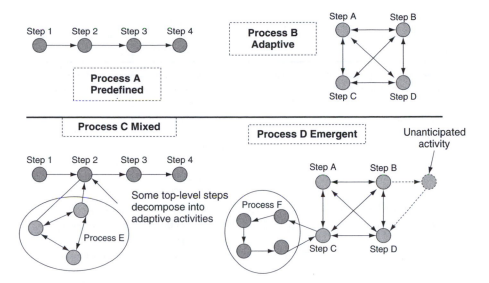

Figure 9.6   Predefined and non-predefined processes

operations. The transactions here are well defined have a clear objective and each causes a specified change to the database. As business systems are becoming more complex, the sequence of steps often has to adapt to changes in the situation. Such changes can often be following a different option in the process. However, if the situation changes in unexpected ways then process themselves have to continually change or emerge and process objectives themselves evolve. Such emergent processes focus on integrating knowledge work into everyday work where processes continually improve to deliver new products and services in large-scale collaborative environments. For example, mass customization processes will often have to adapt to the changing needs of the client as described by Hall and Johnson (2009).

The difference between the different kinds of processes is illustrated in Figure 9.6.

Each circle in Figure 9.6 represents a business activity. A directed line between two circles shows how one activity follows another. 'Process A' in Figure 9.6 is a predefined process. It has four activities, Step 1, Step 2, Step 3 and Step 4. The arrows show that the activities are executed in sequence. When one step finishes the next step commences. Step 1 finishes then Step 2 commences, when Step 2 finishes then Step 3 commences and so on.

However, processes like Process B or C in Figure 9.6 are now becoming more common (Hall and Johnson, 2009). In Process B activities may be carried out in a variety of sequences depending on how a situation develops. In fact many of these may be continuous activities as described in Chapter 2. In Process C, the top level may define broad process goals and follow a predefined set of steps. The detailed process followed in each step, however, may be non-predefined.

Table 9.1   Classifying processes

Activity	Type of Process
Tendering process to respond to a client request for a complex product or service	Process C, which follows a set of steps each of which have to be customized to the tender requirement
Product customization	Process C as the production usually follows a standard design process although individual steps may be adapted to a special client need
Help desk	Process D, where a non-predefined process is used to identify a problem, but the problem solution is predefined
Processing financial transactions	Usually process A as the funds have to be
Coming up with ideas	Process B as the process is spontaneous and cannot be predetermined
Coming up with ideas and evaluating them	Process D, which uses a standard predefined evaluation process to evaluate the ideas

For example, Step 1 may be to get an order from a client. How this is done can depend on the client. Step 2 may be to identify the requirement, which may follow a non-predefined set of steps to gather the necessary requirements. Then Step 3 may be to satisfy the request, which itself may need to adapt as requirements may change or new ideas come up. Finally Step 4 is product delivery.

In process D the top-level process is not predefined but the steps themselves may follow a predefined sequence. This often happens in strategic planning or product design applications. New ideas may come up depending on the situation. Each idea may be evaluated using a prespecified procedure. These processes are commonly found in knowledge-based environments. Some examples of these kinds of different process are given in the Table 9.1.

3.1   Modeling methods for predefined processes

The methods used to model predefined processes include structured systems analysis and object-oriented methods. They use well-defined modeling methods such as dataflows, database design methods, or object models to precisely define process flows and data needs (Hawryszkiewycz, 2001). These models are then converted to implementations in another design step. Requirements analysis for predefined processes focused on what are sometimes referred to as mechanistic systems that almost follow a precise set of steps. Fulfilling an order and sending out an invoice is a typical example. The analysis determined the details of each step, how to fit it into the process and how to support each step with technology. Each step was thus precisely defined and usually required only one person to carry out the task. The techniques used in structured systems analysis and object modeling were well suited to model well-defined business processes.

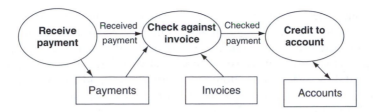

Figure 9.7   Describing a process by a dataflow diagram

The most common way to describe processes is by diagrammatically showing the process steps using dataflow diagrams such as that shown in Figure 9.7. It shows the process steps and their sequence. The label on the arrows describes the information moved between the process steps. It also shows the data stores used in each process step. Thus when a payment is received in the step 'receive payment' then process step 'Check against invoice' is activated. Once checked the payment is credited to an account.

Dataflow diagrams are fine for describing predefined process, which have well-defined flows. Events in one activity such as 'receive payment' result in messages such as 'payment received' sent to subsequent activities. Dataflow diagrams can get clumsy when we have non-predefined processes.

3.2   Methods for non-predefined processes

Here there are a large number of situations where processes depart from a pre-defined path. One way to use dataflow diagrams to describe a non-predefined process is by a set of contingencies as, for example, shown in Figure 9.8. Here there may be a number of dataflows from each activity depending on different

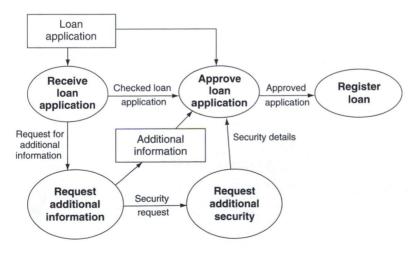

Figure 9.8   Adding contingencies

possible outcomes in the activity. Thus in Figure 9.8 the process step 'Receive loan application' may have two outcomes. One is a 'request for additional information' and the other a 'Checked loan application'. Each of these then go to a different activity. It is of course possible that there are so many contingencies that the dataflow will mainly show the contingencies and the main purpose of the process may not be obvious. Furthermore, anticipating all possible situations is often difficult and alternate methods are often sought here.

3.3 Informal methods

BAMs are one informal way to describe business processes at a high level. There are others. Sometimes all that is needed are some sketches to describe a system. These are often sufficient to facilitate discussion on ways to improve a system. Initially people often use informal sketches to do this. Figure 9.9 illustrates a typical sketch. For example, many medical processes that include many non-predefined activities. They may carry out a diagnosis or examination and then choose a procedure that fits the diagnosis. It is not likely that a totally new procedure would be created for a patient, although some tasks like a pathology test are more structured.

Work in the test laboratories tends to be more deterministic. Other dimensions of the process show the transitions between the different activities and the relationship between the different roles. Figure 9.10 shows a number of activities with transitions between them. Here there is the process that starts with admission, which is predefined. Examination follows. This can include any number of tests – (TEST A, TEST B, TEST C in this case). Each test usually follows a predefined set of steps, for example TESTB B follows STEP X, STEP Y, STEP

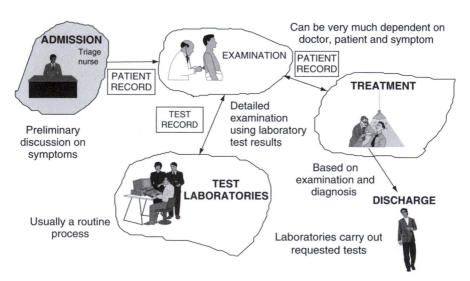

Figure 9.9   Health systems

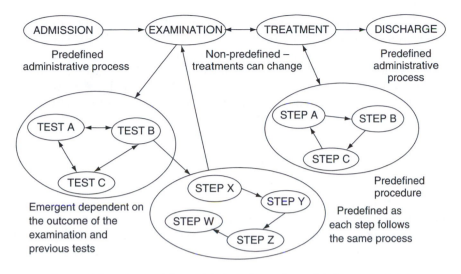

Figure 9.10   A mix of deterministic and non-deterministic process steps

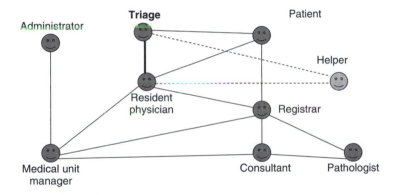

Figure 9.11   The work connections

Z and STEP W. After the tests, treatment begins. This itself can follow a number of steps – in this case STEP A, STEP B and STEP C. The double arrow shows that an examination can be commenced from treatment leading to more tests.

Figure 9.11 shows an initial sketch of the personal relationships between the different roles in a system. It is an ESN that can be expanded into more detail as more information is gathered through interviews, studies of procedures and observations where possible. It shows, for example, that a patient contacts a triage nurse, who is responsible for admission in the hospital system. It can be extended to show the knowledge needed by each role, its responsibilities and ways they share knowledge through their interaction and collaboration.

The ESN is sometimes relevant when discussing value. One is to consider any system changes as providing value to the patient – that is, to provide the best medical services as quickly as possible. A design will then proceed by looking at ways for roles to work together to provide the best value for the patient.

Such criteria can be satisfied by providing services that can be easily rearranged as the situation changes. Each service can be used by different units and they can communicate flexibly between the units and provide abilities to reorganize connection through changing communication paths between the services. The design outcome is to identify such services for particular applications.

4   Modeling the organizational perspective

The book also occasionally uses the organizational perspective where it describes relationships between businesses or business units within the same organization. Figure 9.12 shows relationships between organizations in the apparel industry. There is a symbol (in this case a house) showing each business unit or each organization, their responsibility and the interactions between them. This is similar to an ESN but at an organizational level. The detail of such interactions and responsibilities appear in detailed documents.

Cross-organizational activities here would include the following:

- Agreeing on the designs to be adopted that requires participation from the retailer, marketing and apparel company;
- Arranging production, which principally involves the manufacturing and apparel companies; and
- Arranging distribution, which is an arrangement between the transporter and the apparel manufacturing.

Figure 9.12 is of course a broad level model from an organizational perspective. Details of the interaction are documented as contracts, agreements and plans.

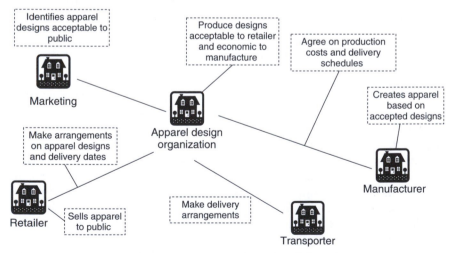

Figure 9.12   The organizational perspective

5 Modeling the knowledge perspective

The knowledge perspective is often complimentary to the other perspectives. It is, however, more difficult to show in highly structured forms as the definition of knowledge is not very precise. Knowledge can be associated with each object in the rich picture. For example, tacit knowledge can only be shown in terms of who possesses it and how they are willing to share it. Again free diagrammatic ways are useful here. Modelers are completely free to choose the symbols they use on a rich picture. They can draw symbols, show documents, building, computers and any kind of object that is important to the system. The idea here is to express in the most obvious way the system works. It includes what different people do and what they value. Figure 9.13 is one example of a rich picture illustrating the apparel industry.

Here the designer, manufacturer and retailer work as individual entities. There is also a transporter. The designer and marketing are all part of the apparel organization. The rich picture illustrates the broad relationships between the different stakeholders and their values and objectives within the system.

Rich pictures like that in Figure 9.13 show one perspective of process design and they indicate both the knowledge people need and their various relationships. They can be combined with the social perspective to indicate the kind of knowledge to be created in interactions between the people in the system. For example, negotiations for material purchase must resolve the issues of high volume of quick moving stock that has to be met through arrangements between the purchaser, retailer and materials manufacturer.

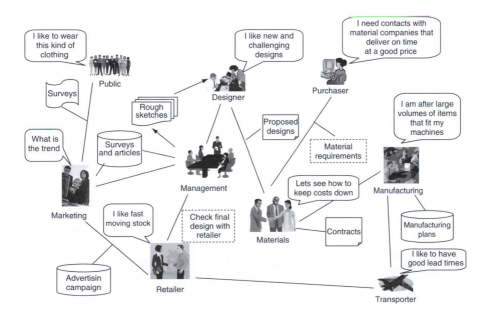

Figure 9.13 Rich picture of the garment manufacturing industry

Rich pictures are a diagrammatic tool often used with soft systems methods (Checkland, 1981) to describe unstructured systems. It is like a diagram without rules. It can include any kind of object although most contain people and their thought processes. Figure 9.13 shows rich picture model from the knowledge perspective, although it would be possible to have a rich picture for each perspective and then use these in the design process.

6 Modeling as part of system development

So far the models described can be used to model the new business architecture from a number of perspectives. Modeling is also used in developing new computer systems to support the business architecture. The use of modeling for computer system design commenced in the early 1980s and has evolved in line with changes to the business environment. Early models mainly focused on controlling projects to deliver the requirements expected by users. They could be used to clearly show how, for example, to reduce the cost of everyday activities, such as financial transactions or inventory movements. Modeling has changed and developed over time as new modeling techniques evolved in line with changing business requirements. Figure 9.14 illustrates the trend in modeling. This trend at the same time follows the changes in value systems in design. The earliest models were aimed at improving processes. They were aimed initially at delivering value to business units or process by clearly defining the process steps and finding ways to improve flows through these steps. Now the trend is more to systems that focus on using knowledge to improve the quality of services and products.

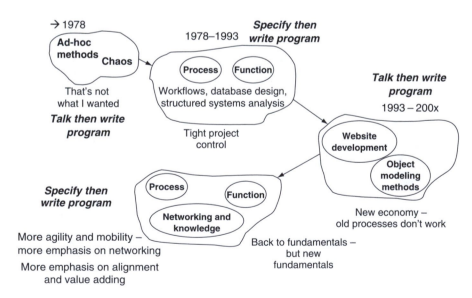

Figure 9.14 The range of modeling methods

Values delivered have also changed. First the emphasis was on cost reduction by reducing the amount of routine work by system users. Then there was an increasing emphasis on maintaining contact with clients and improving client reach using the WWW. Now the emphasis is increasingly on using knowledge to increase innovation and competiveness.

6.1 System development methods

There are a number of terms that are often used to describe processes for developing computer systems to support a business system. The most common is system development methods. A system development method (SDM) is itself a business process used to develop a computer support system for a business architecture. The ways to describe a system development method are illustrated in Figure 9.15. The description includes:

- The *design steps* that are followed in a systematic way to create a new system.
- The *design tasks* and *design methods* used in the step. For example, a task may be to create a team and the design method may be to create a team structure with technology support. Or it may be to develop a client interface and the method is to build a Web program.
- The *design process*, which defines the sequence of design steps.
- The *design phases* which are grouping the steps into *manageable phases*. These group a number of design methods with a similar high-level objective into a manageable activity.

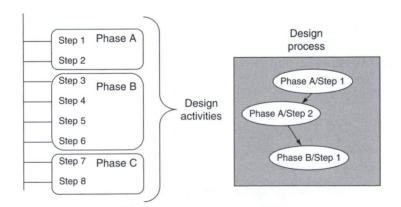

Often phase B is logical design and
Phase C is physical design.

Figure 9.15 System development processes

A system development method includes both the design process and the ways to manage it. Thus in the left-hand-side figure, design steps 1 and 2 make up phase A of the design process. Then steps 3, 4, 5 and 6 make up phase 2 and so on.

By this definition, each step in Figure 9.15 is included in a phase of the design process. Each step often requires different kinds of knowledge. This chapter will describe the design methods and the design knowledge needed in them. It is important here to distinguish between modeling methods and SDMs. The modeling methods are used to represent systems. The SDM includes modeling methods as part of the business process to create a system. It may use different modeling methods in the different steps of the design process.

Consequently there is a distinction between two kinds of design processes, namely:

- SDMs that focus on predefined processes and develop systems for transaction management without excessive human interference. The process here is well defined and follows a precise number of steps in a strict sequence, and
- SDMs that focus on complex adaptive processes and the needs of knowledge workers, who do not in most cases follow predefined processes. These design processes allow designers to select steps depending on the current situation. Consequently they are known as *open methods*.

6.2   System development methods for predefined processes

Most SDMs for predefined processes follow a predefined set of steps. The most commonly known SDM here is the *waterfall cycle*. The steps that make up this cycle are the following:

- Concept formation that defines the scope of the project and broadly what it is to accomplish;
- Feasibility analysis to determine whether the project will deliver benefits, in this case, usually financial benefits;
- Developing the specification, which produces a model that shows exactly what the business architecture will look like;
- System design, which defines the various parts that will make up the system;
- System development and construction, which constructs the various parts of the system;
- System testing.

There are variants on this cycle, as for example staged development, where parts of systems are built in successive stage. Here the same design process is repeated a number of times, which is appropriate in large systems, as for example large-scale ERP systems. Each stage still follows the same set of predefined steps. For example, the first stage may be to build a system to keep track of material purchases. Then a module is added to assist material planning.

6.3   Open methods

Methods for predefined systems are often not suitable for knowledge-based processes. Knowledge-based processes tend to be ill-defined and hence require design methods that are also adaptive. There are now many suggestions that rather than following a fixed number of steps an alternate can be adopted. The alternate comes under the general heading of *methods engineering*. Here the step chosen and the modeling method used in the step depend on the current situation. Here:

- The emphasis is on what is to be done and not the SDM. However, the tools that are used in pre-specified systems are also needed here but they must be sufficiently adaptive and to be used.
- The designers are often the users who must quickly change the process as needs arise and choose the design methods needed to do this.
- The methods and processes must be goal oriented to allow goals to evolve and for processes to be aligned to these goals.

An open method would need to provide design steps for the different perspectives and combine the steps in ways that ensure that all perspectives are included in the final design. Such methods are described in the next chapter.

6.4   Notification schemes

Notifications are often used in non-predefined processes Usually an outcome or event in one business activity needs to be analyzed to determine what other activities must be notified about the event. Such notification may depend on the entire context of the enterprise. They usually take the form of messages sent to individuals. For example, in a business process once a business task is completed a message is sent to people responsible for the subsequent task. An important concept in non-predefined processes is maintaining awareness, which requires people in the process to be aware of what is happening within the process. Messages must thus be sent to all members of effected groups or communities.

6.5   Implications for managing system development

Predefined systems usually support major enterprise processes and are developed by information technology units using SDMs that follow precise set of steps to ensure system quality. Requirements are precisely defined and are verified at different stages of system development. These systems usually stay in use for a long period of time and once installed need little change. SDMs use precise project management methods. There are project stages that have intermediate goals and there is a final handover to user units. People who developed the system can now move to a new project.

With emergent or adaptive systems the situation is different. The requirements cannot usually be defined in detail at the start of development and even change once the system is put in place. Hence the project is never really complete and requires continual interaction between users and information technology people even after the system is put into operational use. Design methods used here are often referred to as agile development methods. They include extreme programming, which are used to respond to changing user needs, as well as feature-driven development where features are added to systems as the system grows.

Emergent business processes support knowledge workers and require a combination of emergent analytics work combined with operational processes. Hence systems that combine both are increasingly in demand. The different management styles, however, make it difficult to support for development processes in the same project. Vinekar et al. (2006) describe the challenges of supporting both kinds of SDMs within the same organization. They identify the management, organization, people and process issues. In particular they focus on culture where traditional methods focus on projects and are primarily hierarchical requiring planning, organization and control with facilitation at the work level. Agile methods (Meso and Jain, 2006) are people oriented, flexible and focus on achieving user satisfaction. Managing this dual culture in the same organizational unit often presents difficulties.

This dual nature of development has implications on choosing support for collaborative systems and leads to tradeoffs in choosing technologies to support knowledge-based processes. These are discussed later in Chapters 13 and 14 when choosing technologies to support knowledge processes. The remainder of the chapter describes modeling methods which are often the first phase of system development.

7 Summary

After readers have read this chapter they will have the knowledge to model business processes in terms of the major perspectives covered in this book. ESNs that model the social perspective were described earlier in Chapter 3. This chapter focused on the business activity perspectives as well as introducing the organizational perspective and knowledge perspective. Rich pictures were used to show the knowledge requirements of different roles. The latter is the least structured given the nature of knowledge itself. The modeling tools including rich pictures are proposed mainly as communication tools to clearly describe in unambiguous ways the business process in terms of its perspectives. The modeling methods described in this chapter are used in the following chapters to define business system requirements.

8 Exercises

Develop a business model for each of the following exercises. In doing so identify the kinds of processes in the system and choose appropriate methods to model the different system perspectives. Identify the knowledge requirements of each of the roles.

Exercise 1 (from 6/GS98)

Product selection in an organization includes a number of activities. First of all a MARKET REPORT is produced. This requires consolidating information received from *salespersons* as sales reports as well as from discussions between salespersons and the *marketing manager*. A product selection committee of *department heads* together with the marketing manager produces a list of POTENTIAL PRODUCTS. The list of potential products is used by *design engineers* to develop PROTOTYPE DESIGNS. The designs are evaluated by the marketing manager, who works together with *external experts* and the design engineers. Evaluations often lead to design changes prior to going on to project selection. Their DESIGN EVALUATIONS are then made available to the product selection committee. This committee selects a number of projects for production based on the design evaluation.

Exercise 2

Business analysts develop software specifications with clients. These specifications are approved by the software development manager (SDM) and used by developers to develop the software systems. Once approved, a project plan is created through discussion between the SDM and developers. Development is broken up into a number of development activities, each of which produces a software module. The modules are tested together as a total system. Project progress is monitored by the SDM, developer, client and business analyst, and records of progress are made on the project plan. In addition developers often contact clients during development to clarify the requirements specifications.

Once the system is delivered the organization is responsible for fixing any faults found after delivery. A liaison officer receives reports about any faults from clients, records them into a fault report log, identifies the possible location of the fault, and contacts the relevant developers to fix it. Fixing of faults requires clarifications between the developers and client. Where faults are seen to be significant they are also reported to the SDM by the developer.

Exercise 3

Worldlink Enterprises have found that they are often developing proposals that require contribution from widely distributed experts in their organization. A proposal brief is prepared by the project manager together with a client. The brief is then used to prepare a proposal plan by a coordinator working together with the project manager. A proposal is divided into parts. Different parts are assigned for work by different experts. Experts work on each part, and each part is then reviewed by reviewers.

The coordinator regularly assembles the different parts into a project draft. The coordinator checks the parts for consistency and may request changes to selected parts. Changes made to the different parts must be consistent with each other, and experts must agree on the changes before the whole document is issued. The coordinator then requests the experts to make any changes. Changes may also be requested by the client.

Exercise 4

You are getting requirements from a client.

The requirements are analyzed with a designer to determine what parts are needed and the tasks to assemble the parts.

Define a plan and schedule.

Identify the work to be contracted out to the contractor.

Organize the work to be carried out internally.

The internal and external work has to be coordinated and the different components need to be assembled.

Once assembled, the product is delivered to the client.

Choose your activities so that they mostly cover one kind of work. Describe the kind of work in each activity and what you need to support them with technology.

Some further readings

Checkland, P.B. (1981) *Systems Thinking, Systems Practice* (John Wiley & Sons Ltd).

Hall, J.M., Johnson, M.E. (2009): 'When Should a Process be Art', *Harvard Business Review*, Vol. 87, No. 3, March, pp. 58–65.

Hawryszkiewycz, I.T. (2001) *Introduction to Systems Analysis and Design* (Prentice-Hall, Sydney).

Meso, P., Jain, R. (2006) 'Agile Software Development: Adaptive System Principles and Best Practices' *Information Systems Management Journal*, Vol. 23, No. 3, Summer, pp. 19–30.

Wilson, B. (2001) *Soft Systems Methodology* (John Wiley & Sons Ltd).

Zhu, H. (2008) 'Roles in Information Systems: A Survey' *IEEE Transactions on Systems, Man, and Cybernetics – Part C: Applications and Reviews*, Vol. 38, No. 3, May, pp. 377–396.

The First Design Step: Defining Requirements

10

Deciding what you want to do

Learning objectives

- Combining perspectives in design
- Requirements analysis methods
- An open method approach to combine perspectives
- Some principles and guidelines
- Socio-technical criteria in design
- Design phases.

1 Introduction

The book now continues to describe design processes for business systems. This and the following chapters build on earlier chapters, and describe how to combine the four perspectives into a business system design process. The chapter provides an organized way for design by focusing on different perspectives and socio-technical issues. The focus of the design process is to:

- Clearly define goals of the new system and the business activities needed to achieve the goals;
- Develop ways to support business activities with social relationships and build communities of practice where needed;
- Define knowledge requirements and how knowledge will be captured and used;
- Consider socio-technical aspects in design to ensure that collaborative systems are adopted with minimal disruption and new technologies are introduced in ways that are seen as beneficial by the participants.

At the end of the chapter readers will be able to see how the perspectives can be incorporated in designing systems. It will also describe how to choose a design process that is most appropriate to their application.

2 The evolving business architecture

Requirements analysis defines what a business system must do to achieve stakeholders goals and the business architecture needed to achieve this. To do this we can look at the trend in business architectures. Previous chapters described the trend in business processes as one where ERP systems provided value by reducing human intervention in business processes. Then additional benefits were obtained by electronic exchange of transactions. The trend now is towards greater innovation by harnessing knowledge to continually satisfy new customer requirements. This in turn leads to more emphasis on people and the way they interact to share and create knowledge. This trend has an important impact on the design of business architecture. A typical business architecture is shown in Figure 10.1, which shows the complex relationships now found in many enterprises. It shows the following:

- Activities that form a dual-core structure of two often separate activities, namely, knowledge activities and structured ERP processes;
- Knowledge activities where people collaborate to generate new ideas and ways of doing business;
- Services that support collaboration in knowledge activities and capture knowledge in collaborative databases,
- Participants take on roles, which have specific responsibilities in each activity, and participants can dynamically change their roles;
- Participants collaborate to share knowledge to develop innovative products;
- ERP databases, which share information about enterprise processes;
- Support for business analytics, such as evaluating acquisitions or new projects;
- Lightweight technology to support colloboration between knowledge workers.

Architectures such as that in Figure 10.1 are commonly found across larger enterprises. For example, in large systems there are often many teams. The teams are often autonomous and must themselves coordinate their activities as now often occurs in alliance or outsourcing situations, or indeed in large enterprises. The relationships within teams can change dynamically requiring team activities to be coordinated towards wider organizational goals. The complexity of such changing relationships has made design more challenging. Any proposed changes must support and whenever possible enrich such relationships, not only automate or simplify well-defined tasks, as has been the case in much earlier design.

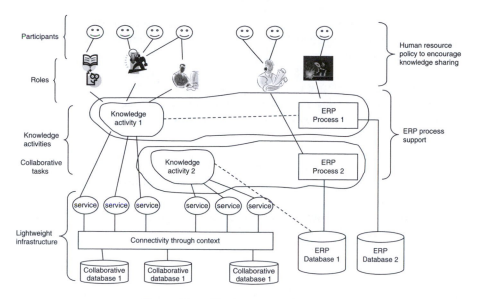

Figure 10.1   The business architecture

Business system design processes must create workspaces that:

- Provide ubiquitous access to corporate intranet and extranet to harmonize what is viewed by some as a dual-core structure of knowledge activities and ERP systems.
- Provide an interface that supports the capability for analytical and decision services, by providing access support to corporate data and support the interaction between knowledge workers.
- Provide the capability to dynamically identify knowledge requirements and share knowledge between these two core activities and the ability to change the ERP system.
- Support through policy and technology, the dynamic development of communities, which focus on specific goals and share knowledge to develop innovative solutions.

It is becoming evident that to design systems with dynamic capabilities it is necessary to place more emphasis on communication and collaboration between business users. Here, in contrast to mechanistic processes, different people will often organize different ways to carry out the same task and the way they collaborate in each task. Designers must identify the ways people organize their work and provide solutions that enable new relationships to be easily created.

Hence socio-economic issues come into prominence because any change results in some disruption to existing work patterns and in new socio-technical gaps created within the system. Designers must be aware of such gaps and ensure that any disruption is carefully considered, and gaps are reduced through discussion of business system stakeholders. Chapter 2 discussed the idea of gaps between structure, people, technology and task as measures of acceptance of systems. Gaps can arise in many ways:

- A change in the structure of a new system can require people to assume new responsibilities and relationships creating potential conflict;
- Introduction of technology may not fit with knowledge workers tasks; and
- Changes to tasks themselves may not be acceptable to people.

Any design must provide people with the tools to manage complexity and ways to quickly adapt the tools to changing work patterns. Business architectures in this case provide ways to change processes using business activity, social structure and knowledge management perspectives, thus providing more flexibility in managing change.

3   Methods for defining requirements

Requirements analysis determines what the new business system must do. Traditionally requirements analysis is made up of three steps – elicitation, modeling and specification. The goal of these three steps is to decide what the design is to achieve, and how to arrange our business activities to achieve it. Different stakeholders can put in their requirements at each phase, resolve their differences and set priorities.

One method for requirements analysis is the i* method, which was defined by Yu in 1995. Such methods focus on capturing the detailed needs of different stakeholders. i* identifies the stakeholders and their responsibilities as well as relationships between them. It identifies the ways stakeholders interact and the information that they exchange. Designers often assume that there is a high-level goal with defined stakeholder responsibilities and design the system that realizes the goal. The process is sometimes called as defining the strategic dependency model between the stakeholders to realize the overall goal. One characteristic of these methods is that stakeholder values and goals are assumed to be fixed. In complex adaptive systems stakeholder goals and values can change. The focus is primarily on the business activity perspective ensuring that any outputs satisfy stakeholder needs.

New teams can quickly emerge to solve some new issues and the responsibilities of team members be defined by agreement between them. The ways they interact can also change. The term often used here is goal-oriented requirements engineering – it implies that the high-level business goals are actually defined as part of the requirements process. This can redefine the responsibilities of the system stakeholder.

3.1   Choosing your own design process

Often new design processes are needed to change all perspectives in design. Most current design processes focus on the business activity perspective.

However, it is increasingly found that other perspectives begin to play a more important role in some industries. Zhang et al. (2002), for example, have developed applications in the medical profession where they found that the social perspective is important to improve the acceptance of systems by professionals in the health area. Commonly many systems focusing on the business activity perspective expected health workers to adopt a structured approach to tasks, whereas professionals here require a more flexible collaborative and expert approach, which is usually found in knowledge work. Hence a gap emerged between health workers and the developed systems, which as a result are not fully utilized.

As a result, Zhang recognized this gap and emphasized user practices in its early stages using a design process known as HCDID (Human-centered distributed information systems design). The primary reason for developing this design process was to go beyond the focus on the interface, but also include users, functions and tasks that are fundamental to the process. Many human-centered methods focused in interface design whereas HCDID goes beyond focusing on interfaces but considers the capabilities of users and their interactions. Its goal is to reduce the gap between users and the technology by an in-depth evaluation of user capabilities and responsibilities and their interactions in a complex system.

The HCDID design process is described by Rinkus and others (2004) in more detail, which is shown in Figure 10.2. The HCDID design process follows the idea of methods engineering by providing a set of design methods and grouping them into four phases. The early emphasis is on the social perspective. The four phases are the following:

- User analysis: A social perspective to collect information about how users work. Identify user knowledge and abilities and social relationships within the system to understand its culture. This phase examines the knowledge possessed by users, their goals, the way they improve their knowledge and create new knowledge, and the way they work together.
- Functional analysis: A business activity perspective, that identifies the critical top-level domain structures – goals to be met independent of implementation. It defines the business activities required to accomplish these goals and relationships between users. Here it is necessary to analyze each activity to determine what is happening in the activity.
- Task analysis: A more detailed activity perspective that identifies specific business activities. Identifies system functions, task procedures, input and output formats, communication needs, organizational structures and information flow. The goal of any design here is to provide the tools and other guidelines for people carrying out the tasks.
- Representational analysis: Focuses on socio-technical aspects by defining interfaces between system and users. Defining the services to be provided to users to improve their work practices. These services can of course be provided by computer systems.

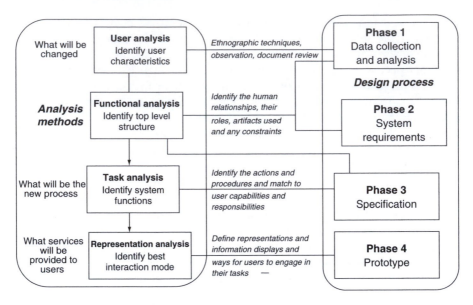

Figure 10.2   Including user analysis in the design process

The first phase of this design process focuses on what knowledge workers have, and their responsibilities and capabilities. These workers are often autonomous and follow personal practices but must collaborate with others in their work. This is the major difference from methods that focus on information flows and data. Functional analysis then places increased importance on communities of such workers and their collaboration. The way they work together and carry out their tasks now often is the first step of the analysis. Primarily the goal is to align social, economic and information technology structure while causing least disruption to existing relationships. Specification then integrates the user information with the tasks to be carried out to create a specification.

Finally phase 4 develops a prototype that can be further refined based on user feedback and experiences. The idea of a prototype that evolves corresponds to the changing nature of knowledge work, which calls for adaptable interfaces. Ultimately what is needed are systems that can be changed by the knowledge workers themselves and thus further reduce the socio-technical gap between people and technology. The important difference here is the emphasis on user analysis at the start of the process.

3.2   Design choices – Who is the driver

One important aspect of choosing a design process is the way that new systems evolve. Figure 10.3 shows a classification of design processes. They are the following:

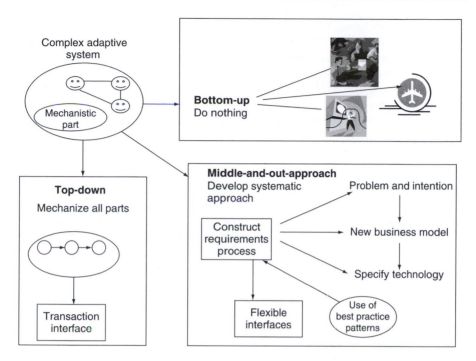

Figure 10.3   Design options

- Top-down design processes, which are driven by a high-level definition of requirements and systems, are built to exactly meet these requirements. These are often driven by management with long-term goals in mind. They try to mechanize all social relationships and record any knowledge created through the relationships – something that has been proven not to work. Mechanizing social relationships implies that people's interactions are all planned and predetermined, which is really not a realistic approach. These are characterized by design methods used in predefined processes and developed within information technology departments.
- Bottom-up design processes that evolve by users themselves adding components to a system. These are driven by users often addressing a shorter-term goal. Enterprises often do nothing but just provide facilities for e-mail and other tools, support meetings and travel. Here users gradually discover and use technologies and adapt them to their work practice. The idea here is that through both meetings and exchange of messages, the participants will themselves create any new knowledge and share it with others. This, however, may take some time and may not develop the same productivity gains than adopting a more systematic approach.
- Middle and out methods that center on defining broad-level functional needs that are adopted by top-level management but lead to the development of

lower level systems that can be adapted by users. They adopt a systematic approach that defines intentions and business value and ways to realize these through a collaborative infrastructure. It is appropriate to the large collaborative networks described earlier in Chapter 8. It is often seen as a top-down approach to design. Here designer or designers of a system choose the critical stages that become the phases, at which stakeholders must reach some decision. Often they base the design at each stage on previous experience based on patterns, guidelines or metaphors.

The current situation as regards support for collaboration and knowledge sharing is thus quite fluid. There is no such thing as a standard design process for knowledge-based processes and people often borrow design methods from other design processes to use in their design process. This is because each knowledge-based process is to some extent special and different. It often requires more focus on some perspectives when compared to others. Whatever the choice, however, the method must result in systems that support communication, and knowledge sharing.

This chapter describes a systematic approach which:

- Provides a choice of perspective to be used in the design;
- Develop an infrastructure that can provide the foundation for quickly reconnecting existing activities, or creating new ones in ways that maintain connectivity and support interactivity within the organizational context;
- Provide ways to rearrange services within activities decided by users themselves.

The systematic approach thus provides a combination of top-down and bottom-up. The systematic approach provides the infrastructure within which users can choose their ways of interactivity but within the context. It can provide a platform that incorporates ERP systems and databases combined with collaborative services and can result in improved productivity through quicker access to information.

3.3   Cross organizational issues

The methods described here apply equally to collaboration within a business to collaboration between businesses. Stakeholders can come from a number of businesses and relationships between them can change as the relationships between the businesses evolve. The business activity diagram can show activities in different organizations and ESNs that include roles responsible for cross-organizational collaboration identified. There are many more issues faced in developing cross-organizational systems when compared to systems within one organization. The sharing of resources, distribution of any income as well as contribution are just some. Generally top management is more likely to be involved and there is more emphasis on the financial perspective and the relative importance of different enterprises.

4   Some techniques being proposed for open design processes

Requirements analysis methods for knowledge-based processes is different when compared to predefined processes. They are more lightweight in that precision is not as critical as in predefined processes. We look at relationships and identify their general interactions but not in terms of elementary transactions, as is the case when designing structured processes. Analysis and design of knowledge-based processes goes beyond looking at the functional needs of different activities. The processes must:

- Place greater emphasis on knowledge creation and the social structure to achieve it;
- Support agility by responding to changing requirements;
- Support complex and changing relationships between process participants.

Thus, for example, the increased collaboration in a complex outsourcing arrangement can require people to collaborate more intensely and furthermore change their collaborative processes as different issues come up. An unanticipated problem may need a new transient team to be quickly set up to address it.

Open design processes can be organized in systematic ways. They are fundamentally based on methods engineering approaches where methods are chosen based on the situation as one proceeds through a design. Open design processes provide a set of design methods but allow them to be used as needed. The design methods can provide guides on using these methods by suggesting a systematic way to proceed through them. Designers, who use the open approach in a systematic way, must themselves choose the design process and methods depending on the problem at hand. The more open approach to design provides opportunities for designers to:

- Bring in facts, opinions, ideas, theories, models, principles, their insight and experience as well as contextual information into the design process;
- Bring in informal methods while combining them with the methods used in mechanistic processes and provide a more adaptive approach where and whenever needed;
- Bring this information together using metaphors, concepts, diagrams, models or prototypes from earlier experiences and designs.

4.1   Metaphors

Metaphors and patterns also help designers to come up with good ideas. They can in fact be one dimension of design knowledge. A previous chapter described knowledge and innovation metaphors that can be used in design.

More background here can be found in the literature from researchers from a more theoretical perspective (Morgan, 1986), who proposed organizations as living organisms, or knowledge as water flowing as the metaphor for system design. Morgan's metaphors include organizations as:

- Working as machines, with all parts working together to achieve a goal working in routinized and well-defined ways;
- Being an organism that exists flexibly in its environment that satisfies its needs but in which it must compete for resources;
- Being a tribe of people with customs, rituals, ideas, beliefs that guide its practice and behavior;
- Political system where a loose network of people with different goals striving to achieve the goals in the context of conflict and power issues;
- Continuing transformations that emerge in new forms from chaos and complexity resulting from internal tensions and conflicts.

Some of these metaphors, as for example organizations as living organisms that continually evolve or continually transform, correctly reflect the dynamics of the more agile and knowledge-based systems today. Oates and Fitzgerald (2007) go further and recommend a multi-metaphor approach be adopted in the design of systems where designers choose metaphors as needed to combine ideas or serve as a communication tool. They can use these techniques to simplify the complexity and in this way assist in the understanding of ways to resolve complexities.

4.2   Design knowledge and patterns

One consideration for complex adaptive systems is that it is not possible to redesign the system in traditional ways. Going to the IT department every time a change is needed is not practical. What is needed is for users to actually change the system themselves. This requires guidelines on the best ways to create change and services to support change. Such guidelines themselves are based on earlier design knowledge.

Design requires both design knowledge and knowledge about choices that can be made in particular situations. It also requires design rationale to make the best choice. Design knowledge often comes from experience and one goal of any process is to build on such experience and use it to guide designers in making choices. This chapter will suggest such guidelines for different design steps. Such guidelines result from knowledge gained through earlier experience, or from best practices that have been recorded for particular applications. They often serve as a good start to design and can suggest initial alternative designs that are then adapted to a given situation. They are equally useful for small- and large-scale collaborative processes.

A complimentary approach is to use 'patterns' (Rizzo et al., 2004) in design. Basically design requires users to identify 'patterns' and use them as templates to implement system components. Patterns or templates can also be seen as design knowledge. We discussed many such patterns before. Chapter 3, for example, outlined some social networks and roles. Such social patterns include both those found in small team environments and in exchanges between groups within large enterprises or for applications (Herrman, et al., 2004). The challenge is to merge the open activities into the high-level activities that define the major outputs required of the process. We are in fact moving from standard design processes to what can at best be called flexible design processes or in some other domains as methods engineering – that is choosing the method that best matches the problem at hand.

The book has already described a number of patterns. There were a number of social structures described in Chapter 3. They defined different role structures and later in Chapter 4, it was described how these apply to knowledge sharing. This chapter describes how some of the techniques and methods covered in previous chapters can be combined into a design process.

4.3 The importance of having a vision

The term 'vision' is also often used in developing new systems. It states what the long-term goal of any new system is, or where we want to be in the future. For example, we want to become competitive in the high fashion industry through establishing better links with high fashion houses. We think that this is achievable as we have some of the best designers. Metaphors provide a good way to describe a vision – for example, 'we wish to improve the flow of knowledge'.

The question then is how to implement the vision. This calls for the setting of objectives. One way to define a set of objectives is in terms of value chains. This identifies new objectives. Then it is necessary to look for manufacturers that produce quality outcomes. Ways then have to be developed for these parts of the value chain to be coordinated.

Visions can take many forms. Social visions can, for example, be ways to support an aging population, improvements to transportation systems.

4.4 The importance of alternatives

Any design must consider a number of alternatives. The very act of looking at alternatives leads to more ideas being considered and ultimately a better system being built. The alternatives can be systematically varied to:

- Look at alternate business value expected, as for example, should we build a customer base or get greater value from existing customers;
- Changing the scope, as for example outsourcing different non-core operations;
- Considering different application patterns; or
- Look at alternate business emphasis, as for example focusing on developing best practices.

5 Option 1 – A totally open and bottom-up approach

Patterns, metaphors and other guidelines assist designers to make sense of process complexity and simplify the cognitive processes to design new systems. The way all of these are put together is shown in Figure 10.4. Figure 10.4 illustrates the combination of patterns with other design methods. It most closely corresponds to the ideas proposed in methods engineering, where designers select the design method depending on the situation at the time. Each circle in Figure 10.4 represents a design task and can be a step in the design process. The numbers on the design tasks are more indicative as a reference point rather than in any way implying a series of steps. Each of the steps in Figure 10.4 has a set of guidelines attached to them. For example, method 5, 'design for networking', has collaboration patterns, or method 10, 'specify technical support' has 'lightweight workspaces' as its guideline. These guidelines are in fact design knowledge as they bring together earlier experiences.

The design process itself is totally open. The design process is actually not defined as a set of steps but is seen as the central element. You can envisage the designer as being in the center choosing design methods as needed. The designer is central and can carry out any number of design steps selecting the most appropriate method for each step. They select the methods as they need them. The designer can use the guidelines and methods attached to the step. Typical design tasks include the following:

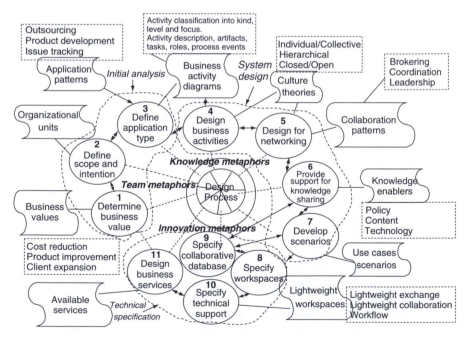

Figure 10.4 Design tasks for an open design method

- Identifying the business values to be achieved;
- Identifying the application patterns that were found in Chapters 7 and 8;
- Defining the work and social patterns, and ESNs, which were described in Chapter 3;
- Selecting the knowledge enablers described in Chapters 4 and 5.

Metaphors can also play a part here. Sometimes one can start with Morgan's metaphors to define a vision of how the system will work. Then other metaphors can be used to structure the vision. These metaphors were identified in Figure 10.4 – knowledge and innovation metaphors. These metaphors can serve as communication tools and as guidelines in design. We can be talking about knowledge design and using the knowledge as water metaphor to illustrate a broad objective. This can be used to check the ways to get knowledge to all people involved in some processes. Usually they can raise questions such as "is there a way to let all our global team know about the new product as quickly as possible?"

Alternatively we can be using any of the innovation metaphors discussed in Chapter 4. Their role in asking questions is particularly important. For example, if we use the idea of innovation as a journey then it should be possible to show how this journey takes place through the proposed activities. For example, has an idea been commented on by all those that can be involved in developing a new service for a client? Or the metaphor of knowledge management is "like facilitating water flows" can lead to a question like "is information flowing to all people involved in a new strategic initiative?".

Those metaphors proposed by Morgan can also serve as general descriptors of the whole system. For example, we want to be efficient, as a machine can mean more emphasis on defining formal work processes.

Designers must continually elicit information from people in the system. Elicitation can take many forms. It can be discussions with stakeholders or even taking part in the business activity. It can be with the analyst spending some time working in the organization to understand the way processes work and relationships are formed and grow. Ethnographic studies and focus groups can also be used in the elicitation process. In ethnography studies, analysts study the way people work with the goal of providing them with services to support their work practices. Focus groups, on the hand, provide analysts with information on particular aspects of the work situation.

Activity diagrams and social patterns can be gradually developed as elicitation proceeds. Metaphors can also often help in communication that is part of the design process. For example, the metaphor 'knowledge flows like water' can be used to check whether knowledge is being passed between different activities.

6 Option 2 – A systematic (Up and Down) approach

Systematic approaches usually tend to be more organized and view design in phases. Hence we organize the design steps into a more formal process. There is

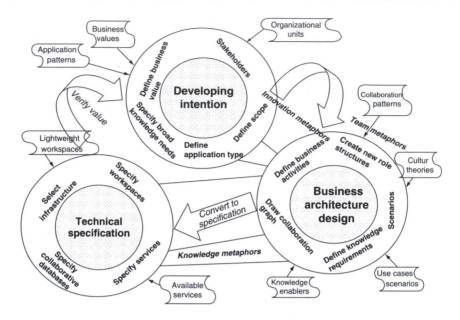

Figure 10.5   A more systematic description of design tasks

often a role that sees the whole picture and guides various groups to follow the systematic path but with the same top view. We thus organize the design steps in Figure 10.4 into three phases as shown in Figure 10.5. The most common way is to start with the phase 'developing the intention', then follow with the 'business architecture design' phase and then the 'technical specification' phase.

The design methods and guidelines used here are the same as in Figure 10.4 – how they are grouped into the phases to provide a better way for managing the design process. It is of course possible to move between phases as new issues arise. Thus if architectural design identifies some new opportunities the intention can change. The process thus becomes goal-oriented rather than one of creating design for a particular goal.

It is also perhaps interesting to note the close correspondence to the HCDID design process. Phase 1 in Figure 10.5 is different as its goal is to define the goals of the project, something that is given in HCDID. Architectural design in Figure 10.5 strongly corresponds to phases 1 and 2 in HCDID and focuses on user and functional analysis, providing ESNs and scenarios for this purpose. It also provides a number of methods that focus on user activities with the process rather than focusing on interface design. Technical specification corresponds to phases 3 and 4 in HCDID.

6.1   The systematic approach – What are the design steps

The requirements analysis process provides a systematic way to determine what to do to improve the business – to think before you leap. Business system design is a very creative process and requires people to use their creative abilities to determine new ways of carrying out their business activities. The three phases in Figure 10.5 follow the traditional approach in requirements analysis. The first phase starts by looking at the current situation and then analyzing and deciding what to do – that is stating your intention.

Phase 1 – Developing the Intention – Developing an understanding of stakeholders and the kind of environment they work in. Phase 1 clearly identifies the following:

- The business value that is expected of any change;
- The kind of application that will be developed, especially identifying the knowledge activities and knowledge requirements;
- The scope, or what part of the existing system will be effected;
- The impact of current stakeholders;
- The intention of a new design as agreed to by the various stakeholders;
- Broad ways for enabling knowledge sharing and creation and possible changes to the organizational and social structure.

Phase 2 – The Business Architecture Design – Proposes the business architecture. It is a top-level logical design, which describes the following:

- The new business activities;
- Any agreed relationships between the users, and the information they need to carry out the business;
- The acceptance of systems in the socio-technical sense often using scenarios to describe any new ways of working;
- Relationships to any ERP databases;
- The kinds of knowledge created and proposed social structures needed to enable and support knowledge creation.

Phase 3 – Technical Specification – Specifies the software architecture. This is usually a definition of a platform and associated services. An important consideration here is to design a workspace that provides the services needed in the different business activities.

The phased approach also provides a systematic way of considering the different perspectives in design.

- Phase 1 emphasizes the knowledge perspective by identifying the major activities and their knowledge needs;
- Phase 2 emphasizes the social perspective by going into a more detailed analysis of businesses activities and the social networking needed for knowledge sharing;
- Phase 3 emphasizes the technical perspective by choosing technologies to support the business activities.

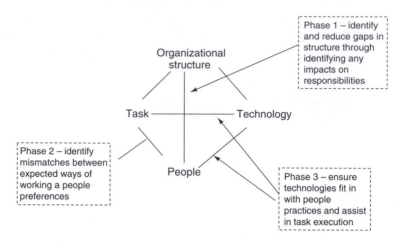

Figure 10.6   Addressing the socio-technical gaps

6.2 Integrating socio-technical analysis into the systematic approach

The three-phase design process also provides a systematic way to address the issues faced in accepting new ways of working usually required from new systems. The phased approach addresses the socio-technical gaps described in Chapter 1 in the systematic manner shown in Figure 10.6. Here:

- Phase 1 predominantly looks at the impact on people's responsibilities and relationships within a changed business structure and seeks agreement on any changes to responsibilities;
- Phase 2 then looks at any gaps between the new proposed tasks, their relationship to the new structure. It looks at more detail at business activities to match social structures to these activities and that the proposed tasks fit in with people responsibilities and capabilities; and
- Phase 3 looks at ways on introducing technology in ways to support people carrying out the new tasks.

7 Developing intention (Phase 1)

This phase uses the methods in steps 1, 2 and 3 in Figure 10.4. It also often proposes possible solutions in terms of business activities, collaborative networks or knowledge enablers. The general process followed in phase 1 is illustrated in Figure 10.7. It includes the following:

- Develop an understanding of how the business works now and its vision of the future. This vision is almost an essential part of any design. The vision sets the general direction that can be used as a benchmark for any proposed changes. It identifies the business values important to the enterprise, takes into account stakeholder values, and the scope of any changes. At the same time it is also necessary to understand how the current business works. This includes the predefined ERP systems and their databases as well as the social issues in their development and change, and any changes to responsibilities of knowledge workers.

- Propose a number of alternatives of varying application types, knowledge enablers and expected business value. To do this it may be necessary to identify the current problems and how they will be solved. Metaphors can also be quite useful here.
- Select one alternative. The selection is often based on both quantitative issues, like cost and risk, and the values placed by different stakeholders on each alternative.

The detailed steps are described below.

7.1   Phase 1 Design steps

The phase 1 steps are discussed in some more detail in the following section. They commence with stakeholder analysis and then proceed to propose alternatives, one of which is eventually selected.

Step 1 – Stakeholder analysis

Stakeholder analysis is seen as one of the most crucial issues in ensuring the success of a project. Stakeholders are considered as the people who can be positively or negatively impacted by any systems changes, or can influence, or sometimes oppose, the system changes. Any analysis must:

- Identify the stakeholders and rank them in their importance to the project. There are many ways suggested for this ranking.
- Define their values, their primary concerns and their position in the enterprise.

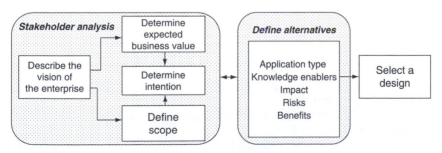

Look at links to existing system

Figure 10.7   The goal setting process

Table 10.1   Stakeholder matrix showing values to each stakeholder

Objectives	Stakeholders			
	Warehouse manager	Production manager	Marketing	Client
Minimize inventory holdings	Reduced inventory costs	Ensure items are available when needed		
Ensure on-time part delivery	Improved ability to manage storage space	Reduced delays in production	Improve delivery times to client	Improves chances of earlier delivery
Keep track of production	Advance knowledge of item requirements	Better planning and manufacturing control	Ability to keep customer informed of progress	Ability to plan for delivery
Ensure quick delivery of product		Eliminate production delays	Better client relationship	Improve chances of early delivery

There are many ways to do this. The most common way is to develop lists that show the stakeholders, and their relative importance and values and their expectations. One possible list is illustrated in Table 10.1. It shows the stakeholders along the horizontal dimension and the potential objectives in the vertical direction. The table shows the value expected by each stakeholder from each of the objectives.

Step 2 – Determine business value

The design step 'Determine business value' is generally a discussion with stakeholders and their expectations. It often requires negotiation to resolve the different priorities of each stakeholder group. Stakeholders can include key clients, management and personnel responsible for tasks in the system. Collaboration is particularly seen as providing the following kinds of business value:

Dimensions of business value

- Improve productivity of existing business processes to get additional business at small incremental cost
- Encourage innovation through collaboration to quickly create products that satisfy client needs
- Improve delivery times through improved processes by supporting communication
- Improve relationships and task management to collect and analyze information

- Improve customer service and satisfaction
- Improve team performance
- Create new partnerships
- Reduce training costs
- Expand customer reach.

Generally the outcome is an agreement between the stakeholders on the expected benefits. It should be expressed in a way that can be measured. Often there can be more specific focus on broad ways to achieve business value. Examples include statements such as 'improve the process by facilitating process innovation and integration', 'maintain relationships', 'facilitate the emergence of new communities', 'raise effectiveness of carrying out tasks', 'add new capability', or 'support some particular task'.

Step 3 – Determine scope

The design step 'Determine scope' defines the scope of the project, what is to be achieved, and what part of the current system is affected. It identifies those parts of the existing system that will be directly affected by any proposed changes. These can be team, the whole organization, size of organization – does it cover the entire organization, or part of the process, or part of the organization? At this stage there is often considerable discussion between the stakeholders to determine the scope that has the best potential to improve business value at minimum cost. Parts where agreement is reached can be identified. The scope should also include specifications of any cross organizational activities. Setting the scope is seen as important in large-scale systems as it is often seen as setting priorities.

Step 4 – Define the intention

One common approach here is to start with problems in current business activities or in challenges coming from changes in the business environment. It is important here to focus on business intention not technological intention. Thus an intention like 'develop an intranet' or 'provide a groupware system' is not a business intention. The technical solutions are something that may be needed to satisfy a business intention and may be proposed as part of phase 3 of the requirements process. Any choice of technology must be shown to realize business value, rather than simply be based on the particular properties of the technology.

The first step here is to identify the problem – that is why requirements analysis is initiated in the first place. It is also important to focus on the main and critical problem and not be side-tracked on peripheral issues.

The intention is often used to identify the alternatives, as each alternative usually supports a different intention.

Step 5 – Determine application type

The process step 'Determine application type' is to find the kind of application that most matches the expectations of the stakeholders. The list of different applications was described earlier in Chapters 7 and 8. It is usually the first step as it can be used as the foundation for quickly developing an understanding of the current business and how it will be developed. This is a relatively common cognitive approach. We say the application 'is like something we know' and this leads to a quicker and better understanding of the current system. Usually the analysts use their experience to identify the kind of application that is most likely in this situation. This can then provide a good basis for starting a solution.

Step 6 – Determine knowledge requirements and support for knowledge sharing

This design step identifies the knowledge needed by different roles. It selects the knowledge enablers, which were described earlier in Chapter 5, to provide ways to access and create knowledge. Rich pictures can be quite useful here to define the knowledge requirements. The support must take into account how knowledge should be managed and the activities to be supported to manage knowledge. The choices here include the following:

- The activities, artifacts or roles that are selected for knowledge capture.
- The knowledge management process goals, including any new roles or changes to role responsibilities. Are these just to capture articulated knowledge in an application and use it in that application or for enterprise wide purposes?
- Identifying and creating communities of practice.
- How the captured knowledge is to be stored including any technologies to be used.
- How to distribute knowledge throughout the enterprise. This will determine both the technologies provided and the necessary roles.
- Ways to link to ERP systems or existing database systems to support knowledge work.

Step 7 – State the impact

One important part of phase 1 is to state the impact on the existing system of any proposed changes. This is one of the first steps in addressing social acceptance of the new system. It identifies new things to be done and who will be responsible for them. Important parts of the impact statement must include the following:

- Effect on current clients;
- Changes to any existing processes and activities;
- Change in people networking; and
- Changes in the responsibilities of current system participants.

The effect on the way people work, or the culture, must be considered in the impact statement to ensure acceptance. These again can be used in discussions with stakeholders to suggest the impact of any new work structures. The main impacts are often expressed in terms of:

- Changes in system goals – explicit definition of what is expected of the new system;
- Changes to processes – or how new processes will work including any changes to process type;
- Social networking – any new roles and changes in relationships and how people communicate and use services;
- New communication services and tools – specify what new tools and services are needed in the new system.

Step 8 – Identify risks

The risks of a proposal are also identified and evaluated. Generally economic, technical and business risks must be assessed. Economic risks are evaluated to ensure that the new system will generate economic profits. Business risks include assessing the reliability of any alliance partners, or evaluating the risk. Technical risks include evaluating the suitability of new technologies and their acceptance of proposed social structures.

This step also includes stating any negative effects of the impact analysis and suggesting ways to minimize them. The possibilities of any socio-technical gaps should be identified here.

Step 9 – Evaluate costs and benefits

Costs and benefits must always be included when proposing an alternative. Estimate the costs of new people, premises and any equipment. Estimate differences in costs of running the new system and compare to current costs.

These steps are now illustrated with an example in marketing.

8   Example – A global marketing services (GMS) organization

The example shows the ways that requirements analysis is used to set the goal. It not only implements a selected goal, but focuses on the initial setting of business requirements and the determination of the goal itself. It is important to consider a number of alternate solutions to identify alternate business activities and select the one that most fits the current culture of the organization. Alternate solutions can actually change the responsibilities of the different stakeholders and the business activities.

The GMS organization provides services for developing marketing plans for their clients. It is principally made up of a small number of partners, highly skilled in developing marketing materials and strategies. The partners have a very busy schedule keeping track of current contracts and very little time for work other than their current projects. They realize that time spent on looking for new clients will take them away from work in which they possess the best expertise – marketing plan development – and which is the core of their business.

The current system is described in Figures 10.8a and 10.8b using the symbols described in the previous chapters for business activity modeling and ESNs. Again as a remainder the pictorial model gives an overview and there is often

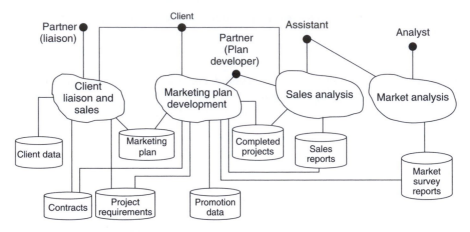

Figure 10.8a   Business activity model of existing system

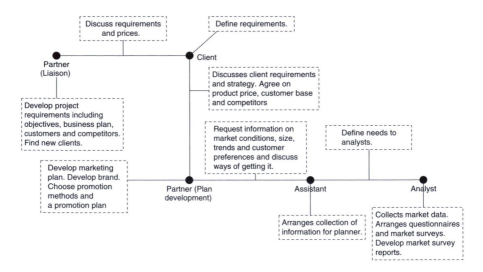

Figure 10.8b   Enterprise social network

substantial documentation about the responsibilities of people and rules to be followed.

8.1 Business activities

To elaborate, the business activity model shows four main business activities:

1. Client liaison is keeping in touch with clients and their requirements. There is a liaison role that is taken by the partners. Each client in general liaises with one partner. Usually work is divided into projects. This is usually taken

on by the partners with each partner responsible for one client project. A contract is developed and client requirements are defined. These include things like the client product strategy, their current sales, customer base and competitors.

2. Marketing plan development where the partners develop the marketing plans. Here one partner works together with clients to develop a plan. Usually a partner takes the role of plan developer. The partner has their own experience to draw on as well as information such as sales and marketing surveys, previous similar projects, and access to cost data on use of alternate promotion channels.

3. Market analysis determines the current trends in the marketplace if needed by a new project.

4. Sales analysis considers the effectiveness of the plans. The monitoring is usually carried out by the partner, who was initially the plan developer for the project.

8.2 Information

The business activity model also shows the major information used in the system. These include contracts, project requirements for a client, various market survey reports, which are used by the planner to develop the plan. There are also records of previous projects, and the corresponding sales reports, which provide knowledge of what worked in the past.

8.3 Social networking

The ESN shows the main responsibilities of the different roles and the way they interact. It shows that:

- The partner (plan development) develops the marketing plan. This partner chooses the promotion plan and develops the costs for discussion with the client.
- The assistant carries out sales surveys to evaluate the outcomes of earlier plans.
- The analyst is responsible for carrying out market surveys, which may be necessary for a new project.

The ESN also shows the interactions between the roles. The client and partners take part of each of these activities. The closest relationship is between the client and the plan developer for the client requirement. This takes place during plan development and later in monitoring the effectiveness of the plan. The requirements analysis then identifies ways to reorganize these activities to improve operations.

Step 1 – Stakeholder vision and values – The major stakeholders here are the business partners. Their vision is to create an organization where they continue to focus on applying their expertise to development but at the same time grow both by expanding their client base and perhaps going global. There are of course other stakeholders, in particular the clients, who would expect improved service from the company. Based on this vision it seems appropriate to start by looking at non-core activities that can be outsourced.

Step 2 – Defining the business value – As a first step, the partners are considering outsourcing some of their activities and supporting the outsourcing with collaborative technologies. They feel that their marketing expertise is the core value of the business and can be further developed by outsourcing other parts. It is thus important to ensure that they continue to make a substantial contribution to system development.

Step 3 – Setting the Scope – There are a number of potential non-core enterprise processes that can be outsourced in organizations. They can include human relations or finding new clients or one of a number of other functions. Not all of them apply to this organization. The potential activities that can be outsourced are shown in Figure 10.9. There are many options and ways to generate business value. In an actual situation there would now be considerable discussion on what is to be done and what to outsource.

Step 4 – Intention – This is where the alternatives come in. In general the partners are looking at outsourcing, some on the non-core activities while they apply their core skills to developing new systems. The alternatives are often what to outsource.

8.4   Alternative 1 – Outsourcing selected non-core processes

The alternative suggested here is to outsource marketing and possibly evaluating the effect of the marketing plan. This is outsourced to a 'search manager'.

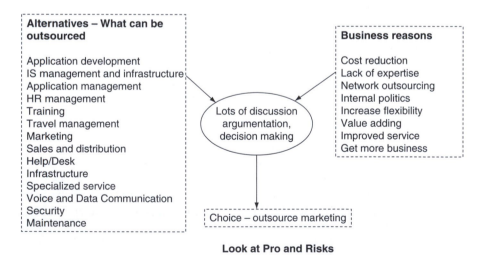

Look at Pro and Risks

Figure 10.9   Discussion to determine scope and strategy

Step 5 – Defining the application type – in this case it will be an outsourcing application.

The design patterns are chosen from those described in Chapters 7 and 8. The result of adopting alternative 1 can then also be outlined on the business activity model shown in Figure 10.10a. The decision here is to outsource searching for new clients as well as some of the evaluation work. The impact of the decision is shown in Figure 10.10a. It shows the activities and roles that are affected by the strategic decision. The arrows on the diagram identify the effected activities. Figure 10.10b includes an initial ESN showing the proposed new work relationships. It proposes that partners can now take different roles. For example, one partner, here called liaison, can maintain contacts with any new clients. Other partners can focus on development. These would have been agreed upon during stakeholder discussion and now require partners to assume roles for maintaining contacts with the manager of the marketing partner, and with maintenance groups. The partner, who prepares a plan, then maintains a relationship with the evaluator of the plan.

Step 6 – Define Knowledge Requirements – In this case the intention is to capture the knowledge articulated during interactions between people. The next question is to how to identify the sources of the knowledge and the way it is to be captured and distributed. Often drawing a picture like that shown in Figure 10.11 helps to see what people need to know. It also identifies the relationships through which much of the knowledge is developed.

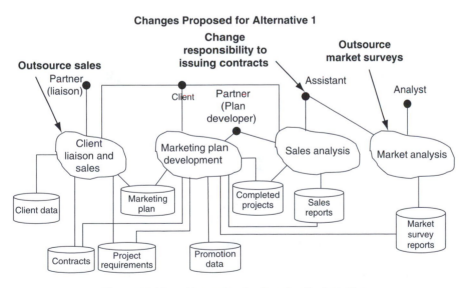

Figure 10.10a   Alternative 1 – Showing the intention

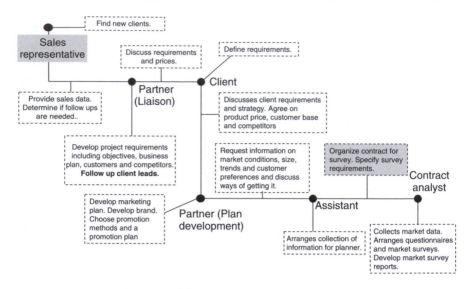

Figure 10.10b   New enterprise social network

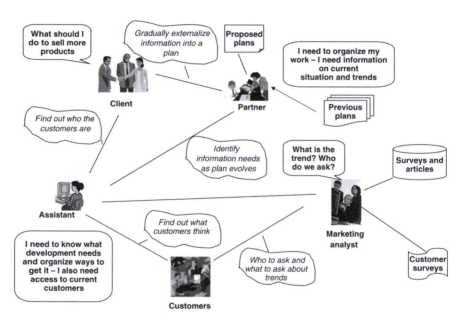

Figure 10.11   Knowledge requirements and sharing

The following kinds of knowledge need to be gathered:

- Knowledge about customers and their preferences. It is the responsibility of the assistant who interacts with clients and their customers and the marketing analyst to gather such knowledge.

- Knowledge about market trends.
- Knowledge about the client's vision and capabilities.

At this stage the proposal is to simply gather articulated knowledge through social relationships which are also shown on the ESN. This will indicate the kind of social software, which will be selected during subsequent phases to facilitate the interactions and to capture some of the knowledge created during the interactions. Information about clients and sales performance, however, will be captured for later use in making new marketing plans.

Step 7 – Stating the Impact – The impact of this alternative is mainly to require existing partners to liaise with an external sales representative and the contracted analyst of sales data. The responsibilities of these external parties are shown in Figure 10.11. There has to be agreement that the partner will carry out such liaison or else the system will fail. This impact can be minimized by the development of formal reporting processes with appropriate documentation and technology support.

Step 8 – Evaluating Risk – The risks here are mainly in difficulties of maintaining contact with the search manager.

Metaphors can eventually play a role here in design. The knowledge metaphor can be used as a guide to identify ways for information to flow through the system. Thus information gathered by the marketing group must flow through to the developers and also be collected and analyzed to assess any trends.

8.5 Alternative 2 – Specializing internal operations

Another alternative is to reorganize activities by identifying routine tasks and hiring additional staff to carry them out (see Figures 10.12a and 10.12b). Some of the steps in this alternative are described below.

Step 3 – Intention – The intention now is to hire assistants to carry out some of the routine work involved in developing marketing plans and to carry out the evaluation. This decision could be made as part of a cost-benefit analysis where the salary and associated costs of a new person is more attractive than outsourcing some of these activity. The partners have now agreed that they will take on the responsibility of supervising the assistant.

Step 7 – Impact – The impact now can be more serious in that the partner's time will be taken up in supervising the junior people. This may include training, explaining how existing applications work, or discussing alternate ways of change, all of which can take considerable time. Again existing partners must agree to participate in these new activities. There is also some impact on the way knowledge is captured and shared.

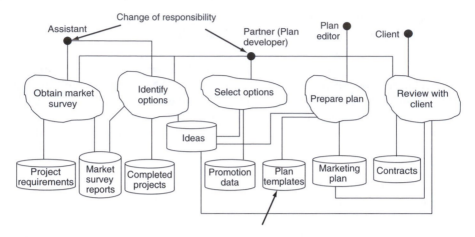

Figure 10.12a   Alternative 2 – Changing the Organization of Market Plan Development

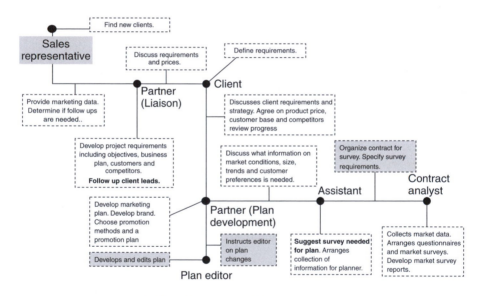

Figure 10.12b   Enterprise social network – Alternative 2

8.6   Alternative 3 – A strategic change – Opening branches or franchises

A more innovative alternative is illustrated in Figure 10.13. It is based on the observation that the team to date has developed a number of general marketing strategies that are reapplied in many situations. In fact in their completed projects they have a knowledge base of successful marketing and proforma that can

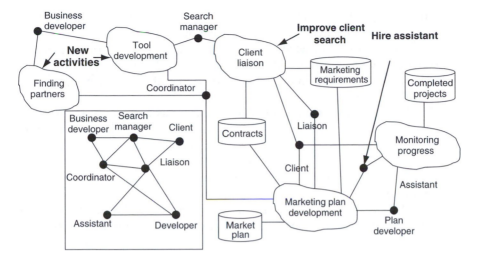

Figure 10.13 Alternative 3 – A strategic change

be used to develop new plans. This can give them an advantage over their competitors as well as the ability to set up new global businesses based on these plans.

This alternative is to package some of the marketing formats. It perhaps needs an approach such as that suggested by the innovation journey metaphor. Perhaps a start should be made with selected franchises, tried and tested, and the feedback should be used to amend the product and then go on to other customers, before attempting mass marketing. Some selected steps follow.

Step 2 – Defining new business value – Here there has been a proposition to hire a business developer to market some of the methods developed by the partners. The intention now is to create two new activities – one to package the tools into a marketable format and the other to find business partners to use these plans.

Step 3 – Changing the scope – In this case, in the work relationships one or more of the partners is assigned a role to coordinate the development of the products.

Step 4 – Additional intention – The new intention here is to franchise the methods developed by the partners globally. It will mean setting up a relationship with a business developer to find business partners that are ready to adopt the methods in their practices. It will require the development of guidelines, packaging the methods, agreeing on intellectual property rights, and commissions to be paid.

Step 5 – Additional application pattern – Currently the process followed is the traditional product development process. Now there is the additional emphasis on product development to package the methods used by GMS. A possible business activity diagram is shown in Figure 10.13

Step 6 – Additional knowledge – Now it becomes necessary to maintain knowledge about locations and branches in those locations. Sales data may now have to be captured and codified to see different customer preferences in different locations.

Step 7 – Impact – The impact now is much wider as a there can be extensive negotiations involving preserving intellectual property rights and commissions paid to any partners. It also requires one partner to almost make a commitment to work full-time on the project. This alternative presents the most challenging of the three as it requires a shift in the culture of the organization.

Step 8 – Risks – The risks can also be perceived to be higher especially in maintaining intellectual property rights globally of the methods developed by the stakeholders.

8.7   Making the decision

Once the alternatives are agreed to be feasible a decision to select one must be made. A final decision will be made by the stakeholders. Their opinions and values as well as preferences come into play. Cultural aspects can also be important. The analysis will also contain a cost-benefit analysis as well as risk analysis. In our case the stakeholders may agree that to minimize the impact of any change is their highest priority. In that case alternative 1 would be most probably selected. If the priority is on growth then other alternatives may be preferred, in which case priorities will have to be set on whether local or global growth is preferred.

9   Summary

This chapter continued to stress the need to create a business architecture from all perspectives. It suggested an open method approach that clearly identifies the perspectives and can emphasize selected perspectives depending on the application. The method identified three phases where each phase emphasizes a different perspective but places it in the context of the entire process. The method also focused on socio-technical issues and identified the socio-technical gaps to be addressed at each phase. The chapter identified the design tasks and the design knowledge needed in each task and concluded with an example.

The chapter outlined the first phase of the design method in detail. This phase defined the requirements of the process. The next chapter will use the requirements model produced in this chapter to design a business architecture.

10 Questions and Exercises

Question 1

What perspective would you emphasize for the following:

- Designing a system to capture best practices for client relationship management.
- Designing a system to process travel arrangements.
- Designing a system to support outsourcing of cleaning services.
- Designing a system to capture feedback about products and use it to redesign products if necessary.

Case study VII

Organizing experts

An organization, Expert Solutions Z (ESZ), develops marketing plans for its clients. The clients come from a number of industries. ESZ prefers to employ external experts that have the core knowledge and skills needed for a particular client assignment. These experts may be sole traders or small enterprises. They may be experts in particular media or industry sectors. Generally ESZ sets up a project team and monitors project progress. It provides the project manager for the project who coordinates the external experts in completing the project. Figure 10.14 shows the ESZ business model in terms of business activities.

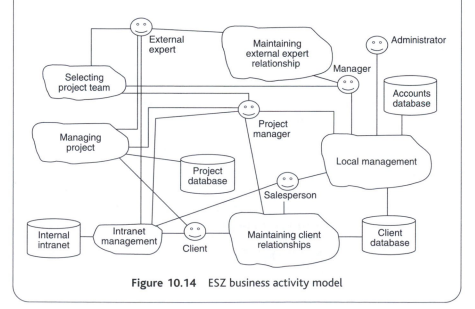

Figure 10.14 ESZ business activity model

Case study VII

Continued

Brief descriptions of the business activities are given in Table 10.2, which also describes the major tasks in each activity.

Table 10.2   Business activity descriptions

Activity	What happens in activity	Communication Method Used
Local management	The group responsible for the business. It includes salespersons, project managers and administrative staff. Tasks include: • keeping track of the organizations financial status, • developing strategy, and • managing accounts.	Generally personal contact or e-mail. Use ESZ database systems.
Maintaining external expert relationships	Experts are usually kept aware of organizations activities through e-mail mailing lists. Tasks include: • Finding new experts, • Updating expert background, • Circulating information about ESZ to experts.	Contacts made by e-mail but followed up with face-to-face discussion. New experts often found through informal external contacts, such as attending conferences or Web searches. Mailing lists used for circulation.
Maintaining client relationships	Mainly the responsibility of salespersons. Tasks include: • Negotiating new projects, • Arranging contracts. • Distributing marketing information.	Mainly through face-to-face meetings or discussions. Marketing information distributed through mailing lists or the Intranet.
Selecting Project Team	Mainly the responsibility of the manager. Tasks include: • Approaching experts with offers for a particular project, • Assigning a project manager, and assigns experts to the project. This can be a very time-consuming process especially to arrange time commitments with suitable experts.	Often initiated through telephone calls, followed by e-mail and face-to-face meetings.

Managing project	Mainly the responsibility of the project manager. Tasks include: • setting time schedules, • coordinating the work process, Usually requires I day per week for each project.	Usually through e-mail notifications or phone calls or brief notes. This is often a time-consuming process especially when managing a number of projects at the same time.
Intranet management	Outsourced to external party. Tasks include: • Updating files, • Maintaining contact addresses	Using the Intranet interface.

Some statistics are as follows:

Local management – 15 (Project managers – 5, Salespersons – 6, administrative staff – 3)
Clients – around 200 (up from 150 last year)
Experts – around 150
Projects at any one time – around 30
Average project duration – 3 months
Average project size – 3 experts

The process followed is broadly illustrated in Figure 10.15 and described in Table 10.3.

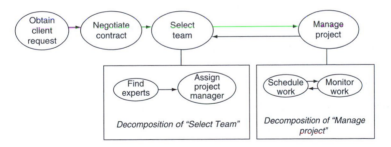

Figure 10.15   High level process perspective

Table 10.3   Process description

Process	Description
Obtain client request	Mainly the responsibility of salespersons. Projects obtained through visits by salespersons or responses to requests.
Negotiate contract	This is done mainly face to face perhaps with an exchange of documents using e-mail. Has to be approved by manager.

Case study VII

Continued

Table 10.3   Continued

Process	Description
Form team	Mainly done by the manager who maintains contacts with the experts. The manager finds experts and assigns the project manager. Communication is usually by phone or e-mail. Usually takes about 4 hours of time to find an expert. Usually a face-to-face meeting to assign responsibilities and define a work schedule.
Manage project	Project manager schedules the work and coordinates activities.

Current situation

The system has now grown significantly with the growth of clients from 150 to 200 this year. Further growth both in clients and in volume of work per client is expected. However, due to competition margins have decreased making it difficult to increase staff to cater for the increased activity. Hence improvements in operational effectiveness are needed by reducing time spent on each project. Hence improvement in communications is needed both to:

- Reduce the workload on staff in maintaining all communications through e-mail; and
- Improve knowledge management and sharing by facilitation sharing of knowledge between the various stakeholders in the system.

Your project

You are required to improve the business processes. Possibilities are as follows:

1. Reducing overheads working with e-mail;
2. Expedite the process of finding experts;
3. Improve knowledge sharing between project teams.

Your output should include the following:

1. An enterprise social network showing the formal communication between the roles in the system and the information flowing between the roles.
2. Your proposed solution including definition of purpose, scope, business value.
3. A new business activity diagram.
4. A set of three major use cases describing the way the new system will work.

Some further readings

Boonstra, A., de Vries, J. (2008) 'Managing Stakeholders Around Inter-Organizational Systems: A Diagnostic Approach' *Journal of Strategic Information Systems*, Vol. 17, pp. 190–201.

Herrman, T., Kunau, G., Loser, K-U., Menold, N. (2004) "Socio-technical Walkthrough: Designing Technology along Work Processes" Proceedings Participatory Design Conference 04, Toronto, Canada.

Holland, J. (1995) *Hidden Order: How Adaption Builds Complexity* (Cambridge Perseus Books).

Morgan, G. (1986) *Images of Organization* (SAGE Publications, Beverly Hills, California).

Merali, Y., McKelvey, B. (2006) 'Using Complexity Science to Affect a Paradigm Shift in Information Systems for the 21st. Century' *Journal of Information Technology*, Vol. 21, pp. 211–215.

Oates, B.J., Fitzgerald, B. (2007) 'Multi-metaphor Method: Organizational Metaphors in Information Systems Development' *Information Systems Journal*, Vol. 17, No. 4. October, pp. 421–449.

Rinkus, S., Walji, M., Johnson-Throop, K.A., Malin, J.T., Turley, J.P., Smith, J.W., Zhang, J. (2004) 'Human-centered Design of a Distributed Knowledge Management System' *Journal of Biomedical Informatics*, Vol. 38, pp. 4–17.

Rizzo, A., Pozzi, S., Save, L., Sujan, M. (2006) 'Designing Complex Socio-technical Systems: A Heuristic Schema Based on Cultural-Historical Psychology' *Proceedings of the 2005 Annual Conference on European Association of Cognitive Ergonomics*, pp. 71–81.

Yu, E. (1995) *Modeling Strategic Relationships for Process Engineering* (PhD Thesis. (Department of Computer Science, University of Toronto, Canada).

Zhang, J., Patel, V., Johnson, K., Smith, J. (2002) 'Designing Human Centered Distributed Information Systems', *IEEE Intelligent Systems*, Vol. 17, No.5, September/October, pp. 42–47.

Creating the Business Architecture: Combining Activities, Knowledge and People

11

Organize how we want to work together

Learning objectives

- Design of business activities
- A guiding blueprint for design
- Criteria for selecting business activities
- Choosing the enterprise social network for business activities
- Extending with knowledge capture

1 Introduction

This chapter continues from the previous chapter to describe how to use system requirements to create the business architecture. It defines ways to organize business activities to realize the intention defined as part of the requirements. It creates the new business architecture, which includes ways to organize business activities, propose an ESN and ways to share knowledge. Design of the business architecture places emphasis on social structures at initial stages of design as has been proposed by many writers, as for example Prahalad and Krishnan (2008). Socio-technical considerations continue to play a part here as any new activities must align people to the task and ultimately to the business intention. Defining role responsibilities is one way of achieving such alignment.

Furthermore the activities are designed to operate in complex environments, which require abilities such as quickly creating or rearranging activities to create new value chains. One way to simplify rearrangements is to align social structures to the kind of work, which was described in Chapter 3. Business activities require clear expertise in one kind of work that can contribute to many value chains. It also provides greater flexibility for rearranging the activities.

Design always improves with experience as new knowledge is created and shared through the design process. Previous design knowledge can help to identify both the activity structures and social patterns. Some design knowledge is found in Chapter 2 together with ESNs described in Chapter 3 and 4. This is used in this chapter.

2   A Blueprint to describe the business architecture

The design follows an open method where designers choose the design tasks as needed for selected perspectives. One way to support an open method is to define a blueprint as a design guideline, especially in using all perspectives in process design. The blueprint is shown in Figure 11.1.

Blueprint components

- The business activity diagram that precisely defines how the business activities will be organized including the artifacts and the roles that are needed to carry out the work in each activity and the information they need. A community of practice can be one of the activities as can be a knowledge hub.
- The ESN to model the relationships between people in the activity and across activities.
- The knowledge structure that initially focuses on capturing articulated knowledge, but can include ways to more formally codify this knowledge in organizational memory. One goal here may be to make each activity exhibit the characteristics of a community of practice or a knowledge hub.
- Scenarios to define in detail what people in the business activity will do.

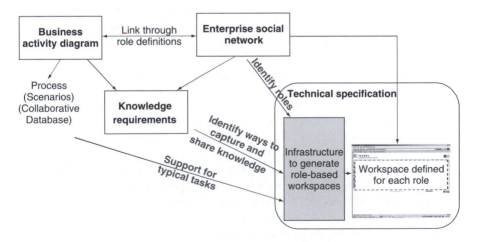

Figure 11.1   A blueprint for the business architecture

This blueprint provides the overriding guideline in design. It provides the key dimensions to organize processes, the activity that produces some outcome, the ESN that defines how people communicate, and the knowledge they use and create.

Furthermore, models based on this blueprint can be directly converted to implementations. Figure 11.1 also shows how the major blueprint modeling components are converted to the technical specification. The conversion to an implementation is made up of a number of steps and described in detail in later chapters.

- First a technical infrastructure, which may be the corporate intranet or some middleware, is selected. This infrastructure is then used to create any number of workspaces.
- Electronic workspaces for selected roles can be generated from the infrastructure for each business activity. The workspace includes the roles and knowledge requirements shown on the business activity diagram. It uses role responsibilities to define the tools needed by people assigned to the role.

The guidelines provided earlier in Chapter 4 are useful for choosing collaboration networks. This is to recognize that the new system may "be something like an earlier system..." and use the good ideas from that system to choose a collaboration structure while adopting them to the current situation.

3   The design process to specify new business architecture

How to create the new design? Stakeholders often identify the needs, designers often provide ideas and suggestions while the stakeholders evaluate them and ultimately decide on a solution. Systematic design follows the idea of methods engineering. Designers can choose different sequences of design steps and can revisit design steps of earlier stages if new possibilities become evident.

The phase 2 design tasks outlined earlier in Figure 10.4 in the previous chapter are repeated in Figure 11.2. A decision can be made here on the perspectives to be used in design.

The design process goes beyond applying the design steps in a deterministic sequence to develop the design. It is more one of doodling and sketching as designers together with stakeholders investigate different possibilities and look for realistic answers. Such discussion involves the different stakeholders and their priorities. Socio-technical considerations come into play here especially in aligning role responsibilities to business tasks. Step 5 – design for networking – defines any new relationships and responsibilities and reaches agreement about them with stakeholders. Step 6 ensures that support is provided for knowledge sharing, using the guidelines in Chapters 4 and 5. Step 7 – developing scenarios – has the express purpose of describing how the business processes will work in business terms and how the different roles in the social structure carry out their responsibilities and interact.

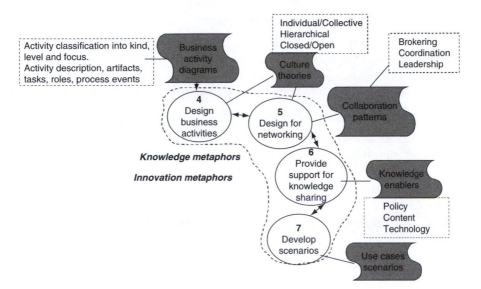

Figure 11.2   Phase 2 – Design tasks to define the business architecture

Figure 11.2 also shows the design knowledge that provides guidelines in design.

Design knowledge

- Knowledge on choosing social structures for business activities can be found in Chapter 3 and also later in this chapter.
- Knowledge of typical business activities can be found in Chapters 7 and 8 used as guideline to create the top-level business activity diagram.
- Knowledge about collaborative structures, especially the patterns can be found in Chapters 3 and 4.
- Knowledge about support for knowledge management can be found in Chapter 4, which describes knowledge processes and enablers and in Chapter 5, which describes ways to facilitate knowledge sharing.

Design includes concept formation, which describes how a system will work. Metaphors are useful here as statements such as 'process will be like a machine' or 'knowledge will flow from the client to all stakeholders within minutes' can be quite useful. Role patterns also play a role here as statements such as 'strong leadership is required in this activity' or 'we need expert advice at this point' are often very relevant and indicative of the direction in which design is heading.

4   Starting with business activity design

The creation of any new activities or changing existing activities is usually a creative process. One way to start design is shown in Figure 11.3 by looking at ways to change activities. We look at intention and the impact of any proposed changes on activities. The objective then is to realize the intention while minimizing the impact.

The process in Figure 11.3 starts with a sketch of the business activity diagram and then looks at each activity in turn to design the individual activities. This divides design into two manageable parts. They are the following:

- The overall structure where we identify the main enterprise activities, followed by
- More detailed design of each of the different high-level activities.

The design of lower level activities can then also call for changes in both the work network and knowledge requirements.

4.1   Developing the top-level activity diagram

The top-level business activity model is created by separating business functions into manageable units. Thus, if enterprise work is organized in functional units, as for example marketing and accounting, then the high-level activities will correspond to such units. For a project-based organization, the high-level

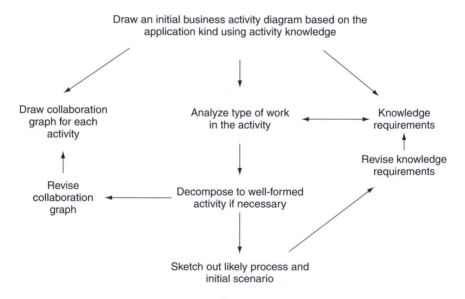

Figure 11.3   Suggested design steps

activities may be projects, whereas the lower level activities will correspond to typical organizational functions, such as client liaison, invoicing and so on. For example, here we look to separate functions like marketing from production, or product development from project management.

The best way is to think about similar applications and say the 'new system will BE LIKE one of the application types' as described in Chapter 8. So we might say that the new business activity will be like a best practice application. This then indicates the kinds of roles that will become part of the system. For example:

- Best practices are usually captured by sharing of knowledge, through team coordination and sharing knowledge about their tasks. Good practices are ideatified and documented. Collaboration is undertaken to get feedback on other people's use of this practice to see if it should be widely adopted.
- Product design is more focused on task management with some coordination when the scope gets larger. It will require ways to coordinate a large number of experts. Similarly a small local team will need less support than a large distributed team.
- Agile supply chains are more process-oriented, especially as the scope or number of participants gets larger. In general irrespective of the size some coordination will be needed and this will become increasingly formal as the size grows.

Once the top-level activity diagram is completed then the activities can be refined in more detail.

4.2   Refining the activities

The strategic objectives and the impact statement are then used to define the business activity model. Typical activities here may be to:

- Split up existing activities, combining them and refining them, changing some of the work practices within the activity through the use of information technology. One goal here is to create activities that include only one kind of work.
- Reorganize people within the activity depending on the social pattern most suited to the kind of activity.
- Create interfaces across different cultural groups.
- Expand the activity into detail including roles and their collaboration.
- Clearly define knowledge management needs.
- Identify links to existing database and ERP systems.

Some rules that can be used in making choices include the following:

- Identify routine parts of work and provide ways to simplify or automate them.
- Ensure that reporting is manageable by avoiding large numbers of relationships for roles. The larger the number of people the more time is needed for

coordination. However, this is modified by the other factors. For example, as the problem becomes less-defined, collaboration becomes more important as changes must be agreed upon to carry out a specific task. Similarly as the team becomes more distributed then collaboration needs to be more formalized. As the scope of the activity becomes larger, then a higher level of collaboration is required.

• Create activities that only have one kind of work, one focus and are carried out at one management level. In complex situations it may be necessary to qualify this by a flexible coordination structure that allows easy reassignment of tasks.

4.3   Look at alternatives

Design creativity is often improved by considering alternatives with one alternative eventually selected by the stakeholders – coming up with alternatives that can involve discussion with people that are part of the business process and bringing together the knowledge of many individuals. During the discussion it is common to:

• Look at the effected activities, compare them to earlier models and suggest new ones.
• Look at the knowledge needed in the activities and ways to capture it.
• Combine the activities into one business activity diagram,
• Propose some scenarios to illustrate different alternatives
• Get stakeholders' opinions on the alternatives and their suggestions to improve it.

As design proceeds, individual activities may be changed, the scenarios redesigned, the system again evaluated until a satisfactory solution is achieved. This can happen a number of times. Finally, what if we start with no existing system. There are no existing activities, and designers must propose the needed activities. One way to begin is to define what outputs are to be provided to satisfy general strategic objectives. Then work backwards to see what needs to be done to produce the output given the strategic objectives.

4.4   Including the social perspective

The standard ESNs described in Chapters 3 and 4 provide broad guidelines for choosing the ESN for a particular business architecture. First, the ESNs are identified for each activity and then these are combined. Figure 11.4 illustrates the process with a simple example. Here, Task A and Task B are identified to be transactive activities and leadership patterns are proposed for them. Project coordination is defined as collaborative in nature. It includes a coordinator as well as the team leaders of Task A and Task B. Project coordination requires a collaborative pattern. Project planning is also seen as a collaborative activity

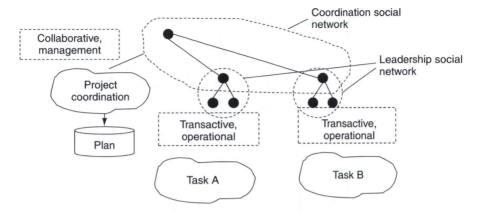

Figure 11.4   Create the enterprise social network

and made up of the same roles. The whole process is iterative and activities are refined as the design proceeds.

5 Designing individual business activities

Activity design concentrates on improving work practices and often requires a detailed understanding of social relationships within the activity. It emphasizes knowledge management and ways to share knowledge in the activities. It is necessary to go into the kinds of things people actually do when they work (how they communicate, how they get information etc.) Much of this calls for *making work visible* through precise definitions of how people will interact by writing scenarios. It requires a detailed specification of what people will actually do in terms of business scenarios. These scenarios will indicate the information and knowledge used and created during the process.

One way to start is to classify an activity in terms of the kind of work, and the management level in the organization. This again is done with the express purpose of reducing any gaps between social structure and task. Identifying the kind of activity provides guidelines for the social structures that suit this activity, and thus reduces the probability of the creation of a socio-technical gap.

Ultimately a good balance must be chosen given the description of the activity in terms of all the parameters. Table 11.1 provides some rough guidelines for choosing ESN for activities. It also suggests that where the type of activity is not clear, then it should be decomposed into simpler activities. The goal to some extent is to create or identify activities that usually support one kind of work and are consistent with the focus and management level.

Table 11.1 Guidelines for choosing enterprise social network

Work kind				Management level			Enterprise social network
Transactive	Integrative	Collaborative	Expert	Strategic	Management	Operational	
	X					X	Set up leadership or coordination structure depending on size
			X	X			Facilitation to devise plans to bring expert advice into plan knowledge sharing
X						X	Most probably leadership structure
	X	X				X	Self-organizing group working on multiple task – may need splitting if large
			X		X		Usually a personal relationship but may need facilitation if large number of experts to be coordinated
		X				X	Self-organizing group working on one task will need some coordination if gets larger
	X				X		Coordinate ways to combine documents into strategic planning

For example the table shows:

- That where the activity is integrative at a management level then a leadership or coordination pattern is probably most appropriate.
- Collecting expert opinions from many sources for strategic planning will probably require some facilitation.

Some guidelines used to design an activity include the following:

Guidelines for activity design

- Clearly define the kind of work supported – Identify whether the activity is transactional, integrative, collaborative or expert to choose the ESN.
- Knowledge requirement – Knowledge of specific task including ways to carry out the task and knowledge of how to do things.
- Collaboration structure – Define the ESN for the activity, and the responsibilities of different roles.
- Define enablers for knowledge sharing and creation including building relationships, especially people getting to know each other, building trust and the ability to work in teams.
- Provide social support for: negotiation, idea generation and selection, reflection and evaluation of past experiences.
- Identify the kinds of services and tools to be provided for the activity.

There are other guidelines for defining collaboration requirements. These include the size of the collaborating group, its geographic distribution, the complexity of their goal, and any time constraints placed on getting some outcome.

During design some scenarios can be sketched as the process proceeds, especially those applying to knowledge management. They should describe where knowledge is found, how it is used and stored. References should be made to the capture of tacit knowledge that builds with the experience of group members for it to be shared between the members and to be retained as group memory. Often important knowledge sharing happens informally and knowledge is retained by individuals and not made widely available. What is now needed are precise ways to collect and use such knowledge and codify it into explicit knowledge whenever possible.

5.1 Questions to ask during activity design

One important component of design is how to include knowledge management components in each activity and in fact make them an integral part of the activity. Some questions that can be asked here include the following:

- What must be done to improve the quality of future actions? This question will indicate the kinds of information that needs to be captured during the activity.

- What kind of information is available to simplify peoples' work and reduce the time for them to reach a good decision?
- How to record information for future use as part of the process?
- How to make existing databases and ERP systems available to knowledge workers?
- What tools and services are to be provided?

Further questions result from guidelines about good structures. For example:

- Integration work requires some coordination focus, or
- Collaboration work can have a task focus.

5.2 A simple example – Part ordering

One simple example is ordering parts from inventory. The problem and intention are shown in Figure 11.5. The problem is that there are a number of transactional tasks, which are carried out to purchase a part but there are very weak linkages between the roles responsible for these tasks. It is "like a sequential set of transactional steps" discussed in Chapter 5. Confusion can arise because of the weak linkages no one really responsible for keeping track of a purchase request. There is thus a gap between the task and the social structure. The activity is integrative but the implementation is collaborative. Basically the intention here is to make it easier to track the flow of orders by either changing the role relationships or changing the activity.

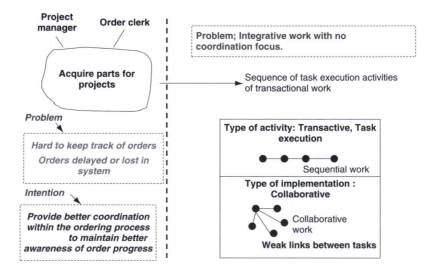

Figure 11.5   Initial analysis

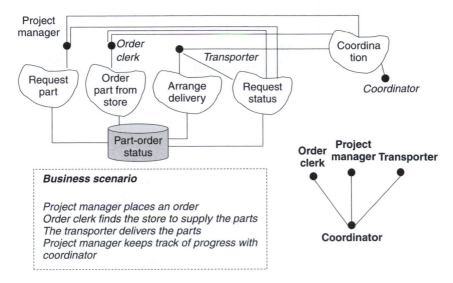

Figure 11.6   A solution to keep track of orders

The proposed change to the role relationships is shown in Figure 11.6. The new activity is described by a predefined workflow of a number of transactional activities. These are shown in Figure 11.6 as 'request part', 'order part' and 'arrange delivery'. A role is defined as responsible for each activity and progress is stored in 'Part-order status'. A coordinator role is defined to keep track of progress of orders through the activities. A project manager can check progress by accessing 'Part-order status'.

The design also identifies the process steps and who is to carry them out. A workflow system and electronic mail can be used to implement the system. Some awareness features must also be provided. For example, the status of the order should be available to the whole group. It would of course be possible to propose alternate solutions.

An alternate approach is to change the activity into a collaborative activity. In that case the solution is shown in Figure 11.7. It now sees an executive assistant position created for the project manager. The project manager and executive assistant work closely together to keep track of project progress. The executive assistant will be responsible for keeping track of project status.

The second solution creates a collaborative activity where the executive assistant plays the role of a facilitator to maintain track of progress. The option that is accepted is often determined by the culture of the organization.

5.3   Another example – Consulting services

Suppose now we are organizing a way to install specialized services for clients requiring the preparation of a market report. The activity is shown in

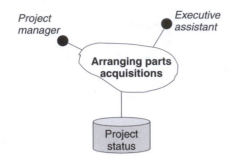

Figure 11.7   An alternate solution

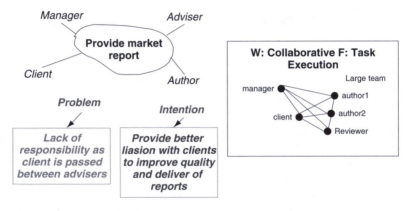

Figure 11.8   Analysis for specialized services

Figure 11.8. The activity appears to be one of an expert nature, where a number of expert authors add sections to the report, there are advisers to comment on the report and the client has to monitor progress through this maze, something that should not be expected of a client. The manager's role is to find the client and initiate the process. The authors here can be considered as experts but their individual work is not in any way coordinated or facilitated. However, the work network is such that the client has to pass any formal requests to an author. In fact the client is in some way expected to coordinate the work of the authors. That author can pass their work to other authors and as a result the client can lose track of what is going on. The activity therefore probably needs a facilitator.

A proposed solution is shown in Figure 11.9. Here it is proposed to organize a new service for each specialized customer report request. There is an 'Analyze client problem' activity. A client liaison officer is assigned to the client and oversees the completion of the report, guiding it for comment and contribution through a number of experts. Three activities are identified with different people assigned specific roles in each activity. A new role of client liaison officer is

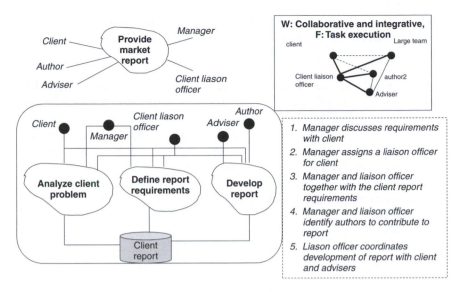

Figure 11.9   Proposed system

created to facilitate report progress. The client liaison officer participates in all activities in a given client service and is aware of its status at all times. The liaison officer is directly responsible for working with the client and passing formal client requests to the authors, although there is social contact between the client and the various authors. It is also proposed to record the final outcome of the report so that any comments can later be made available when preparing similar reports.

One alternative here is that one of the authors could be designated a lead author and delegated with the responsibility of coordinating with the other authors and interacting with the client.

6   Designing the top-level structure – GMS example

Many designs commence with high-level activities. Let us now consider a more complex example and return to alternative 1 in our outsourcing example. The blueprint shown in Figure 11.1 serves as the design guideline.

6.1   Identifying and organizing business activities

Initially, each activity in the system is classified by its kind and level. This classification is shown in Figure 11.10. 'Client liaison sales' business activity is seen both as integrative and collaborative. In this activity people work together to develop contracts but it has some strategic impact as it determines the future direction of the firm. Similarly 'marketing plan development' includes both an expert and collaborative kind of work. The collaborative work is to gather all the information, whereas the expert work is to make the decisions on design. These activities are decomposed into those that have the majority of work as one kind. Thus:

- 'Client liaison and sales' is decomposed into 'developing contacts', which is collaborative, to find clients, and 'client liaison' to develop requirements and contracts once a client is found.
- 'Marketing plan development' is decomposed into 'information collection', which is mainly routine integrative work to collect information, and into 'marketing plan development' which is the expert work carried out by the planner. The integrative work is delegated to the assistant.
- Sales analysis is decomposed into arranging contracts and carrying out the sales analysis.

The design becomes more detailed now and the figures are somewhat more complex. The proposed system now looks something like Figure 11.11.

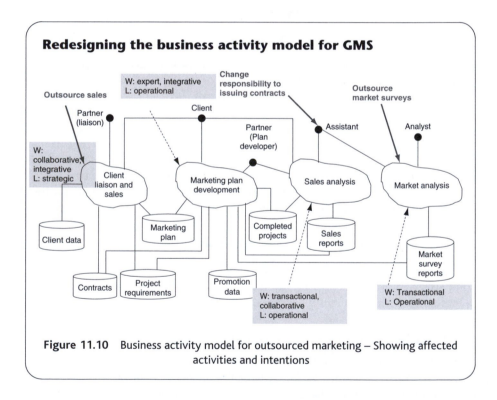

Figure 11.10   Business activity model for outsourced marketing – Showing affected activities and intentions

The new activities in Figure 11.11 supports one kind of work. Such activities can also be quickly reconfigured into a new business structure as the interfaces

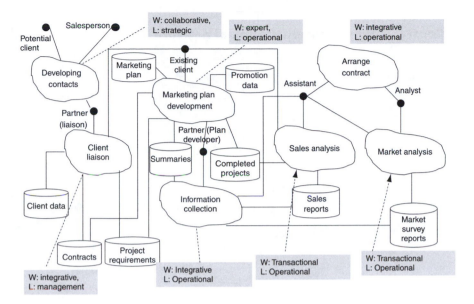

Figure 11.11   New business activity architecture with activity descriptions

are usually through data and information and the kind of work carried out does not depend on how this data is derived. For example, a change to the way 'market analysis' is carried out does not necessarily require changes in market plan development as the interface here are the summaries.

The activities in Figure 11.11 follow the approach of separating cultural groups into their activities and providing interfaces between them. In these cases cultural distinctions are based on professions, such as developing clients, sales analysis, contract management all identified as separate activities. Interfaces are through roles that span more than one activity.

6.2   Defining the enterprise social network

One approach is to look at the kind of work performed in each activity and use guidelines described earlier to choose a work network for the activity.

In our case study, for example, the fact that contract development is integrative work suggests a facilitator role, which in this case may be taken by the liaison officer. Part of such decisions must describe the impact on current networking on organizational governance. An ESN is now developed showing all relationships. This can proceed in two steps. First the relationships between roles are shown for each activity as shown in Figure 11.12. Then responsibilities and interactions are specified as shown in Figure 11.13.

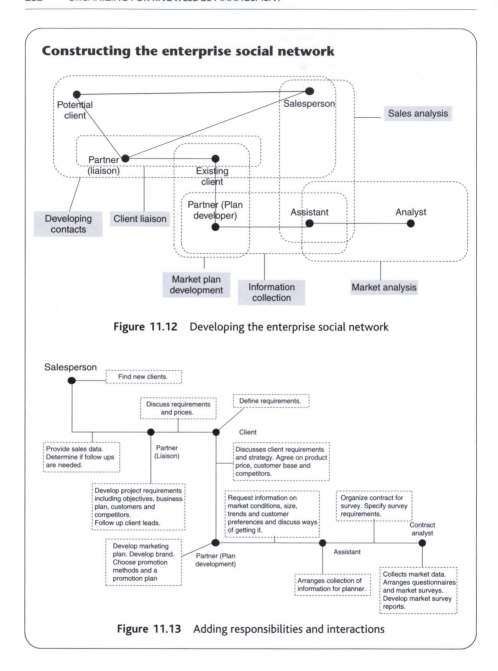

Figure 11.12   Developing the enterprise social network

Figure 11.13   Adding responsibilities and interactions

6.3   Designing the database and collaborative knowledge base

Now the information needed is defined without going into its detailed structure.
There are two components here:

- The information contents needed in each activity. These are various databases that are created and updated during the activities – things like client information, payroll or inventory records.
- The collaborative knowledge base keeps track of issues raised, records of good ideas or program records for people to keep track of progress on various tasks or programs. Often knowledge is captured here using social software.

Table 11.2 describes some of these activities. Thus there is an issues board for developing client requirements and a program board for project development. An issues board is also provided for contract development. For example, contract development is classified as being operational in nature and integrative in work. It is operational as only a few people are involved and does not require extensive management planning or support. It is integrative as it includes contract parts that may require input from more than one person exchange information with

Table 11.2 Logical requirements of the new activities

Activity	What happens in activity	Kind of work	Knowledge capture
Developing contacts	Salesperson is kept informed of capabilities and services being developed by the organization by the liaison officer. Salesperson uses this information in their contact with clients	Collaborative Loose relationships between the salesperson and potential client. This gradually evolves as the client is converted to an existing client.	Develop contact details and capture stories about clients including their views
Client liaison	Salesperson arranges with potential client to initiate formal agreements with the partner. Formalize client requirements and define the cost and time for providing a marketing plan.	Integrative The relationship is basically a negotiation over a contract and agreeing on requirements.	Capture issues that arise in contract discussions and how they are resolved
Information collection	Preparing information in ways required for developing the marketing plan.	Integrative Assistant in consultation with the planning partner collects all information needed by a project and develops interpretations.	Notes on ways sales and marketing information is interpreted.
Marketing plan development	Develop a plan to meet contract requirements.	Expert Client and planner work together to develop the contract with guidance from the salesperson	Strong relationship between client and planner partner to develop marketing plan. Capture of issues raised by client and the responses.

Table 11.2   Continued

Activity	What happens in activity	Kind of work	Knowledge capture
Arrange contract	Arrange a external analyst to carry out market analysis	Collaborative A partner develops contract with the client	Information on meeting deadlines. Good sources of information.
Sales analysis	Analyze sales following Implementation of earlier plans.	Transactive	Organizes the collection of sales data from salespersons and develops summaries.
Market analysis	Develop future prognosis of marketing developments.	Transactive	Assistant arranges for the analyst to conduct market surveys.

the marketing people. Project development itself requires some coordination support and is integrative in nature.

7 Defining scenarios

The last part of the design is to define typical scenarios. The scenarios are consistent with the ESN and as they are developed they provide further insights that can lead to further design refinements. They define what different roles will do and how they interact with others. They are also important in further clarifying how any system will ensure that stakeholders do not have any surprises as a new system evolves and are less likely to reject it.

7.1 Scenarios

Scenarios describe the steps that illustrate how the new system will work. There are a large number of possible scenarios. What we need to do is look at each activity and write scenarios of how people will carry out the work in the activity. In the GMS example, these scenarios include the following:

- Salesperson discussions with client;
- Search manager contacting the market liaison person;
- Discussion with client to decide whether to proceed;
- Negotiations in contract development;
- Process followed in system development.

There are some good practices to follow when writing scenarios. These include the following:

- Each step should be just one simple action;
- Define the business activities included in the scenario;

- Steps should refer to the artifacts in the business activity when appropriate;
- Use same names as on the business activity model.

One good way to start is to look at each activity in turn.

7.2   Scenario for activity in contract development

Scenarios can be used to describe business activities at detailed levels. A scenario is made up of a sequence of statements where each statement of the scenario is usually some action taken by one or more roles. One such simple form is:

<role> <takes action> on <document, task> as for example, or <role> <interact> with another <role> about a <artifact> suggesting some <action.

Such simple statements are easy to make sense of. Later they can be used to choose the tools and services needed to carry them out. It provides a basis for discussion about what people will actually do and the services that they will need. One example of a scenario for contract development is given in the following.

Salesperson sends record of discussion with client and issues raised to liaison officer.
Liaison officer creates new draft contract and stores it in the contracts file.
Liaison officer enters initial information into draft contract using information collected by the market analyst.
Liaison officer contacts market analyst to verify draft contract.
Market analyst returns contract with comments.
Liaison officer adds comments to draft contract and posts any issues raised.
Liaison officer sends draft contract to client with a copy to the salesperson.
Liaison officer makes contact with client to arrange a meeting.
Liaison officer and client meet to discuss issues.
Liaison officer makes notes of the issues.
Liaison officer updates draft contract and stores in the contracts.
Liaison officer sends draft contract to client.
. . . .
. . . . the discussion with client may go on for some time
. . . . .
Liaison officer and client agree on contract
Liaison officer prepares contract for signature
Liaison officer meets with client to sign contract
Liaison officer informs marketing officer about signed contract

The scenarios provide the basis for next step, choosing technology support for the scenario. The next phase can use the scenarios to describe the technology that may be used at each step, again ensuring that stakeholders are involved in the design and are likely to accept and use any new facilities as early as possible.

8   Summary

This chapter described the important first steps of creating the business architecture. It defined a blueprint for the architecture composed of three parts – business activities, social structure and knowledge management. It then described a process that starts with defining the business activities and extended these with the social structure and knowledge structures. The chapter provided some guidelines for design. One was to ensure that each activity be made up of one kind of work and then choose the social network that matches that kind of work.

The chapter then described the kinds of choices made in designing a business architecture and illustrated by developing a business architecture for the GMS example. The business activities and roles that are part of the architecture are used to design workspace to support the roles and activities. The definition of the workspaces is covered in the next chapter.

One important design objective was to create business activities that only include one kind of work. This results in better alignment between knowledge worker and task. It also provides better flexibility as the activities can be easily rearranged into new business systems.

9   Continuation of case studies

1. Develop a business architecture for alternative 3 of Chapter 10.
2. Define a business architecture for case study VI.
3. Define a business architecture for case study IV.

Some further reading

Prahalad, C.K., Krishnan, M.S. (2008) *The New Age of Innovation* (McGraw-Hill).

Part IV
Supporting Technologies

Specifying Electronic Workspaces for the Business Architecture

12

Designing workspaces to support peoples' work practices

Learning objectives

- Specifying a workspace
- Workspace components
- Workspace actions
- Workspace governance
- Converting models to workspaces

1 Introduction

This chapter describes how to specify workspaces to support the newly designed business architecture which was specified in the previous chapters. Electronic workspace is used as a generic term here; it can be an interface in a Web-based or ERP application, a workflow interface, or an interface produced by any other software. Increasingly, it can be the interface of a mobile device. At the conclusion of this chapter readers will be able to specify workspaces needed to implement the business architecture. In the next chapter readers will be able to select technologies to implement the workspaces. Workspace design follows the traditional computer systems design in two design steps – logical design and physical design. The two steps also apply to workspace design. Here:

- Logical design specifies the structure of electronic workspaces. It addresses all the perspectives of process design including the information and knowledge in the business activity as well as supporting the links in the enterprise social structure for the application. This includes the various documents as well as services needed to improve work practices and productivity.

- Physical design determines the technology needed to create workspaces. Many factors influence the choice of technology to create workspaces. One is whether people work at a distance and whether they work in enterprises that follow different practices. Another is user abilities and their familiarity with technology. Another is the kind of work supported by the workspace.

This chapter describes logical design and defines the services to be provided to the different roles. The next chapter introduces physical design.

2 Networks of electronic workspaces

An organization supports a large number of workspaces. This workspace architecture reflects the structure of the business architecture in the enterprises. It supports the activities, social structure, process flows and knowledge requirements. All enterprises now have a number of workspaces for people to share artifacts and communicate. They are often linked to the enterprise database. As an example, some workspaces for the business system described in Figure 11.11 are shown in Figure 12.1. These include the following:

- The enterprise workspace, which is usually the enterprise home page, and is not shown in Figure 11.11 for the GMS system.
- Role support workspaces. Figure 12.1 shows some workspaces for the roles in Figure 11.11 including the client support workspaces, which provide customized support to individual clients. A separate workspace would be provided for each client. There is also a role workspace for the assistant and plan developer.
- Business activity workspaces, as for example marketing plan development, that allow team members to maintain awareness of the current plan status and documents. It includes a market analysis workspace that is provided for the external analyst.
- The role workspaces are linked to the business activity workspaces in which the roles participate.

Apart from the workspaces shown in Figure 12.1 other workspaces can include the following:

- Personal spaces for individuals where people can see what is happening in their environment and nominated sites. These are often on mobile devices and increasingly have links to their role or business activity workspaces.
- Community workspaces, which are usually communities of practice or people's organizational units.
- Workspaces that support communities of practice.

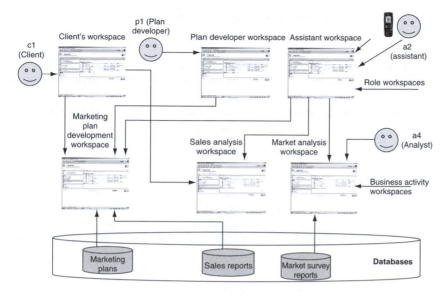

Figure 12.1   A workspace architecture for GMS

Readers should note that Figure 12.1 is a more detailed example of the business architecture outlined in Figure 10.1. Figure 10.1 outlined the general business architecture, whereas Figure 12.1 is an instantiation for a particular business application. It shows the workspaces specific to an application and derived from the BAD and ESN diagrams in the previous chapter. The design considers all the perspectives. For example:

- From a knowledge perspective, Figure 12.1 databases store explicit knowledge used in business activities. The workspaces focus more on sharing tacit knowledge in the business activity. Figure 12.1 does not show the collaborative databases but these are part of detailed workspace design, which is described in this chapter.
- From the social perspective each workspace includes all the roles identified for an activity but can also include people from outside the activity to provide expert knowledge.
- From a business activity perspective, the workspace includes roles to access the artifacts and services needed to carry out their responsibilities.

Detailed workspace design, which is described in this chapter, identifies the specific services for knowledge management and networking.

Typical workspaces in industry provide services that allow knowledge workers to easily interact, share and create knowledge. It includes artifacts and tools to support their work. The workspace specification defines interfaces that can be customized to particular roles and the services needed to maintain enterprise collaboration. Examples of workspaces typically found in practice include the following:

- Configuring and maintaining a customer order;
- Planning which requires capturing expertise and commitment from many people;
- Analyzing competitor strategies, the risks they pose and responses to them;
- Providing educational services especially those customized to individuals or small groups.

Communication of course takes place not only through workspaces but also through devices outside workspaces and in person-to-person meetings. Research indicates that the most common uses of technology in collaboration are in communication and document sharing. Hence complex negotiation processes and conflict resolution often occurs in face-to-face meetings, although preliminary documents can be exchanged prior to a meeting.

3 Specifying workspace requirements

Each of the workspaces in a workspace architecture like Figure 12.1 must be specified in more detail. Workspace is a general term that defines the place where people work and interact. An electronic workspace is an attempt to replicate electronically or complement a part of a physical workspace. Thus an electronic workspace should be more than just a place to retrieve and store information. It is a place where existing knowledge is shared and new knowledge is created to see what works, where people use their tacit knowledge or make comments, suggest ideas or in general contribute to the discussion. The workspace must be personalized to users or user groups. It must thus complement people's natural work connections and ways to collaborate with others. Conceptually the electronic workspace can be seen as part of an office, which provides a space to store information and to discuss ideas and suggestions with co-workers. It includes people, interactions between the people, papers, designs and the other kinds of objects commonly found in an office. Furthermore it should be possible for users to themselves change their workspace as the task evolves.

The business system architecture is the input to the process of workspace design although it is possible even at this stage to return to earlier steps and make further refinements to the design. Workspace specifications are made up of a number of parts shown below.

Structure of a workspace specification

- Major business components of the workspace;
- Commands provided to workspace participants to create and operate on the components, often provided as electronic buttons in the workspace;

- The collaborative services to support interactions between workspace participants;
- The services, often social software, to capture knowledge;
- Ways to define workspace governance through providing different permissions to workspace participants;
- Commands that provide ability for the workspace to evolve and for the evolution to be driven by users; and
- The technology platform that supports the workspaces.

3.1 Specifying workspace components

The main question is what to include in the electronic workspace and how to use it. The major components of a workspace are the components that make up the business activity. In most cases a workspace supports a role or an activity. This implies that the workspace will contain most of the information and contacts needed in the activity or by the role. The workspace provides easy access to this information and keeps it up to date. This is particularly the case where people may be in different places or highly mobile.

Major workspace components

- The documents and other objects used in the workspace. These correspond to the documents used in the business activity;
- The roles in the workspace that correspond to the roles in business activity;
- The people assigned to the roles and their responsibilities;
- The services to support interaction between the roles;
- The services to capture knowledge;
- Access to corporate databases;
- Links to related workspaces and roles.

It is important to remember that electronic workspaces not only include the necessary components but also present them in a work environment that is supportive of people's work practice. Workspaces must support privacy, sharing in a controlled manner, and allow the unstructured and often informal communication that is part of the normal work environment. Of course not all workspaces need to be group spaces. People also need some personal spaces that can be accessed through the Internet to support their community or personal contacts.

3.2 Workspace dynamics

The kinds of commands provided to workspace users are also important. There are two kinds of commands. One is to set up and change the workspace; the

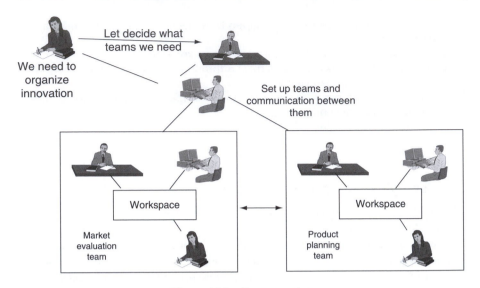

Figure 12.2   Team creation

other is workspace governance that is used to give participants permissions to take actions within the workspace. Workspace commands can be used to change workspaces so the workspace evolves as the nature of interaction changes. Thus often we hear things like "Bring Jim and Jill together to work on the marketing problem". This means creating teams that focus on a task and supporting these teams with appropriate tools. The goal of workspaces is to bring such teams together across distance so that they can work together from any place at any time. Hence it must command to add new roles and people to the workspace. Figure 12.2 illustrates a typical first step for team formation. This, for example, may be to set up teams for market evaluation and production planning.

Just as is the case in a workplace, people in each team may then build up their work environment. The steps followed to define a team workspace are as follows:

1. Create the team workspace;
2. Invite team members to the space if needed;
3. Bring in any information into the workspace;
4. Set up services for interaction;
5. Assign team members to the services to support collaborative interaction;
6. Provide team members with access to the documents.

A good workspace will thus evolve as an activity proceeds. It should be possible for users to invite new users into the workspace, create new artifacts and provide communication facilities as the need arises. It is important that such changes should be made by system users, rather than by information technology experts. The support here should include semantics like:

'I will set up a workspace for my team and invite team members into the workspace'

'I will go to the enterprise workspace and bring some information into my space'

The activity can go further and often requires the team members themselves to dynamically create a process. It may even go further where teams have meetings to address issues and want to keep track of these meetings over time.

3.3 Managing workspaces

From a knowledge and social perspective it is desirable for users themselves to create their workspaces – a process known as mashing up workspaces. Mashups means that workspaces evolve by continuous change through the addition or deletion of components to the workspace. There are a number of levels of mashing up, namely:

- Presentation level, that simply presents services in a unified interface;
- Data mashups that present information in a unified view; and
- Process mashups that allow users to construct processes as an activity proceeds. This is perhaps the most complex level as it must include negotiation between process participants on actions to be taken.

The ease of use is also an important consideration as the goal is for users themselves to change the workspace as their work evolves. To do this requires technologies that provide users with the command needed to change workspaces.

3.4 Workspace governance

Workspace governance commands are used to assign responsibilities to roles. Initially the owner is the only person who can give permissions. Once a role creates an object it can then assign permissions to this object to other roles. Permissions are needed for two reasons. One is to preserve confidentiality where some people in a workspace are restricted to what they can see. The other is to assign responsibility for particular objects, in which case only some people have the ability to change these objects.

Figure 12.3 shows the permissions granted to roles to apply actions to artifacts. This defines the responsibilities of different roles, especially their abilities to change or create documents. For example, a partner can update a plan but the client can only read a plan.

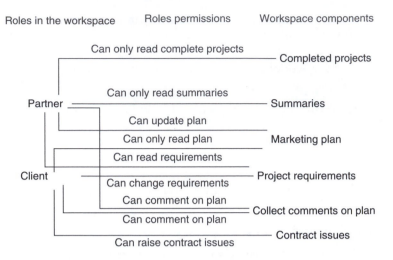

Figure 12.3   Showing permissions

Often designers needed to choose technologies to support the workspace. Often the commands provided by the technology provide a good basis for the comparison. A summary of commands is given in the following table.

Summary of workspace commands

- Commands for constructing or mashing up the workspace;
- Commands to give permissions to people or roles to change the workspace;
- Commands to install communication services in the workspace;
- Commands to follow links to other workspaces;
- Commands to give permissions to roles;
- The tools provided by the workspace.

Commands for constructing workspaces

- Create <object type: object-name>; object can be artifact, role, or the other concepts of the semantic model supported by the workspace.
- Create <social-service : service-name>; social-service can be forum, blog, wiki or other social software.
- Provide <tool : tool-name>; tool can be word-processor, CAD or other tools used in everyday work.
- Delete <object> from workspace.
- Invite <participant>.
- Assign <participant> to <role>.

Governance commands for assigning responsibilities

- Allow <role> to execute <command> – the commands can be <invite participants, create objects of a particular type>.
- Allow <role> to <access> <artifact> – the different kinds of access include <read only, update, delete, and assign access to other roles>.

These commands are listed here as statements but normally they would be affected through selection options provided by technical workspace interface.

4 Using business architecture models to specify electronic workspaces

There is a structured way to use business architecture models to specify workspaces. The most common conversion is to create a workspace for an activity. The conversion guidelines are given below.

Conversion guidelines

- The business activity becomes a workspace;
- Roles in BAM or ESN become roles in the workspace;
- Databases become artifacts in the workspace;
- Interaction in the ESN identify the communication services, as well as any social software to capture knowledge;
- Role responsibilities identify the tools needed by the roles.

An example is given in Figure 12.4. It shows the BAM and ESN for the enterprise. The business activity is converted to the workspace. The database 'Marketing plan' becomes a document in the workspace. The ESN is used to identify the roles and communication services in the workspace. It also identifies the workspace participants.

Figure 12.4 shows how the business activity model and the ESN provide the guidelines for constructing workspaces. You should also note that the specifications focus simply on the content of the workspace and not the layout and other presentation objects associated with workspaces. There are numerous books in the area of interface or interaction design that cover detailed layout designs.

4.1 Example – GMS – Marketing organization

Figures 11.11 and 11.13 together with Table 11.2 defined the business architecture in the marketing organization and suggested the articulated knowledge

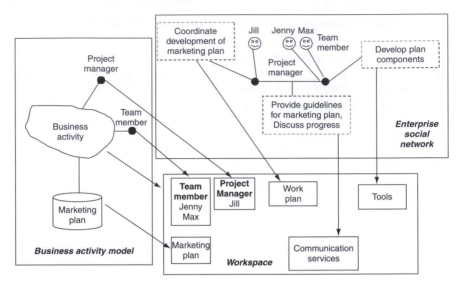

Figure 12.4   Principles of implementation

to be captured. It is possible to define a workspace for each activity or for particular roles. Figure 12.5 illustrates two such workspaces, one for 'marketing plan
development' and another for 'information collection'.

It shows the structure of the workspaces. The other part of the specification
are the commands to be made available to each role, with governance determining including commands provided to different roles. Thus, for example, the
client in the 'marketing plan development' workspace would not gain access to
'completed projects' but have the permissions to comment on 'contact issues'
and enter comments in 'client comments on plan'. The permissions given to
roles is generally determined by role responsibilities. Workspaces place greater
emphasis on the social perspective with the ability to create new relationships and
bring new people into the workspace when needed. For example, the partner will

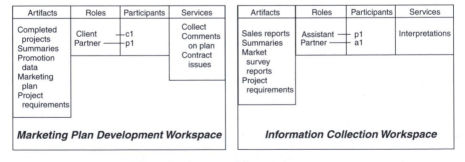

Figure 12.5   Initial workspace specifications

probably have the ability to create new roles and invite people into these roles. An expert might be invited to comment on the plan with a discussion board created to collect these comments with the partner, the only person able to interact with the expert.

Services at this stage are defined in logical terms, with specific implementations described in the next chapter.

4.2 Creating the workspace

Once a workspace is designed it can be created.

A scenario for creating a new market plan workspace

Plan developer creates a new workspace.
Plan developer invites an assistant into the workspace.
Plan developer creates a new marketing plan document.
Plan developer provides a link to the contracts.
Plan developer creates blogs for collecting client comments.
Plan developer authorizes assistant to enter documents into the workspace.
The assistant enters links to the sales and marketing databases and authorizes participants to only read these databases.
Plan developer authorizes client to read the market development plan and make comments on the blog.

It is possible to look at the scenario and select a specific service for each action. For example, recording a story may use a blog, whereas client details are obtained through discussion or through a portal.

5 Summary

The chapter described ways to specify workspaces to support the business architecture business developed in Chapter 11. It used conversion rules that used business activity models and ESNs to define the components of the workspace.

A separate workspace was proposed for each activity or role. The chapter then also described the kinds of commands that are needed to create and manage workspaces. These included both ways to bring components into the workspace and the governance structures needed to control access to these components. The next chapter will describe ways to implement these workspaces using information technology.

6   Questions and Exercises

Question 1

The business model and ESN are shown in Figure 12.6. Provide workspace specifications (using the notation in Figure 12.5) for the role of 'our manager' and for the 'system development' business activity.

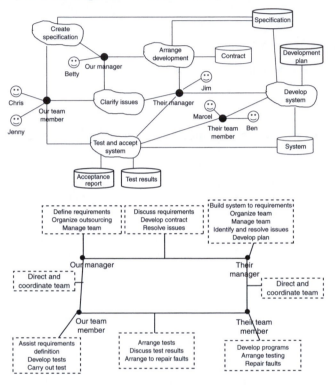

Figure 12.6   A model for Question 1

Question 2

Convert the model in Figure 12.7 to a workspace specification.

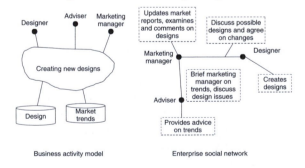

Figure 12.7   Model for Conversion

Question 3

Sometimes it is necessary to create special workspaces for particular purposes. A model for the apparel industry is shown Figures 12.8 and 12.9. The ESN identifies three special requirements:

1. Maintain contact with retailers about trends including salesperson, retailer, manager and designer;
2. Keeping track of design issues for new designs;
3. Maintain liaison with contractors about their availability, including interactions between contractors and the manager.

Specify workspaces for the three special requirements.

Business Activity Model

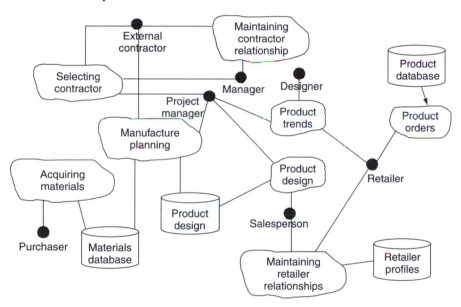

Figure 12.8 Activity model for question 3

Enterprise social network – showing the roles involved for the three special requirements.

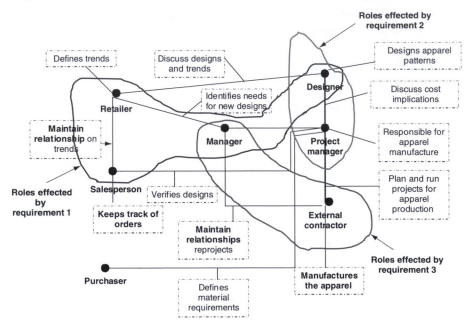

Figure 12.9   Enterprise social network for the apparel industry

Some further readings

Andriessen, J.H.E. (2003) *Designing with Groupware* (Springer-Verlag, London).

Saffer, D. (2006) *Designing for Interaction: Creating Smart Applications and Clever Devices* (New Riders, Berkeley, California).

Technologies for Business Processes

13

Learning objectives

- Choosing the workspace architecture
- Current technologies
- Paths to evolution to dynamic systems

- Extending ERP capabilities
- Lightweight technologies
- Combining lightweight and ERP
- Selecting technologies

1 Introduction

This chapter follows on from Chapter 12 by describing the technology options to support the workspaces specified in the previous chapter. Technology often places limits on support for workspaces and the perspectives it presents to users. One limitation is the cost of actually building the workspaces. The other limitation is on the ability of users to change the workspace structure at reasonable cost. Usually the greater the flexibility, the greater the cost. However, technologies that overcome these limitations are becoming more common giving designers increasing choice of technology to use in their implementation. Managers can now choose between a number of different technologies to find a balance between cost and change. These kinds are the following:

- Traditional mainframe technologies. Here workspaces have to be developed by information technology professionals and are usually closely linked to corporate databases and ERP systems. Workspaces that use these technologies are costly to change.

- Middleware used to construct workspaces where workspaces can be specially constructed and changed by information technology professionals. These provide some support for change while providing more flexible links to corporate databases. In most cases they need to be developed by information technology professionals.
- Lightweight technologies that provide good abilities for adaption with limited connections to corporate databases. This is usually through what is commonly becoming known as mashing up a workspace. Most of these possess interfaces based on generic terms that can confuse all but the technologically savvy user. Mobile technologies are playing an increasing role in providing lightweight interfaces.

Because of these differences in the capabilities of technology, business architectures like that shown in Figures 10.1 and 12.1 require different technologies to implement its various parts. Many of these workspaces can be implemented using different technologies. The kind of technology often depends on the kind of work supported by the workspace. This chapter will identify the kinds of choices available to designers for the different kinds of requirement. They should allow knowledge workers to continually change their workspace as their work practices.

2 Defining Technology Requirements

Workspace requirements reflect business needs and a business must make decisions as to what workspaces to support, and the technology to implement them. There are often many strategic options for choosing technologies to implement workspaces with options defined by business priorities and technology availability. Primarily the choice of technology depends on the kind of business activity represented by a workspace. Thus a transactive workspace to update databases will require a different technology when compared to a collaborative workspace to evaluate an idea. Transactive interfaces usually take a business activity perspective, where collaborative interfaces take a social perspective.

Figure 13.1 illustrates various criteria that can be used in making the choice. The two dimensions in Figure 13.1 are the following:

- Segmentation of content – or the selection what to include in the workspace and to customize the workspace to roles or individuals supported by the workspace; and
- Customization – the degree to which users themselves can compose, change and organize the layout of their workspaces.

Primarily the choice is one of how to select the content and whether to specialize by function or by individual. The vertical dimension in Figure 13.1 is

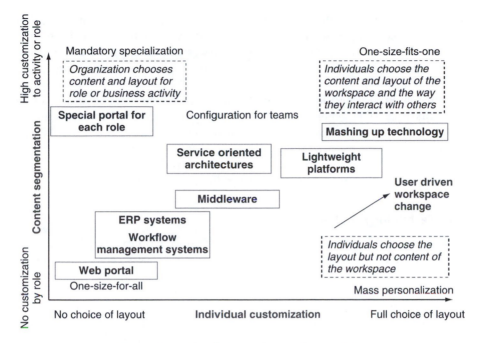

Figure 13.1 Identifying workspace characteristics

specialization by function and the horizontal is customization by individual. The options here are the following:

- At the bottom left-hand corner is the 'one size fits all' – everyone has the same workspace, which is often the organization's portal. These are provided by mainframe technologies usually through Web portals. They include the databases that are part of any system and mostly focus on business activities.
- As one proceeds up vertically the workspace is specialized to roles. Thus, for example, there may be a different interface for a customer and another one for the marketing department although they all share the same database. Again often business systems based on traditional technologies are used to provide such workspaces for specific roles. One common example is workspaces that allow clients to make on-line purchases. These are developed by IT profession-als and mostly use Web portals combined with ERP technologies. Middleware is now increasingly used to provide greater flexibility.
- At the top right-hand corner is the one-size-fits-one, a special interface for each person. Here the user or group of users can choose what is to be included in the workspace. Technology is provided for the user to create and change workspaces themselves. There is a growth of technologies that allow users to 'mash-up' workspaces for their individual use. The workspaces usually sup-port collaborative activities and integrate the knowledge, social and business perspectives.

- At the bottom right-hand corner there is the mass personalization option which allows people to customize the presentation of the provided information. Here technologies that allow workspaces to rearrange the components specified for the workspace but not change the workspace components.

Another important consideration in Figure 13.1 is who creates and changes the workspace. The general trend is that anything developed on the left side of the graph is carried out by information technology professionals. As one moves towards the right of the graph, then user involvement increases. These options are not mutually exclusive and a variety of workspaces can often be made available within the enterprise, often using different technologies.

2.1 Technology trade-offs

Designers have to choose technologies to support workspaces. The requirements of an entire business or even one business process cannot be met by one technology alone. Transaction-based activities require greater emphasis on the business activities and are most often implemented using ERP systems. Requirements for knowledge workers cannot be met by ERP systems alone and require more emphasis on the knowledge and social perspectives. These are met by technologies on the top right-hand corner of Figure 13.1. They need more control over the work process than that provided by a workflow management system. Most business systems require support for different kinds of activities and hence need different kinds of workspaces. Technological developments were to initially provide different technologies for the different workspace requirements. There are now trends to create technologies that integrate the different requirements. There are two options to provide adaptable workspaces, namely:

- Middleware – this provides a solution where workspaces can be customized to roles with links to corporate databases. They can be used to develop special interfaces for roles or activities. However, middleware change is more difficult than change using lightweight technologies, and the expectation is that change would not happen frequently. In most cases it would require information technology specialists to construct an interface for each individual and change it as needed.
- Lightweight technologies – these provide better abilities for change but in many cases cannot easily connect to corporate-wide databases or other lightweight systems. They can be used to develop the one-fits-one option or for mass personalization, which is ideal for knowledge workers. Many allow users themselves to create and manage their workspace.

A solution is needed to combine the two approaches – traditional and agile. Vinekar et al. (2006) see this as impractical more from the standpoint of managing information technology given the different cultural and technical dimensions of the two. Usually major software for traditional systems and middleware is chosen by information technology departments, who do not have resources to develop personalized interfaces, whereas technology is not yet at the stage where it can easily be adapted by its users to their work practices.

3   The ERP component

Any system has a number of databases that store earlier transactions, various policy documents and general information about its environment. Returning to Figure 12.1, the GMS system included databases on market survey reports, earlier plans and sales surveys. These represent explicit knowledge about the organization, which must be made available to any knowledge workers. In this case the ERP approach is implemented either by organizations writing their own software or using that provided by a software vendor. In either case the ERP approach is generally characterized by:

> Document management sharing between applications, and Workflow management systems for managing predefined processes.

3.1   Document management systems

The most common function that is widely adopted in collaboration is that of document sharing. Knowledge workers use document systems to access current information relevant to their project. Designs and plans created by project teams are now commonly available on Internet sites to all team members. These may be specially developed websites or project management packages. Many organizational Intranets now provide the ability to share documents within groups using software such as Sharepoint. These documents can be placed on Intranet sites and downloaded when necessary. The most important business advantage of document management is as a central repository of information. One example here is the use of document management systems in the building industry. Here there are many plans, contracts and other documents that must be constantly available to site workers. Furthermore, it is important that people always have access to the latest copies of such documents.

Many commercial document management systems go beyond simple storage of documents and can include access controls and versions of documents. Anyone with access to the document site can only access those documents they are authorized to access. Most such document repositories store codified knowledge but do not capture articulated knowledge.

The workspaces here are usually of the one-size-fits-all variety. They provide commands to access the databases, and allow some of the roles to update the databases.

3.2   Workflow management systems

The idea of workflows was defined earlier. They define the steps followed by a business process. Workflow management systems (WFMS) were developed initially to support predefined workflows. Their main advantage is that they ensure that once a transaction starts it is traced right to the end. Apart from completing the transaction, good workflow management systems ensure that it is possible to see the status of any initiated transaction at any time. Typical workflow systems were described in Chapter 7. The most common kinds of workflow are transaction systems in particular financial, payroll or inventory transactions. Portals that support purchases on the Internet are another example. These provide workspaces customized to the role and focus mainly on the business activity perspective.

3.3   Setting up a process workflow

The major activities in setting up a workflow are the following:

- Design the workflows. Here the roles, artifacts and processes needed in each step are defined.
- Implement it on a WFMS.
- Executing the defined workflow, by passing messages from one step to the next.

Workflows are set up using software known as WFMS. A WFMS must have a number of components. Typical components are defined by the Workflow Management coalition and shown in Figure 13.2. These include the following:

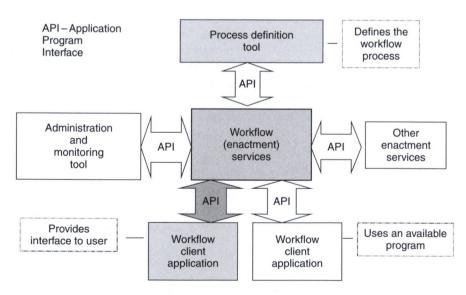

Figure 13.2   Technical components of a WFMS

- A process definition module;
- A workflow processor uses the definition to direct messages to client application interfaces;
- Client application interfaces that are the workspace provided to users.

3.4   Setting up ERP systems

ERP vendors provide methods for both modeling and implementing applications. The setting up of ERP systems is a topic in its own right and out of the scope of this text. It requires an analysis of the data structures of databases, and model of process steps. These then go through a design process, often requiring the selection of a vendor and software, detailed design of system modules, and their implementation by information technology professionals.

3.5   Extending ERP

ERP implementations in most cases focus on the predefined aspects of a business system. Many ERP systems are extending their capabilities to move into the knowledge management and social networking space. There is an increasing growth of technologies provided by ERP systems vendors through what are here called middleware technologies for knowledge support.

4   Middleware technologies for knowledge support

Middleware provides a link between ERP systems and knowledge-based systems. It provides the flexibility needed to customize workspaces to collaborative needs and as such extend the capability to place greater emphasis on the social and knowledge perspectives. Middleware provides support for creating workspaces for knowledge work with links to ERP systems. There is a range of middleware technologies. Middleware is computer software that can be used to create workspaces that connect to ERP applications and communication systems. Figure 13.3 shows where middleware can be used to create workspaces. Figure 13.3 shows the following:

- The IT infrastructure that includes the network, access to the WWW and various communications services.
- ERP systems and databases, which are provided by ERP vendors. These are used to develop ERP applications.
- Middleware for knowledge support. This software generates workspaces that can include access to a number of ERP databases. Often these are through using the SQL language.

Many vendors are now focusing on the middleware layer, as for example IBM's Websphere (Ding, 2008) or SAP Netweaver. That can be used to create specialized workspaces. These must be developed by information technology

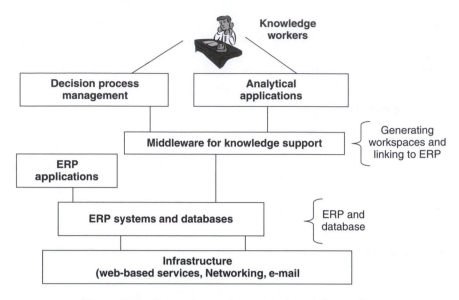

Figure 13.3   Generating workspaces for knowledge workers

professionals with expertise in the use of the middleware and not by general users. It is possible here to develop special portals for selected roles, or portals for activities. Such portals can be developed by information technology professionals, who are also required to carry out any changes to the portals. They are somewhere in the middle in Figure 13.1 where they segment often a large content and allow minimal customization.

5   Trends to fully customizable technologies

There is an increasing emphasis on providing software that allows both full choice of content and layout and lets users themselves create workspace that include support for business activities, support knowledge creation and the formation of evolving social relationships. This software is primarily based in the WWW and is increasingly known as Web 2.0 technology.

5.1   Web 2.0

Web 2.0 is being proposed as primarily to improve connectivity and support the social perspective. It uses the Internet as the infrastructure and is now being seen as the wave of the future. Its goal is to create an infrastructure that incorporates the kind of social software described in Chapter 6 and thus supports the kinds of characteristics proposed for Enterprise 2.0. Its goal is to provide the software to interact using the Internet and to capture articulated knowledge. In a Web 2.0 environment the social software described in Chapter 6 becomes part of the standard Internet interface and can be shared between applications. It is almost ubiquitous and can be used without resorting to special setting up as currently required.

The interface will provide commands to easily compose or mash up workspaces using social software. It is expected that everyday users will be able to set up such workspaces thus focusing more on the top right-hand corner of Figure 13.1.

5.2 Service oriented architectures

Another trend is towards service oriented architectures (SOA) (Krafzig et al., 2004). Here the idea is as shown in Figure 13.4. A repository of services is provided in a repository. These may be tools such as budgeting tools, or collaborative services that support the kind of ESNs described in previous chapters. The repository may be a public repository with the tools provided by different vendors. Designers can select any of these components and place them in their workspace, or create a lightweight platform. The challenges here are to develop standards where services from different vendors can exchange information between themselves to provide an integrated platform.

The idea of SOA is closely related to the idea of Web 2.0 where the repository is the social software provided through the Web and selection and composition is provided through the Internet with support for mashing up workspaces. SOA goes further and provides business services. The idea of SOA is also in its infancy and it is tied to simplifying the development of business application like those described in Chapters 7 and 8 applications by reducing the cost of development. Various languages such as BPEL or WSDL are being developed to simplify application development and many vendors. Perhaps one dichotomy here is that Web 2.0 be used to mash up knowledge workspaces by their users, whereas SOA focus more on the development of corporate systems to simplify the work of information technology specialists.

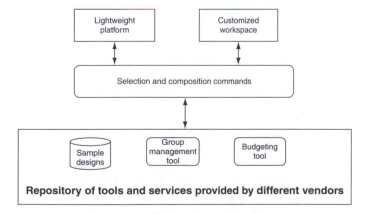

Figure 13.4   A platform of services

Typical business services suitable for knowledge workers through SOA should include the following:

Some team services

Workflow instance – To arrange work actions associated with an activity. Here a workflow is defined in terms of events, which are assigned to roles. A completion event initiated by one role can result in an initiation event for some other role. The process can change dynamically by adding new events dynamically.

Group management – managing a group of people, which may be an organizational unit or people with common interests, usually requires support for sharing information, managing group changes and maintaining group memory in general.

Team formation – requires support for keeping track of activities and responsibilities of individual team members. Important aspects are new members joining teams, resolution of issues and distributing work between team members, including negotiation for assigning and carrying out tasks.

In many cases information technology specialists are needed to develop applications using SOA technologies.

6 Lightweight platforms for constructing workspaces

Lightweight workspaces are those that primarily allow users to select services and include them in a workspace as they are needed. Ease of use is one of the driving factors and the ability to change the interface itself is an important factor. They have three major characteristics. They are the following:

- Low cost to create and set up the workspace;
- Flexibility to easily change the workspace by their users; and
- Web-based implementation to easily support distributed teams from any location.

The most common technology that provides lightweight capabilities is workspace management systems. Lightweight technologies provide capabilities at different levels of sophistication. A broad classification of levels used in this chapter is as follows:

Lightweight exchange, which corresponds to office work, and can easily support facilitation or expert work with small groups.
Lightweight exchange with minimal lightweight collaboration, where documents are exchanged and commented on and can be jointly developed.

This is generally suited for transactive activities within larger projects, which require some coordination between group members.

Lightweight collaboration with minimal lightweight workflow, where work on larger projects and tasks are assigned to roles and tracked for progress.

The classification is made primarily by the kinds of services provided for constructing platforms. The classification is also one that continually increases the level of services available to users.

Mobile devices are also playing an increasingly important role here. Many mobile devices now have the ability to access the WWW and provide their users with access workspaces on computer systems and participate in the business activities from a distance.

6.1 Lightweight exchange

A lightweight exchange platform supports the kind of communication generally found in offices. This platform provides a variety of services to support communication between users. It also integrates the services into a single workspace. Such a platform raises social awareness of what people in a community are doing. The discourses found here are those generally found in normal office work. The kinds of services needed in lightweight exchange are given in the Table 13.1.

Table 13.1   Services for lightweight exchange

User communication	Description	Services provided
Conversational task threading	Intermittent communication tasks with different individuals. System must keep track of the interactions. Both synchronous and asynchronous.	Instant messaging
One way drop	Leave brief message asynchronously	Voicemail e-mail Pager
Quick connection	Quickly contact others in the system	Phone Common media space Video conference
Context preservation and generation	Long delays between interactions requiring access to prior interactions as well as artifacts to maintain continuity.	Shared portal Document sharing WIKIs
Real-time shared objects	Require conversational resources supporting documents that are used to mediate conversation	Shared portal Video conference Blogs

Real-time shared objects are often specialized to some special activity – for example, architectural design. The kind of support often needed includes annotations and structured critique. Most mobile phones now include the kinds of communication services shown in Table 13.1.

However, there are still some issues that are lacking in most systems, such as change meetings in coffee rooms, or seeing who is working on the same thing at the same time (translucency). These are sometimes called non-deliberate sharing methods and it is not quite known how to implement them using computer technologies.

6.2   Lightweight collaboration

Lightweight collaboration requires many additional services. In particular it should use collaborative databases to maintain the quality and effectiveness of collaboration. Lightweight collaboration requires people in communities to make arrangements of who does what. The required services are given in Table 13.2.

Discourses supported here are at a higher level than those found in lightweight exchange. Collaboration here requires a collaborative database. The main

Table 13.2   Additional services for lightweight collaboration

User communication	Description	Services provided
Assignment to tasks	Assign people to tasks	Issues board to select people Calendar to note milestones Program board to record tasks
Agree on completion of task	The person completing a task sends a message indicating completion	Usually a e-mail notification
Create new task	A decision is made on what to do next; the decision can: • Be automatic as defined by some rule, or • Require negotiation Allocate responsibilities for next step	Enter task on program board e-Portfolio to keep track of outcomes
Issue management	Raise and resolve issues	Blogs, discussion boards
Coordinate progress	Identify causes of delays	Video conference Meeting system e-portfolio
Maintain common information	A place where all information is kept	Shared workspace
Task reporting	Task reporting	Program board e-Portfolio
People tracking	Keep track of people activities	Calendar to record activity

difference now is that records of the collaboration are kept – that is to maintain a collaborative database. An example is the following scenario.

A typical scenario for lightweight collaboration

Person X divides a document into parts and stores each part in a document folder.
Different people agree to work on parts of a document.
Person A changes part A.
Person B changes part B.
Person A queries the change made by person B using a discussion board.

6.3 Lightweight workflow

Lightweight workflow (Anderson et al., 2003) includes additional services especially a way to develop and maintain a plan. It requires community members to monitor the progress of processes. They agree on the process steps and follow them. The services needed are given in Table 13.3:

Table 13.3 Additional services for lightweight workflow

Communication service	Description	Service provided
Agree on process	Jointly define process steps	Usually a discussion with a plan entered into project management tool.
Set milestones	Set completion times for tasks	Enter into project plan
Notify task completion	The person completing a task sends a message indicating completion	Usually e-mail to inform about the completion of a task. May be project plan feature.
Decide on next task	Decide what to do next including change of process	
Review progress	Decide if changes are needed	Project plan

The collaborative database must now be extended with events and coordination rules, which can be dynamically changed.

A typical scenario for lightweight workflow

Project workers agree on a process
A program board is set up
The process workers set milestones for each task

A worker signals completion of a task
The group decide on next task and place on program board
Manager tracks progress through a program board
Team review progress using video conferencing
Team decides on process changes using video conferencing.

6.4   Technologies for lightweight workspaces

Software to support lightweight workspaces has been evolving for many years. The range of software includes the following:

- Free services provided on the Web mainly to support lightweight exchange. One example here is Google docs. Users can register on Google and use Google docs to create a lightweight exchange workspace. They can then add any business objects into this space. This workspace obviously does not provide easy access to corporate databases.
- Groupware such as LOTUS Notes, eRooms, Groove, BCSW among many groupware systems. These systems can be set up by users and provide different levels of lightweight support. LOTUS Notes has been on the market place for some time and has the properties of middleware as well as some lightweight characteristics. It can be used to support workflows with links to corporate databases and also provides the ability to customize workspaces. Groupware allows users to change workspaces as their work evolves. Each provides a selection of components and commands to create workspaces made up of these components. In general, the goal of any groupware system is to reduce the cost of customization needed to support specialized needs of business activities. This includes the ability to quickly compose a workspace, invite people into it and define the governance structures that define people's responsibilities. Such software uses generalized semantics that often confuse non-technical users and hence discouragetheir use.
- Groupware for selected industries in terms familiar to that industry. There are also special workspaces designed to support knowledge workers. There are also many specialized workspace systems on the market. There are, for example, systems to support a particular industry. These often come under the banner of business intelligence and allow knowledge workers to mash up workspaces composed of business objects used in analyzing a situation. Microsoft, for example, proposed that sharepoint can be used for this purpose. Word documents, spreadsheets, calendars and other business objects can be brought together here to support some business analytics activity. It is also possible to create a workspace and using permissions create special portals for roles. Other examples of special purpose groupware include business collaborator (www.businesscollaborator.com) and unionsquare (www.union2.co.uk), which provides interfaces in the construction industry.

7 Choosing technologies to support business activities

Chapter 12 developed specifications for workspaces. The next step is to choose the technologies to support the workspaces. This is not a deterministic process and is often influenced by the systems already available in an organization. The first consideration usually is the strategy to be used. Figure 13.1 provides a framework for identifying the technology given the broad capabilities required of the workspace. One way to start is to ask questions such as:

- How to segment and specialize workspaces to individual business activities or roles?
- What technologies to use to create workspaces that can be adapted to changing needs
- How specialized are the workspaces?
- Are links to corporate databases needed?

Where there is need to access databases middleware technologies will be preferred. Otherwise a lightweight platform will probably be chosen. Some further guidelines are the following:

Some guidelines for selecting technologies

- Increasing group size usually calls for more structured support leading to more emphasis on process perspective with some middleware support for specialized roles.
- Collaborative activities in general require lightweight technologies.
- Integrative processes most often require middleware support with access to databases.
- Task execution with repetitive actions and a small group is often supported by ERP systems.
- Coordination, small group can usually be met with lightweight exchange.
- Coordination, integrative work, large group requires ERP with middleware.
- Coordination, integrative work, small group often supported with lightweight coordination preferably with links to databases.

There are:

- The databases that represent stored explicit knowledge;
- The workspaces to support the social networking within the enterprise; and
- The collaborative databases that capture the knowledge created during the interactions and make it available across the enterprise.

Thus lightweight exchange primarily support the kind of discourse found in offices. As collaboration gets to higher levels the discourse tends to focus more on process aspects and the negotiation often needed to resolve process issues. Furthermore it should be noted that higher level of technology do not replace lower levels but simply add additional services to raise the level of collaboration.

7.1   Example – Marketing organization example

Again as in all design it pays to consider alternatives and to remember that good support requires a mix of technologies. This is also the case in GMS as here there are databases that hold explicit knowledge such as sales reports as well as considerable interaction that can provide useful articulated knowledge.

A possible set of alternatives is given in Table 13.4 using Figures 11.10 and 11.11 as guidelines for describing the different activities. The table also uses

Table 13.4   Possible technology options for GSM

Business activity	Selected technology strategy	Workspace operation
'Developing contacts' is a collaborative activity	Lightweight exchange including blogs to collect information about clients or stories of client experiences.	Contacts here are informal with potential with salesperson making blog entries. Partners can refer to the blogs.
'Client liaison and sales' is an integrative activity in managing contract development.	Lightweight collaboration platform with special role for client. Usually has a discussion board to keep track of issues.	Either client or partner raises issues. User permissions are used to prevent client access to past projects.
'Marketing plan development' – generally a collaborative activity.	A combination of ERP and lightweight collaboration with special interface for client and access to databases.	The marketing plan is developed in conjunction with the client. Requires sharing of knowledge and joint development of a plan.
'Information Collection' – an integrative activity with some collaborative components	The group is small. Lightweight collaboration is often sufficient to keep track of work carried out by the assistant.	Setting deadlines with information changing as documents as a plan evolves. Assistant undertaking tasks to collect information.
'Sales analysis'	A transactive activity that can be supported by ERP systems with perhaps customized role interfaces for the roles.	Here the assistant needs to communicate to get further clarifications.
'Arrange contract' is an integrative activity	An integrative activity with transactive components. Often supported by ERP systems.	Arranging collection of market surveys with delivery deadlines defined. Surveys uploaded to the 'sales reports' database.
'Market analysis' is a transactive activity as it is carried out externally.	Supported by ERP systems or simply through lightweight collaboration such as using e-mail to exchange reports.	Often requires exchange of standard contacts for analysis. Results received by e-mail.

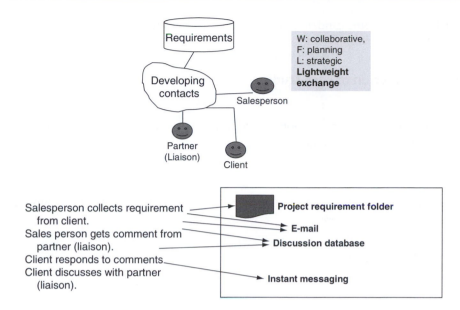

Figure 13.5   Detailed specification of services

the ESN in Figure 11.13 to provide guidelines for selecting social software to capture articulated knowledge.

The choice of alternative is determined by costs and technologies accessible to the designers.

7.2   A more detailed specification of the services required for work processes

In some cases detailed analysis can be carried out on some workspaces. One approach is to look at each activity in turn together with its scenarios and identify the services that are needed at each step of the scenario. Figure 13.5 expands one of the activities in more detail. It illustrates the scenario for the 'Developing new clients' and the services required by the actions in the scenario.

8   Summary

The chapter outlined the choices available to designers to implement workspaces. It provided a framework for choosing technologies based on the degree of segmentation and customization needed for each workspace. It then described the kind of technologies to implement workspaces and the kinds of workspaces that are supported by different technologies. It described the need to integrate ERP systems with knowledge work and outlined ways to do so. The main choice is to use middleware that allow users access to ERP systems but does not provide the ability for user-driven change. The other is to use lightweight technologies, such a workspace management systems. These often cannot be easily linked to

ERP systems. Some guidelines for choosing technologies were also provided in the chapter.

9   Continuation of case studies

Exercise 1

Choose technologies to support the collection of market data shown initially in Figure 2.2 and then in Figure 6.10.

Exercise 2

Continue the case studies from Chapter 11 to propose technologies to support the business architectures.

Some further readings

Anderson, K.M., Anderson, A., Wadhwani, W., Bartolo, L. (2003) 'Metis: A lightweight, Flexible, and Web-based Workflow Services for Digital Libraries' *Proceedings 3rd. ACM/IEEE Conference on Digital Libraries*, May, pp. 98–109.

Berchet, C., Habchi, G. (2005) 'The Implementation and Deployment of an ERP system: An Industrial Case Study' *Computers in Industry*, Vol. 56, pp. 588–605.

Ding, Y. (2008) *Websphere Engineering* (IBM Press, 2008).

Krafzig, D., Banke, K., Slama, D. (2004) *Enterprise SOA: Service Oriented Architecture Best Practices* (Coad Series, Prentice-Hall).

Meso, P., Jan, R. (2006) 'Agile Software Development: Adaptive System Principles and Best Practices' Vol. 23, No.3, *Information Systems Management Journal*, Summer, pp. 19–30.

Connecting
Enterprises

14

Organizing for industry-wide collaboration

Learning objectives

- Extending to the enterprise web
- Typical industry wide networks
- Importance of a cross organizational perspective
- Forming strategic alliances
- Creating collaborating arrangements

1 Introduction

This chapter extends some of the methods described in the previous chapters to cover enterprise-wide collaboration to combine the expertise in a number of organizations in running their business. It extends the description of business networking in Chapter 8, which made a distinction between process collaboration and enterprise-wide collaboration. Chapter 8 focused on process collaboration. This chapter focuses on enterprise-wide collaboration to bring together what are called organizational silos to create new business opportunities. These include bringing together business units within global enterprises that work on their own with minimal interaction with other units. It also includes networking across businesses to provide value by sharing their knowledge and resources.

This chapter describes trends to support enterprise-wide collaboration using the perspectives described in the previous chapters. Organizational and social perspectives play a major initial role in enterprise-wide collaboration to identify the organizational structures to create the benefits of collaboration and the social relationships needed to realize them. Strategic planning is also more prominent.

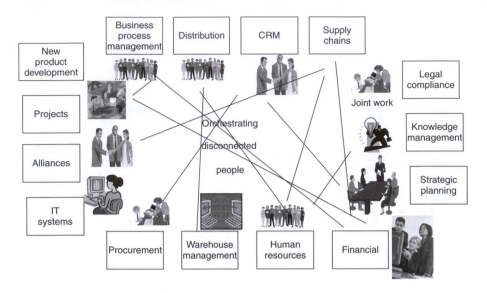

Figure 14.1   Emerging connections

2   Typical industry wide networks

Business networking on a large scale has the potential to realize the goal of Enterprise 2.0. It can facilitate innovation, as new and innovative products can be developed quickly by combining the expertise of a number of businesses. Furthermore change can be accomplished by forming new liaisons with a new business partner or changing existing business partners. This again is seen as increasing organizational agility. The ultimate objective is to quickly create a seamless network that includes the components needed to respond to a particular situation. It is to create the collaborative infrastructures like Figure 14.1 that orchestrate independent silos to work together. Here operating units are increasingly interconnected into enterprise-wide processes to create value in collaborating with other units in the same or different enterprise. Typical networks can be composed of a variety of organizations, including Universities, Government, Small to Medium Enterprises (SMEs) and bigger companies. Examples include the following:

- Health systems (Tan et al., 2006), where processes may involve different enterprises, such as insurance companies, or hospitals. Here information about patient health has to be collected and distributed to practitioners involved with their health care. Tests must be scheduled and assessed and provided to the practitioners in a timely and secure manner. At the same time, hospitals must plan for sufficient beds to cater for patients and the equipment needed for different kinds of treatment.

- Industry parks now increasingly supported by technology to allow companies within the park sharing resources and were described in Chapter 2.
- Global organizations that gain advantage from quickly putting together business value networks made up of operating units from different parts of the organization. Supply chain issues are often dominant here as described earlier in Chapters 7 and 8.
- Global manufacturing and service enterprises (Camarinha-Matos et al., 2009) that have the potential to improve operations through collaboration across the globe.
- Emergency systems (Jacobs et al., 1998), where a number of units have to coordinate their activities to respond to emergencies. Response to emergencies will depend on the kind of emergency and require the quick establishment of communications between units that can respond to the emergency. These units can be medical services, fire brigades as well as other units such as the traffic authorities.
- One stop shops where customers have the one access for all enquiries and dealings with an organization. This is one of the major goals of e-Government. Thus a complex order, for example, may go through a number of departments. Often a customer must interact with one or more of these, as many of these may have their own process. If all processes are combined, then the client can interact in one space but still see the whole picture.

Collaboration is crucial in business networks. People in all networked units must be aware of the entire context and the value to work together and in some way act in unison to respond to any change. They must also respond consistently depending on any change. It often requires some facilitation of the business process. This applies to both networking across large global organizations and networking across organizations.

Many global businesses now have units distributed across the globe and need to maintain collaboration across the globe. Such collaboration impacts on most business processes. The impact depends on the kind of processes especially on whether the process is predefined or emergent. Thus most predefined processes such as payroll, billing and invoicing, bank deposits and withdrawals are now automated. The application processes here are usually supported by ERP systems. Collaborative knowledge networks go beyond ERP systems and include support for change which in turn requires the exchange of ideas and identification of new directions for value networks. Some approaches described in the previous chapters were those of Hustad (2004) and Maybury et al. (2001) for supporting knowledge communities and identifying experts in global organizations.

Networking across enterprises adds a further dimension. Now individual processes, which go across organizations, can be collaborative rather than transaction-based activities as described in Chapter 7. Currie and Guah (2006) describe the complexities in making such interconnections in the UK health service. From an application perspective the strategy is to identify projects to gradually build a complete network. Typical projects include creation of electronic health records, simplify hospital bookings for doctors and the electronic transmission of prescriptions. The construction of such networks involves not only the technical issues of computer communication, but also the management of contractors as well as varying political issues. From the knowledge management perspective they identify applications such as capturing knowledge about service suppliers and contractors to support supplier negotiation. Knowledge gathered in this way is used to create new pathways to improve care delivery. Tsiknakis and Kouroubali (2008) also identify similar application for the island of Crete. These also focus on specific applications such as primary care information as well as a health record system. They also describe the processes involved in implementing the system. These are primarily based on agile methodologies using a Task-Technology-Fit (TFF) model to ensure that the developed system are accepted and used by users.

Hackney et al. (2008) identify the importance of top-level support where managers of car sales companies agreed to exchange marketing knowledge through a website.

3   Creating the business connections

Business networks do not just exist. They are created. How they are created depends on the size of the businesses and the volume of the business. The social perspective is important here. Business networks may be brokered by special brokers whose business goal is to set up and facilitate business networking. They are initiated by businesses themselves. This particularly occurs in industries like the automotive industry where the major business seeks potential partners and form strategic engagements with them.

Small business networks are often arranged by brokers. Figure 14.2 describes a typical situation that was supported by the Norwegian and Australian governments. Thus the activity 'Identifying business opportunities' includes the roles of brokers and external contacts. Here brokers, commissioned by the government, identify opportunities often through international government contact and try to find candidate SME (small to medium enterprise) to work together and take advantage of these opportunities. It should be noted that brokers are the source of knowledge in selecting possible candidate businesses. This knowledge is often in tacit form and gathered by the broker through continuous contact with their clients. In many cases the brokers also keep personal records about their clients. Once interested parties are found a memorandum of understanding is signed followed by a contract if suitable arrangements can be negotiated.

The process followed in business network formation is shown by the dataflow diagram in Figure 14.3. Thus an event like 'opportunity found' initiates the 'Find potential matches' activity to find possible business to exploit the opportunity. Once potential partners are found then an activity to construct a memorandum of understanding between them is initiated. At any point in time

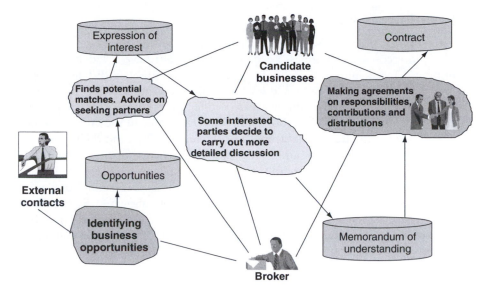

Figure 14.2 Business activities in setting up small business networks

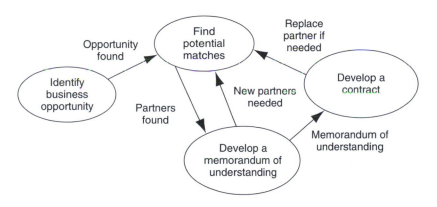

Figure 14.3 Process perspective in creating business networks

there may be any number of such activities going on, one for each identified opportunity.

Thus the major steps are well-defined. An opportunity is found, partners identified, a memorandum of understanding created. Each of the activities, however, follows a non-predefined process made up of meetings, phone calls and so on. Again there may be many similar activities going on at the same time. Thus there may be many memorandums of understanding being developed each with the same roles but different participants. The question that arises here is what kinds of collaborative technologies would effectively support this kind of process?

3.1   Virtual organizations

'Virtual organization' is also a term that has been used to describe a variety of kinds of interconnected business systems, but does not have a widely accepted definition. One definition can simply be people working at a distance. There is, however, the question of how does a virtual organization differ from a distributed system. To answer this we can define some criteria. One especially important is on the kinds of relationships between people in the virtual organization. One measure here is the strength of the relationships and their duration. Another is the extent of distribution of people in the virtual organization.

'Virtual organization' was a term that was commonly used to describe loosely connected individuals sharing knowledge. It is a term that is still commonly used and can in some sense describe the kind of connections shown in Figure 14.1. The general experience is that most networks begin as virtual enterprises but more formal connections are created as these mature and their relationships grow stronger.

3.2   Emerging objectives

In summary, objectives and goals emerge as enterprise relationships mature from simple outsourcing to strategic engagements. There is now agreement that one of the early steps in the creation of a network is a loosely connected virtual organization. In fact there is a trend to encourage such formation by providing what are sometimes called "breeding grounds" where small businesses can make contact and develop the partnerships to provide competitive new services with little assistance from government. The breeding grounds may be supported or facilitated through government. Examples are the various technology parks that are fostered through providing premises in close location, although often not supported by collaborative technologies.

Finally in summary there are two ways for networks to emerge. There are two distinct alternatives:

- One is on an ad-hoc basis where small groups emerge informally and share their knowledge. Often there are two units that get together, work as a virtual team, then another one joins and the virtual system gradually builds up until more formal arrangements are established.
- The other way is through a formal strategic decision to support networking and the creation of policies that guide and support such activities. Such policies would not only include provision of technology and associated services but also training and education to illustrate ways to quickly build relationships.

4   Growing cross-organizational relationships

In many cases business networking commences through outsourcing non-core work to other organizations mainly with the goal of cost reduction. This included outsourcing garment production, marketing or software development.

Such relationships can often grow to a partnering arrangement where enterprises see mutual benefit not only through cost reduction but in value adding through development of new products and services using the knowledge in both enterprises. This can provide competitive advantage through reduced time to market, made possible by more effective partnering arrangements. Relationships thus grow and three levels of cross-organizational networking can be defined, namely:

- Client server sourcing of work, principally concerned with cost reduction;
- Collaborative partnering, where enterprises through relying on their partners improve their services to match each other's needs and hence achieve advantage through reduced time to market and better customer orientation; and
- Joint strategic engagement where they develop new and innovative products through a better understanding of each other's capabilities and leveraging each other's skills.

Organizational factors are often more important than technical factors as developing personal relationships is important in business networking. Stakeholders from different units have to be convinced of the benefits of processes to their unit. They must see how their operating units improve through such connection. These often depend on designing new ways of working as well as new benefits not possible in disconnected systems.

4.1 Strategic engagements

Strategic engagements go beyond carrying out joint projects but require close alignment and common strategic objectives. They require engagement at all levels of the enterprise with almost the commitment to a common brand. Strategic engagement goes beyond simply exchanging tasks but requires relationships to be maintained at the corporate level as well as developing interpersonal relationships and common work cultures at all levels of the enterprise. In our earlier example, the marketing organization could form a strategic alignment with its client. The marketing organization with its knowledge of client preferences could suggest potential product changes knowing the clients abilities. They can then work together to bring their knowledge of marketing and manufacture together to better meet the needs of the market.

Generally stakeholders in a strategic relationship must agree on a strategy, create a project portfolio, and identify potential changes and resultant potential benefits. It is here that alignment of the organization to proposed new tasks becomes important. Such alignment goes beyond simply doing tasks on behalf of each other but includes developing shared vision and objectives including a unified governance model, cohesive teams that include members from different organizations, and aligning incentives and reward structures. Such alignment has to be supported by technology.

How do we choose ways to identify new products for a mass market? Here it is necessary to identify a new product strategy by identifying or anticipating what people are likely to buy. This is a particular problem in electronic devices. For example, what components to include in mobile phones in ways that can still reduce its cost while making it more attractive than currently available devices? Chapter 8 described the ways such decisions are made in some Japanese firms through strategic communities (Kodama, 2005) described in Chapter 4. It focuses on what are known as strategic communities (SCs) which collect, share and interpret knowledge to define new directions. A typical set of SCs would include a marketing community, a production community closely interacting to come to a strategic decision. These communities include people from different organizations and include a leadership group.

5 Business networks planning

Business networks are formed in two ways, either by gradual evolution or as a strategic initiative. Gradual evolution usually commences as a virtual community. Strategic initiatives require a more systematic approach. Thus although most businesses are composed of various organizational units they must present a unified interest to their clients. Figure 14.4 shows a general view of integration in terms of a number of levels.

- The transaction level where predefined business processes exchange transactions;
- The business functions that can be combined across businesses;
- The services provided by the business; and
- The interface level that supports cross process exchange. Here applications have knowledge of other applications.

Businesses can combine their systems at any of these levels. Chapter 7 described combination at the transaction level using electronic exchange of transactions.

Tourism can be viewed in terms of service integration, where services provided by a number of businesses can be integrated into the one package.

Emergency services are another area where such relationships are continually growing. These are usually combined into a core process providing a 'one-stop shop' usually with the same emergency number for any emergency. The services are still independently provided by each provider. There is usually the brand 'Emergency Services' that covers medical, fire, police and other organizations. The members of such organization work closely together in fighting emergencies. Hence they fundamentally adhere to the principles of the one-stop shop, although in most situations the linkages at all the levels are not complete.

Governments are also developing towards the one-stop shop idea. Any citizen requiring a service should ring one number even though the service can be composed of services from more than one government agency.

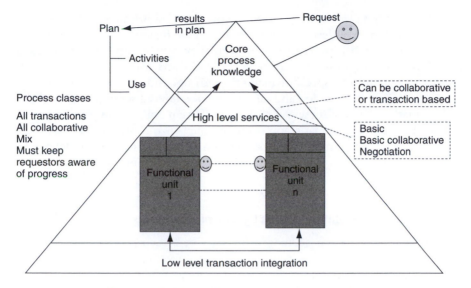

Figure 14.4   Process integration for a one-stop shop

The suggestion here follows that made by King (2006) of starting with a vision. This is followed by a strategy, and then developing the information technology capabilities to support the strategy. The views of stakeholders become more important and diverse now. Stakeholders often perceive any projects from the point of view of the benefit to their own organization and not the project as a whole. One important aspect of developing any vision is to illustrate the direct benefits of any developed system to individual units and stakeholders. The vision then is realized as a set of projects that follow the design methods described in the previous chapters.

5.1   The organizational perspective – Develop a joint vision

A vision as developed by stakeholders is essential in any systematic approach. This may often depend on an industry, as for example, manage mold changes better, improve outsource management. It can be provided a one stop entry to our network. Diagrams such as that shown in Figures 9.12 and 9.13 are very useful here as they can show the main organizational entities as well as the knowledge requirements. In fact rich pictures showing each process perspective are quite useful in making strategic decisions. One could show the stakeholders, their values and how the different units are to be connected. It also provides a structure to identify the benefits for each stakeholder.

For example, in the apparel industry, different combinations of product, brand, retail outlets and customer segment can each result in the different strategy and vision. The choice rests with the stakeholders and their values and knowledge. A retailer aiming to get competitive cost advantage through volume production may develop a retailer brand by forming a partnership with a design group and manufacturer. Or even they may set up their own design group. A fashion house may create special products using one designer with assistants, a sponsor, a specialist marketing group, and one selected manufacturer to focus on the creation and sale of one or a limited set of products within a niche market. Each of these will require a different connection plan.

The three-phase systematic approach outlined in the previous chapters can be extended to larger multi-business environments. It provides guidelines for design but also needs to work within a wider enterprise framework, often guided by a vision.

5.2   Set objectives and priorities by defining projects

Objectives usually lead to defining projects, where each project is designed to meet one or a number of objectives. The objectives define the business value and are developed by the stakeholders. These are generally set as a vision evolves and what is to be done to realize newly identified benefits.

5.3   Define organizational arrangements

As objectives are set, so are organizational arrangements. Here we define the high-level activities and the roles that maintain relationships between these activities. This includes creating roles to coordinate between the units, defining ways of sharing knowledge, and capturing articulated knowledge across organizational boundaries. Here we are modelling a large number of activities across organizational units or across organizations.

6   The social perspective – Developing a connection plan

The social structure in business networks is large when compared with that found for a process. Hence one of the earliest step is to identify communities that will be established to manage the business relationship.

A connection plan identifies the different communities and teams, and defines roles responsible for interactions between the business units. Designers of collaborative support must consider the needs of knowledge workers in the different units, each of whom may work differently over time and even work differently on the same problem. The first step is usually to raise awareness across organizational boundaries.

It is here that some strategic decisions on organization of the communities must be taken. Cultural considerations discussed in Chapter 4 come into play here as it is likely that units in the different connected units follow different cultural norms. Figure 14.5 is a way to illustrate connections using the apparel industry as an example. Each group in Figure 14.5 is a business activity with designated roles to coordinate the activities.

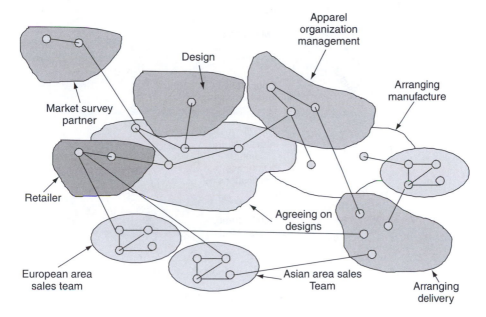

Figure 14.5   The collaborative network

It is here that ways to align organizations must be considered usually by assigning roles to be responsible for the collaboration.

Communities of practice and strategic communities have been introduced earlier and questions arise as to how these can be strategically introduced to support enterprise-wide knowledge networks. The main question is whether these need to be managed and coordinated and if so, what are the ways to do so.

7 Technical architecture to support enterprise integration

The choice of technology must take into account the resources available to the organization and its dynamic nature. It presents problems in that information resident with individual partners has to be shred in the network. Often this may go beyond the support which follows the requirements of supply chains described in Chapter 8, especially if networks are established at the higher levels as shown in Figure 14.4. Where arrangements are stable over periods of time ERP systems using modules like that shown in Figure 8.11 may be implemented. In stable supply chains much transfer takes place at the transaction level. These are usually expensive to implement and require time to get value from the expense. Where the dynamics are high, as for example in the apparel industry, more lightweight approaches are needed. These can be developed as special platforms or using SOA approaches, supported by software houses aiming at particular industries. The use of Vertex PLM by the fashion house Elie Tahari is one example.

Figure 14.6   Integrating business functions

Ultimately an architectural framework like that in Figure 14.6 can provide guidelines. It shows the applications to be supported as the outer shell. These are connected together across a cooperative information system that provides the interfaces between the applications. At the core is the IT infrastructure that provides the hardware and software on which the systems reside. Once the connection is agreed upon the business applications can be connected at the operational level through the exchange of transaction between applications.

Connections across enterprises are more difficult to arrange mostly because of organizational rather than technical issues. The simplest is to create links at the transaction level. For example, many organizations now have transaction links to credit providers. There are also increasing links between insurance companies and hospitals. In most cases such links are at the transaction level using EDI technologies.

8 Summary

This last chapter is more a description of evolving developments rather than current practices. Connecting enterprises places another level on modeling and design – that of developing interorganizational connections, especially on ways to organize systematic collaboration at the organizational level. Designing enterprise networks places more emphasis on factors such as cultural differences, the kind of business relationship. The networks are more likely to gradually emerge through initial formation of virtual communities through to partnerships and strategic engagements. The goal is to reach the ideal where structured processes within and between organizations can be connected and integrated with the knowledge infrastructure.

9 Projects

Select an industry and referring to Figure 14.4 discuss the level at which the industry would get significant benefit through networking. Suggested industries include the following:

Global retail chains – A global retail chain distributes products for a number of different producers in a number of different locations. (You may wish to only consider distribution for only one global company here.)

Engineering construction – Many construction companies are going global and developing partnerships and strategic alliances with companies that have specific engineering capabilities.

Intergovernmental services – Governments are attempting to provide what are known as "one-stop shops" where members of the public need only contact one office to get a service rather than following up a need through a number of departments. This project will develop an architecture to enable such one-stop shops to be achieved. (You may select a particular set of government activities if you wish.)

Some further readings

Camarinha-Matos, L.M., Afsarmanesh, H., Galeano, N., Molina, A. (2009) 'Collaborative Networked Organizations – Concepts and Practice in Manufacturing Enterprises' *Computers and Industrial Engineering*, doi:10.1016/j.cie. 2008.11.024, 2009.

Currie, W.L., Guah, M.W. (2006) 'IT-Enabled Health Care Delivery: The UK National Health Service' *Information Systems Management Journal*, Vol. 23, No. 2, Spring, pp. 7–22.

Hackney, R. Desouza, K.C. Irani, Z. (2008) 'Constructing and Sustaining Complete Interorganizational Knowledge Networks: An Analysis of Managed Web-based Facilitation' *Information Systems Management Journal*, Vol. 25, No.4, Fall, pp. 356–363.

Jacobs, J.L., Dorneich, C.P., Jones, P.M. (1998) 'Activity Representation and Management for Crisis Action Planning' *IEEE International Conference on Systems, Management and Cybernetics*, October, pp. 961–966.

King, W.R. (2006) 'Developing Global IT Capabilities' *Information Systems Management Journal*, Fall, pp. 78–79.

Myers, M.B., Cheung, M-S. (2008) 'Sharing Global Supply Chain Knowledge' *MIT Sloan School Management Review*, Vol. 49, No. 4, Summer, pp. 67–73.

Tan, S.J., Wen, J., Awad, N. (2006) 'Health Care and Services Delivery Systems as Complex Adaptive Systems' *Communications of the ACM*, Vol. 48, No. 5, May, pp. 37–44.

Tsiknakis, M., Kouroubali, A. (2008) 'Organizational Factors Affecting Successful Adoption of Innovative eHealth services: A Case Study Employing the FITT Framework' *International Journal of Medical Informatics*, Vol. 78, pp. 39–52.

Glossary of Some Often Used Terms in Modeling and Design

Artifact	A business model component that is the repository of information.
Business activity model (BAM)	A model of the business activity perspective. Defines the roles, artifacts that make up the activity.
Business activity	The basic construct in a business.
Business Architecture	A combination of objects that describes a business.
Business System Design	A process used to create a new business system.
Collaborative work	Work carried out jointly by a number of people.
Data flow diagram	A method used to model process steps.
Design process	A set of steps to create a new business system.
Design step	A step in a design process.
Design task	Design work carried out at a design step using a design method.
Design method	A method used to carry out a design task.
Enterprise social network (ESN)	A model of the business from the social perspective showing roles in the system, the relationships between them and their responsibilities.
Expert work	Work requiring judgment and expertise.
Integrative work	Systematic work carried out in a number of steps by a number of people.
Lightweight technology	Supports mashups of workspaces by system users.
Participant	A person assigned to a role.
Process	Describes the way work is carried out or a business works. Made up of a number of business activities.
Rich picture	A modeling method from soft systems methodologies that can be bused to model process perspectives.
Role	Responsibility within a business model.
Synchronous communication	Communication at the same time between people.
System Development Method	A process to create a new computer system.
Transactive work	Routine work on a well-defined task.
Workflow	The steps in a business process.
Workspace	A computer screen presenting information needed in an activity or by a role.

Bibliography

Adenfelt, M., Lagenstrom, K. (2006) 'Enabling Knowledge Creation and Sharing in Transnational Projects' *International Journal of Project Management*, Vol. 24, pp. 191–198, Elsevier Press.

Akintoye, A., McIntosh, G., Fitzgerald, E. (2000) 'A Survey of Supply Chain Collaboration and Management in the UK Construction Industry' *European Journal of Purchasing and Supply Chain Management*, Vol. 6, pp. 159–168.

Al-Reshaid, K., Kartam, N. (2005) 'Design-build Pre-qualification and Tendering Approach for Public Projects' *International Journal of Project Management*, Vol. 23, pp. 309–320.

Anderson, K.M., Anderson, A., Wadhwani W., Bartolo, L. (2003) 'Metis: A Lightweight, Flexible, and Web-based Workflow Services for Digital Libraries' *Proceedings 3rd ACM/IEEE Conference on Digital Libraries*, May, pp. 98–109.

Anthony, R.N. (1965) *Planning and Control Systems: A Framework for Analysis* (Harvard University Press).

Aimer, E., Brassard, G. (2005) 'Fostering Interdisciplinary Communication' *IEEE Intelligent Systems*, Vol. 20, No. 2, March/April, pp. 46–53.

Ajmal, M.M., Koskinen, K.U. (2008) 'Knowledge Transfer in Project-Based Organizations: An Organizational Culture Perspective' *Project Management Journal*, Vol. 39, No. 1, March, pp. 7–15.

Akram, A., Afzal, M., Zubari, J. (2008) 'Architecture for extending Agrikiosk Services to Mobile Phones' *Proceedings of the 2008 International Symposium on Collaborative Technologies and Systems*, Irvine, California, May, pp. 144–148.

Allen, P.M., Varga, L. (2006) 'A Co-evolutionary Complex Systems Perspective on Information Systems' *Journal of Information Technology*, Vol. 21, No. 4, December, pp. 229–238.

Andriessen, D. (2006) 'On the Metaphorical Nature of Intellectual Capital: A Textual Analysis' *Journal of Intellectual Capital*, Vol. 7, No. 1, pp. 93–110.

Andriessen, J.H.E. (2003) *Designing with Groupware* (Springer-Verlag, London).

Artail, H.A. (2006) 'Application of KM Measures to the Impact of a Specialized Groupware System on Corporate Productivity and Operations' *Information and Management*, Vol. 43, pp. 551–564.

Artto, K., Wikstorm, K., Hellstrom, M., Kujala, J. (2008) 'Impact of Services on Project Business' *International Journal of Project Management*, Vol. 26, pp. 497–508, Elsevier Press.

Avison, D., Young, T. (2007) 'Time to Rethink Health Care and ICT?' *Communications of the ACM*, Vol. 50, No. 6, August, pp. 69–74.

Barton, M.D. (2005) 'The future of rational-critical debate in online public spheres' *Computers and Composition*, Vol. 22, pp. 177–190, Elsevier Press.

Belassi, W., Kondra, A.Z., Tukel, O.I. (2007) 'New Product Development Projects: The Effects of Organizational Culture' *Project Management Journal*, Vol. 38, No. 4, December, pp. 12–24.

Bellin, J.W., Phan, C.T. (2007) 'Global Expansion: Balancing a Uniform Performance Culture with Local Conditions' *Strategy and Leadership*, Vol. 35, No. 6, pp. 44–50.

Berchet, C., Habchi, G. (2005) 'The Implementation and Deployment of an ERP System: An Industrial Case Study' *Computers in Industry*, Vol. 56, pp. 588–605.

Biehl, M. (2007) 'Success Factors for Implementing Global Information Systems' *Communications of the ACM*, Vol. 50, No. 1, January, pp. 53–58.

Boisot, M. (2006) 'Moving to the Edge of Chaos: Bureaucracy, IT and the Challenge of Complexity' *Journal of Information Technology*, Vol. 21, No. 4, December, pp. 239–248.

Boland, R.J., Tenkasi, R.V. (1995) 'Perspective Making and Perspective Taking in Communities of Knowing' *Organizational Science*, Vol. 6, No. 4, July–August, pp. 350–372.

Boonstra, A., de Vries, J. (2008) 'Managing Stakeholders Around Inter-organizational Systems: A Diagnostic Approach' *Journal of Strategic Information Systems*, Vol.17, pp. 190–201.

Brown, J., Duguid, P. (1998): 'Organizing Knowledge' *California Management Review*, Vol. 40, No. 3, pp. 90–111.

Burrows, G.B., Drummond, D.L., Martinsons M.G., (2005) 'Knowledge Management in China' *Communications of the ACM*, Vol. 48, No. 4, April, pp. 73–76.

Camarinha-Matos, L.M., Afsarmanesh, H., Galeano, N., Molina, A. (2009) 'Collaborative Networked Organizations – Concepts and Practice in Manufacturing Enterprises' *Computers and Industrial Engineering*, doi:10.1016/j.cie.2008.11.024, 2009.

Carrol, J.M., Rosson, M.B., Convertino, G., Ganoe, C.H. (2006) 'Awareness and Teamwork in Computer-supported Collaborations' *Interacting with Computers*, Vol. 18, pp. 21–46, Elsevier Press.

Chaminade, C., Vang, J. (2008) 'Globalization of Knowledge Production and Regional Innovation Policy: Supporting Specialized Hubs in the Bangalore Software Industry' *Research Policy*, Vol. 37, No. 10, December, pp. 1684–1696.

Chang, J.F. (2006) *Business Process Management Systems: Strategy and Implementation* (Auerbach Publications, New York).

Checkland, P.B. (1981) *Systems Thinking, Systems Practice*, (John Wiley & Sons Ltd).

Chen, Z., Li, H., Ross, A., Khalfan, M.M.A., Kong, S.C.W. (2008) 'Knowledge-Driven ANP approach to Vendors Evaluation for Sustainable Construction' *Journal of Construction Engineering and Management*, Vol. 134, No. 12, December, pp. 928–941.

Cova, B., Salle, R. (2008) 'Marketing Solutions in Accordance with S-D Logic: Co-creating Value with Customer Network Actors' *Industrial Marketing Management*, Vol. 37, pp. 270–277.

Currie, W.L., Guah, M.W. (2006) 'IT-Enabled Health Care Delivery: The UK National Health Service' *Information Systems Management*, Vol. 23, No.2, Spring, pp. 7–22.

Davenport, T. (2005) *Thinking for Living* (Harvard Business Press).

Davenport, T.H., Prusak, L. (1998) *Working Knowledge: How Organizations Manage What They Know* (Harvard Business Press).

Ding, Y. (2008) *Websphere Engineering* (IBM Press, 2008).

Dobni, C.B. (2006) 'The Innovation Blueprint' *Business Horizons*, Vol. 49, No. 4, pp. 329–339, Elsevier Press.

Earl, M. (2001) 'Knowledge Management Strategies: Towards a Taxonomy' *Journal of Management Information Systems*, Summer, Vol. 18, No.1. pp. 215–233.

Erickson, T., Kellogg, W. (2000) 'Social Translucence: An Approach to Designing Systems that Support Social Processes' *ACM Transactions on Computer-Human Interaction*, Vol. 7, No. 1, March, pp. 59–83.

Evans, P., Wolf, B. (2005) 'Collaboration Rules' *Harvard Business Review*, Vol. 83, No. 7/8, July–August, pp. 1–9.

Fuchs-Kittowski, F., Kohler, A. (2005) 'Wiki Communities in the Context of Work Processes' *WikiSym 05*, 16–18 October, San Diego, California, pp. 33–39.

Gherardi, S. Nicolini, D. (2002) 'Learning in a Constellation of Interconnected Practices: Canon or Dissonance' *Journal of Management Studies*, Vol. 39, No.4, pp. 419–436.

Goold, M. (2005) 'Making Peer Groups Effective: Lessons from BP's Experiences' *Long Range Planning*, Vol. 38, pp. 429–443, Elsevier Press.

Grant, R.M. (1996) 'Prospering in Dynamically-competitive Environments: Organizational Capability as Knowledge Integration' *Organization Science*, Vol. 7, No. 4, July, pp. 375–387.

Grefen, P., Ludwig, H., Dan, A., Angelov, S. (2006) 'An Analysis of Web Services Support for Dynamic Business Process Outsourcing' *Information and Software Technology*, Vol. 48, pp. 1115–1134, Elsevier Press.

Gruber, T. (2008) 'Collective Knowledge Systems: Where the Social Web Meets the Semantic Web' *Web semantics: Science, Services and Agents on the World Wide Web*, Vol. 6, pp. 4–13.

Guimera, R., Danon, L., Diaz-Aguilera, A. Girral, F., Arenas, A. (2006) 'The Real Communication Network Behind the Formal Chart: Community Structures in Organizations' *Journal of Economic Behaviour and Organization*, Vol. 61, No.4, December, pp. 653–667. Elsevier Press.

Gumm, D.C. (2006) 'Distribution Dimensions in Software Development Projects' *IEEE Software*, Vol. 3, No. 25, September/October, pp. 45–51.

Hackney, R., Desouza, K.C., Irani, Z. (2008) 'Constructing and Sustaining Complete Interorganizational Knowledge Networks: An Analysis of Managed Web-based Facilitation' *Information Systems Management Journal*, Vol. 25, No. 4, Fall, pp. 356–363.

Hall, H, Graham, D. (2004) 'Creation and Recreation: Motivating Collaboration to Generate Knowledge Capital in On-line Communities' *International Journal of Information Management*, Vol. 24, pp. 235–246, Elsevier Press.

Hamel, C.G. (2006) 'The Why, What, and How of Management Innovation' *Harvard Business Review*, Vol. 84, No.2, February, pp. 1–11.

Hansen, M.T., Nohria, N., Tierney, T. (1999) 'Whats Your Strategy for Managing Knowledge' *Harvard Business Review*, Vol. 77, No. 2, March-April, pp. 106–116.

Hansen, M.T. (2009) 'When Internal Collaboration is Bad for Yor Company' *Harvard Business Review*, Vol. 84, No.3, April, pp. 83–119.

Harvey, M., Novicevic, M., Garrison, G. (2004) 'Challenges to Staffing Global Virtual Teams' *Human Resource Management Review*, Vol. 14, pp. 275–294, Elsevier Press.

Hawryszkiewycz, I.T. (2001) *Introduction to Systems Analysis and Design* (Prentice-Hall, Sydney).

Heikkila, J. (2002) 'From Supply to Demand Chain Management: Efficiency and Customer Satisfaction' *Journal of Operations Management*, Vol. 20, 747–767.

Herbslet, J.D., Mockus, A., Finholf, T.A., Grinter, R.E. (2000) 'Distance, Dependencies, and Delay in a Global Collaboration' Proceedings of the 2000 ACM Conference on Computer Supported Cooperstive Work, (*CSCW*), 1–6 December, Philadelphia, pp. 319–328.

Hicks, R.C., Datteroi, R., Galup, S.D. (2006) 'The Five-tier Knowledge Management Hierarchy' *Proceedings of the 35th Annual Meeting of Decision Sciences Institute*, Vol. 10, No. 1, pp. 19–31.

Hislop, D. (2005) *Knowledge Management in Organizations* (Oxford University press).

Hoadley, C.M., Kilner, P.G. (2005) 'Using Technology to Transform Communities of Practice into Knowledge-Building Communities' *SIGGROUP Bulletin*, Vol. 25, No. 1, pp. 31–40.

Holland, J. (1995) *Hidden Order: How Adaption Builds Complexity* (Cambridge Perseus Books).

Howard, M., Vidgen. R., Powell, P. (2006) 'Automotive E-hubs: Exploring Motivations and Barriers to Collaboration and Interaction' *Journal of Strategic Information Systems*, Vol. 15, pp. 51–75.

Hu, C., Racherla, P. (2008) 'Visual Representation of Knowledge Networks: A Social Network Analysis of Hospitality Research Domain' *International Journal of Hospitality Management*, Vol. 27, pp. 302–312.

Huang, S., Fan, Y. (2007) 'Model Driven and Service Oriented Enterprise Integration – The Method, Framework and Platform' *Sixth International Conference on Advanced Language Processing and Web Information Technology*, IEEE.

Hustad, E. (2004) 'Knowledge Networking in Global Organizations' *SIGMIS*, April 22–24, Tucson, Arizona, pp. 55–64.

Ichijo, K., Kohlbacher, F. (2008) 'Tapping Tacit Local Knowledge in Emerging Markets – The Toyota Way' *Knowledge Management Research and Practice*, Vol. 6, pp. 173–186.

Jacob, F., Ulaga, W. (2008) 'The Transition from Product to Services in Business Markets: An Agenda for Academic Inquiry' *Industrial Marketing Management*, Vol. 37, pp. 247–253, Elsevier press.

Jacobs, F.R., Weston, F. (2007) 'Enterprise Resource Planning' *Journal of Operations Management*, Vol. 25, pp. 357–363.

Jacobs, J.L., Dorneich, C.P., Jones, P.M. (1998) 'Activity Representation and Management for Crisis Action Planning' *IEEE International Conference on Systems, Management and Cybernetics*, October 1998, pp. 961–966.

Jones, M.C., Cline, M., Ryan, S. (2006) 'Exploring Knowledge Sharing in Erp Implementation: An Organizational Culture Framework' *Decision Support Systems*, Vol. 41, pp. 411–434.

King, W.R. (2006) 'Developing Global IT Capabilities' *Information Systems Management*, Vol. 23, No. 4, Fall, pp. 78–79.

Kodama, M. (2005) 'New Knowledge Creation Through Leadership-Based Strategic Community – A Case of New Product Development in it and Multimedia Business Fields' *Technovation*, Vol. 25, pp. 895–908, Elsevier Press.

Krafzig, D., Banke, K., Slama, D. (2004) *Enterprise SOA: Service Oriented Architecture Best Practices* (Coad Series, Prentice-Hall).

Krippendorff, K. (2008) *The Way of Innovation Platinum Press* (Avon, Massachusetts).

Kumar, R., Novak, J., Raghavan, P., Tomkins, A. (2004) 'The Structure and Evolution of Blogspace' *Communications of the ACM*, Vol. 47, No. 12, December 2004, pp. 35–39.

Lam, W., Shankararaman, V. (2004) 'An Enterprise Integration Methodology' *IT Pro*, Vol. 6, No. 2, March/April, pp. 40–48.

Leavitt, H.J. (1965) *Applied Organizational Change in Industry: Structural, Technical and Humanistic Approaches* (Handbook of Organization, March, J.G. (ed.), pp. 1144–1170, Rand-McNally, Chicago).

Lee-Kelley, L., Sankey, T. (2008) 'Global Virtual Teams for Value Creation and Project Success: A Case Study' *International Journal of Project Management*, Vol. 26, pp. 51–62.

Leidner, D.E., Kayworth, T. (2006) 'Review: A Review of Culture in Information Systems Research: Toward a Theory of Information Technology Culture Conflict' *MIS Quarterly*, Vol. 30, No. 2, June, pp. 357–399.

Lin., Y-S., Huang, J-Y. (2006) 'Internet Blogs as a Tourism Marketing Medium: A Case Study' *Journal of Business Research*, Vol. 59, October, pp. 68–81, Elsevier Press.

Lings, B., Lundell, B., Agerfalk, P., Fitzgerald, B. (1996) 'Ten Strategies for Successful Distributed Development' *Proceedings of the IFIP TC8 WG 8.6 International Working Conference*, Galway, Ireland, Springer, pp. 119–137.

Lorincz, P. (2007) 'Evolution of Enterprise Systems' *LINDI 2007, International Symposium on Logistics and Industrial Economics*, 13–15 September, Wildau, Germany.

Louridas, P. (2006) 'Using WIKIs in Software Development' *IEEE Software*, Vol. 23, No. 2, March/April, pp. 88–91.

Majchrzak, A., Wagner, C., Yates, D. (2006) 'Corporate Wiki Users: Results of a Survey' *WikiSym 06*, Odense, Denmark, 21–23 August, pp. 99–104.

Martinson, M.G. (2008) 'Relationship-based e-commerce theory and evidence from China' *Information Systems Journal*, Vol. 18, No.4, July, pp. 331–356.

Maybury, M., D'Amore, R., House, D. (2001) 'Expert Finding for Collaborative Virtual Environments' *Communication of the ACM*, Vol. 44, No. 12, December 2001, pp. 55–56.

McAfee, A.P. (2006) 'Enterprise 2.0: The Dawn of Emergent Collaboration' *MIT Sloan Management Review*, Vol. 47, No. 3, Spring, pp. 21–28.

McDermott, R., O'Dell, C. (2001) 'Overcoming Cultural Barriers to Knowledge Sharing' *Journal of Knowledge Management*, Vol. 5, No. 1: pp. 76–85.

McDonald, D.W. (2003) 'Recommending Collaboration with Social Networks: A Comparative Evaluation' *CHI 2003*, April, pp. 593–600.

Milligan, P., Hutcheson, D. (2006) 'Analysis of Outsourcing and the Impact on Business Resilience' *Proceedings of the IFIP TC8 WG 8.6 International Working Conference*, Galway, Ireland, Springer, pp. 199–208.

Ming, X.G., Yan, J.Q., Wang, X.H., Li, S.N., Lu, W.F., Peng, Q.J., Ma, Y.S. (2008) 'Collaborative Process Planning and manufacturing in product lifecycle management', *Computers in Industry*, Vol. 59, pp. 154–166.

Minzberg, H. (2009) 'Rebuilding Companies as Communities' *Harvard Business Review*, Vol. 84, No. 4, July-August, pp. 140–143.

Melville, N., Ramirez, R. (2008) 'Information Technology Innovation Diffusion: An Information Requirements Paradigm' *Information Systems Journal*, Vol. 18, No. 3, May, pp. 247–275.

Merali, Y., McKelvey, B. (2006) 'Using Complexity Science to Affect a Paradigm Shift in Information Systems for the 21st Century' *Journal of Information Technology*, Vol. 21, No. 4, December, pp. 211–215.

Meso, P., Jain, R. (2006) 'Agile Software Development: Adaptive System Principles and Best Practices' *Information Systems Management*, Vol. 23, No. 3, Summer, pp. 19–30.

Morgan, G. (1986) *Images of Organization* (SAGE Publications, Beverly Hills, California).

Morrison, P.J. (2008) 'Tagging and Searching: Search Retrieval Effectiveness of Folksonomies on the World Wide Web' *Information Processing and Management*, Vol. 44, pp. 1562–1579.

Myers, M.B., Cheung, M-S. (2008) 'Sharing Global Supply Chain Knowledge' MIT *Sloan School Management Review*, Vol. 49, No. 4, Summer, pp. 67–73.

Nahapiet, J., Ghoshal, S. (1998) 'Social Capital, Intellectual Capital, and the Organizational Advantage' *Academy of Management Review*, Vol. 23, No. 2, April, pp. 242–266.

Nakata, N., Fukuda, Y., Fukuda, K., Suzuki, N. (2005) 'DICOM Wiki: Web-based Collaboration and Knowledge Database System for Radiologists' *International Congress Series*, Vol. 1281, pp. 980–985, Elsevier Press.

Ni, Q., Lu, W.F., Yarlagadda, K.D.V., Ming, X. (2007) 'Business Information Modeling for Process Integration in the Mold Making Industry' *Robotics and Computer-Integrated Manufacturing*, Vol. 23, pp. 195–205.

Niederman, F. (2005) 'International Business and MIS Approaches to Multinational Organizational Research: The Cases of Knowledge Transfer and it Workforce Outsourcing' *Journal of International Management*, Vol. 11, pp. 187–200.

Nonaka, I. (1994) 'A Dynamic Theory of Organizational Knowledge Creation' *Organization Science*, Vol. 5, No. 1, February, pp. 14–37.

Oates, B.J., Fitzgerald, B. (2007) 'Multi-metaphor Method: Organizational Metaphors in Information Systems Development' *Information Systems Journal*, Vol. 17, No. 4, October, pp. 421–449.

O'Hara-Deveraux, M., Johansen, R. (1994) *GlobalWork: Bridging Distance, Culture and Time* (Jossey-Bass, San Francisco).

Oshiri, I., Van Fenema, P., Kotlarsky, J. (2008) 'Knowledge Transfer In Globally Distributed Teams: The Role of Transactive Memory' *Information Systems Journal*, Vol. 18, No. 6, November, pp. 593–616.

Pisano, G.P., Vergatti, R. (2008) 'Which Kind of Collaboration is Right for You' *Harvard Business Review*, Vol. 83, No. 8, December, pp. 78–86.

Popadiuk, S., Choo, C.W. (2006) 'Innovation and Knowledge Creation: How are these Concepts Related' *International Journal of Information Management*, Vol. 26, pp. 302–312.

Porter, M.E., Millar, V.E. (1985) 'how information gives you competitive advantage' Harvard Business Review, Vol. 79, No. 7, July–August.

Prahalad, C.K., Krishnan, M.S. (2008) *The New Age of Innovation* (McGraw-Hill).

Probst, G., Borzillo, S. (2008) 'Why Communities of Practice Succeed and Why they Fail' *European Management Journal*, Vol. 26, pp. 335–347.

Rajagopalan, R., Sarkar, R. (2008) 'Information and Communication Technology, Communities and Social Capital – How the Digital Ecosystem Approach can work' *Second IEEE International Conference on Digital Ecosystems and Technologies*, pp. 419–425.

Rinkus, S., Walji, M., Johnson-Throop, K.A., Malin, J.T., Turley, J.P., Smith, J.W., Zhang, J. (2004) 'Human-centred Design of a Distributed Knowledge Management System' *Journal of Biomedical Informatics*, Vol. 38, pp. 4–17.

Rizzo, A., Pozzi, S., Save, L., Sujan, M. (2006) 'Designing Complex Socio-technical Systems: A Heuristic Schema Based on Cultural-Historical Psychology' *Proceedings of the 2005 annual conference on European Association of Cognitive Ergonomics*, pp. 71–81.

Rizova, P. (2006) 'Are You Networked for Successful Innovation' *MIT Sloan Management Review*, Vol. 47, No. 3, Spring, pp. 49–55.

Rottam, J.W. (2006) 'Proven Practices for Effective Offshoring it Work' *Sloan Management Review*, Vol. 47, No. 3, Spring, pp. 56–63.

Russell, D., Streitz, N.A., Winograd, T. (2005) 'Building Disappearing Computers' *Communication of the ACM*, Vol. 48, No. 3, March, pp. 42–48.

Rye, K., Lee, S., Choi, H. (2008) 'Modularization of Web-based Collaboration Systems for Manufacturing Innovation' *Proceedings of the Tenth International Conference on Enterprise Information systems*, Barcelona, 12–16 June, pp. 174–177.

Sabherwal, R. (1999) 'The Role of Trust in Outsourced is Development Projects' *Communications of the ACM*, Vol. 42, No. 2, February, pp. 80–86.

Saffer, D. (2006) *Designing for Interaction: Creating Smart Applications and Clever Devices* (New Riders, Berkeley, California).

Sen, A. (2008) 'The US Fashion Industry: A Supply Chain Review' *International Journal of Production Economics*, Vol. 114, pp. 571–593.

Singh, T., Veron-Jackson, L., Cullinane, J. (2006) 'Blogging: A new play in your marketing game plan' *Business Horizons*, Vol. 31, pp. 281–292.

Staples, D.S., Webster, J. (2008) 'Exploring the Effects of Trust, Task Interdependence and Virtualness on Knowledge Sharing in Teams' *Information Systems Journal*, Vol. 18, November, pp. 617–640.

Szulanski, G. (1996) 'Exploring Internal stickiness: Impediments to the Transfer of Best Practice Within the Firm', *Strategic Management Journal*, Vol. 17, Winter Special Issue, pp. 27–43.

Tan, S.J., Wen, J., Awad, N. (2006) 'Health Care and Services Delivery Systems as Complex Adaptive Systems' *Communications of the ACM*, Vol. 48, No. 5, May, pp. 37–44.

Tapscott, D., Williams, A.D. (2008) *Wikinomics: How Mass Collaboration Changes Everything* (Penguin Books, London, UK).

Tsiknakis, M., Kouroubali, A. (2008) 'Organizational Factors Affecting Successful Adoption of Innovative ehealth Services: A Case Study Employing the Fitt Framework' *International Journal of Medical Informatics*, Vol. 78, pp. 39–52.

Vargo, S.L., Lusch, R.F. (2008) 'From Goods to Service(S): Divergences and Convergences of Logics' *Industrial Marketing Management*, Vol. 37, pp. 254–259.

Venters, W., Wood, B. (2007) 'Degenerative Structures that Inhibit the Emergence of Communities of Practice: A Case Study of Knowledge Management in the British Council' *Information Systems Journal*, Vol. 17, No. 4, October, pp. 349–368.

Vidgen, R., Wang, X. (2006) 'From Business Process Management to Business Process Ecosystem' *Journal of Information Technology*, Vol. 21, No. 4, December, pp. 262–271.

Vinekar, V., Slinkman, C.W. Nerur, S. (2006) 'Can Agile and Traditional System Development Approaches Coexist?' *Information Systems Management Journal*, Vol. 23, No. 2, Summer, pp. 31–42.

Whittaker, S., Belotti, V., Gwidza, J. (2006) 'Email in Personal Information Management' *Communication of the ACM*, Vol. 49, No. 1, January, pp. 68–73.

Whittaker, S., Jones, Q., Nardi, B, Creech, M., Terveen, L., Issacs, E., Hainsworth, J. (2002) 'ContactMap: Organizing Communication in a Social Desktop' ACM *Transactions on Computer-Human Interaction*, Vol. 11, No. 4, December, pp. 445–471.

Whittaker, S., Jones, Q., Terveen, L. (2002) 'Contact Management: Identifying Contacts to Support Long-Term Communication' *CSCW*, pp. 216–225.

Wilson, B. (2001) *Soft Systems Methodology* (John Wiley & Sons Ltd).

Wurtz, E. (2004): 'Intercultural Communication Websites' *Proceedings Cultural Attitudes towards Communication and Technology*, Murdoch University, Australia (edited Sudweeks, F. and Ess, C.) pp. 109–122.

Young, R.B., Javalgi, R.G. (2007) 'International Marketing Research: A Global project Management Perspective' *Business Horizons*, Vol. 50, pp. 113–122.

Youtie, J., Shapira, P. (2008) 'Building an Innovation Hub: A Case Study of the Transformation of University Roles in Regional Technological and Economic Development' *Research Policy*, Vol. 37, No. 8, September, pp. 1188–1204.

Yu, E. (1995) *Modeling Strategic Relationships for Process Engineering* (PhD Thesis. Department of Computer Science, University of Toronto, Canada).

Zhang, J., Patel, V., Johnson, K., Smith, J. (2002) 'Designing Human Centered Distributed Information Systems', *IEEE Intelligent Systems*, Vol. 17, No. 5, September/October, pp. 42–47.

Zhu, H. (2008) 'Roles in Information Systems: A Survey' *IEEE Transactions on Systems, Man, and Cybernetics – Part C: Applications and Reviews*, Vol. 38, No. 3, May, pp. 377–396.

Zolin, R., Hiunds, P.J., Fruchter, R., Levitt, R.E. (2004) 'Interpersonal Trust in Cross-Functional Geographical Distributed Work: A Longitudinal Study' *Information and Organization*, Vol. 14, pp. 1–26, Elsevier Press.

Zorn, I. (2005) 'Do Culture and Technology Interact? Overcoming Technological Barriers to Intercultural Communication in Virtual Communities' *SIGGROUP Bulletin*, Vol. 25, No. 2, February. pp. 8–13.

Index

Note: Locators in **bold** indicate figures and *Italics* indicate tables.